SAMA SAMA

COMFORT FOOD FROM MY MIXED
MALAYSIAN KITCHEN

JULIE LIN

INTERLINK BOOKS
AN IMPRINT OF INTERLINK PUBLISHING GROUP, INC.
NORTHAMPTON, MASSACHUSETTS

Introduction 6
In the Middle 14
Substitutes 18
A Glossary of Food Terms 22
Before You Begin 26

Agak-Agak 28
Authentically In-Between 54
Come Over for Dinner 96
One Person's Trash 142
Cook When Nobody's Watching 168
Learnings from the Motherland 200
Not Too Sweet 246

A Love Letter 276
Index 278
Terima Kasih 283
Conversion Tables 286

Me and Mom in Monaco, 1993

Sama Sama
Same-same, but different

"Have you eaten yet?" is a common greeting in Hokkien, one of the four dialects spoken by my family. It's the question my mother asks me most frequently, posed in various languages, and in different tones of voice. Whether I'm happy, sad, frustrated, confused or in a hurry, rain or shine, no matter my mood, it's always, "Have you eaten yet?" By the age of three, I was asking that question in two different languages—my mother taught me a hybrid of Malaysian and English. Although I grew up in Glasgow, Scotland, I was quintessentially Malaysian too, a feeling many mixed children understand, that sense of belonging to multiple places. I would play with a plastic Chinese lantern fish brought back from Malaysia and boast to my school friends about receiving the red packets given during Lunar New Year.

Growing up, we kept in touch with our family over what was known as the "house phone," before we had all of the many different forms of media we use to communicate these days. Back then, there was no internet to help us keep in touch; no option to FaceTime family members, search for images of Malaysia or look up recipes online to satisfy homesickness—it was limited to Saturday phone calls and boxes of printed photos from vacations to gain a visual memory. Connecting to our roots meant drawing on memories passed down through my mom's knowledge and experience of Malaysia. Mom cooked a lot, too, often recreating dishes from memory. My own version of Manglish (Malaysian/English) emerged primarily from food-related words, though there were occasionally some endearing references thrown in.

"Piffy, Big Fat Noodles—ready!"

Little did I know that this phrase would play such a significant role in my life. My mom would bellow it from the bottom of the stairs, and I'd come running down the 19 steps that led to the basement kitchen in our apartment. To this day, I'm not entirely sure why she called me Piffy, but she did all the time. Perhaps I responded faster when she used it (often when I'd done something slightly wrong, or when there was the promise of Big Fat Noodles). Whatever the reason, I'd be there in a flash, sitting eagerly at our dinner table, covered in a wipeable plastic tablecloth featuring images of scoops of ice cream in different colors. Food was always the theme in our house, even when the item wasn't edible food.

For the first 18 years of my life, I didn't know the real name of the Big Fat Noodles. It's char kuay teow (*"char-kway-tee-ow"*) (see page 217), arguably Malaysia's most famous noodle dish. Squidgy, wide flat rice noodles, wok-fried in a treacly soy sauce mixture with chile sambal, shrimp, Chinese sausage, egg and beansprouts. The magic of this dish lies in the "wok hei" (see page 27)—

a concept that holds almost legendary status in the cooking world that my mom is from. Wok hei, which translates as "breath of the wok," refers to the flames that lick up the side of the wok when frying, imparting an inimitable smokiness to the dish. It's something that can't be replicated easily and takes years to perfect, especially with the big wok burners in Melaka, my mom's hometown.

Hawker stall owners would cook this dish repeatedly, with some stalls being passed down through generations, carrying with them decades of cooking skills and passion. The result was a delicious mound of soft, smoky noodles garnished with slightly sweet cured Chinese sausage and juicy shrimp—a dish of sheer dreams. The difference for us was that we were enjoying it in Glasgow, sitting around that small table with the plastic tablecloth, approximately 6,726 miles away from the 100-degree heat of Melaka, where our family resides. The juxtaposition was immense.

My mom's ability to cook and transport you to another place through her food was my initial guide to connecting with Malaysia. When I think about the dish that first introduced me to my heritage, it was Big Fat Noodles. It's become so important to me because my mom made it for me from such a young age. Even the name she gave it was pronounceable for a child. It may seem insignificant to others, but I see it as my mom's way of introducing me to my culture in a way I could understand.

Food has the power to initiate conversation. The nuanced relationship between emotion and food is such a tie when it comes to identifying where you feel like you come from. Scientifically, it's been proven that smell and flavor are the biggest trigger to memory in the brain; there is a true reason for the romanticized feeling of food transporting you to where you aren't. And when we have food in front of us, we tend to slow down and become more relaxed. It doesn't matter what I'm doing, it makes me feel more mindful. Perhaps this feeling extends from my family's link to Buddhism—most of my mom's side is Buddhist. Sitting at the table to eat always makes me pause and politely check in with my organs, brain and mood to assess whether they need sustenance. Do you all require food?

On top of mealtimes being a prompt to check in on my own wellbeing, I find food so symbolic of traditions, culture and identity. I've made it my life's mission to bring together seemingly disparate ingredients to create dishes that are more magical as a whole, greater than the sum of their parts. The alchemy of cooking is combining different ingredients to create a unique bowl of joy. Perhaps this has developed in parallel to my search to understand my own identity. The comfort I've drawn from amalgamating knowledge of the different cultures and cuisines from which I draw my heritage has culminated in an acceptance of something new. And perhaps it doesn't follow the strict rules of the singular culinary identity of each place, but the joy in finding new flavors and gaining an acceptance of sitting somewhere in the middle, has given me a better understanding of how to fuse the knowledge of two very different places.

In recent years, I've found myself connecting with my mixed-race heritage more confidently than ever before by embracing my culture and identity via food. Surprisingly, it's through the creation of my food and the daily operations of my restaurant that I've felt this connection strengthen the most. Food holds an immense significance in defining who I am. Coming from a Malaysian-Scottish background, I've learned to nourish my soul with food and use cooking as a comforting bridge that connects me to my roots. My mom hails from Malaysia and is Nyonya, Malay Chinese, and my father is Scottish, born and raised in Glasgow.

My mom has always and will always be my pillar to feeling grounded and centered. I remember her clearly explaining my identity to me at a very young age. She was proud of it—a feeling I've always emulated from her. She would explain that our cheek bones would be higher than others, sometimes sunglasses will sit slightly differently on me, my hands would look just a little different, we don't have long slender fingers but slightly shorter, my black eyebrow hair grows in a different way from my peers at school, it grows in a slightly downward motion, but these were all part of mixed-race beauty.

Food was also so integral to her teachings. She would teach me how to listen to the sizzle of something we were cooking, how to toss pasta with chopsticks, how to make a full banquet out of leftovers and embrace our no-waste culture. Even when I was just a toddler, my mom cooked dishes that would have been challenging spice-wise had I not been introduced to them from a young age. But outside the security of my mom's home, growing up in Scotland, my appearance often drew scrutiny as people tried to determine my identity and label me. These conversations would often leave me with a simultaneous feeling of "glass half empty, glass half full." With light skin, raised cheekbones, slightly epicanthic folds in my eyelids and deep brown eyes like my mom, my appearance defies easy categorization. It has always influenced my sense of self. I experienced a feeling of "otherness" as I've grown up, but I've discovered it to be my greatest strength, being from two distinct places that have equal significance and influence on me— the "sama sama," or same-same, but different.

It has produced joyous moments, too. Over the years, I would pleasantly surprise visitors from Singapore or Malaysia when I revealed that my mother is Nyonya. We would engage in lively conversations about food, reminiscing about nostalgic dishes that connected us on a deeper level. These moments were pure bliss, a celebration of my heritage and a reminder of the little bits of humanity and common love of food that bind us.

While life has been full of love and joyful influences, the challenging experiences that I faced growing up, running businesses from a young age and learning about myself, have also shaped me, and made me keenly aware of the importance of embracing my own identity and allowing in love to nurture the sense of belonging. I have tried to reflect into my mom's matriarchal resilience in situations I have found difficult. Knowledge is power, and my mind is filled with the intellectual nuances of my Malaysian culture. I adore those nuances deeply.

"I feel that cooking is a way of strengthening oneself: not being able to feed oneself feels like a state of victimhood; being able to sustain oneself is the skill of a survivor. And I am no victim, but very much a survivor! Everyone should be, or make sure they become one."
NIGELLA LAWSON (OBSERVER FOOD MONTHLY, 2014)

These words have become my mantra, a reminder that food is more than just sustenance. It's a source of empowerment, a means to nourish not only our bodies but also our spirits. Through my journey in food, I've discovered that food has the power to heal, unite and remind us of our own resilience and identity. As I continue on this path of self-discovery, I hold onto the lessons learned from the times of love and hardship. They taught me to find comfort, resilience and knowledge within the realms of food. And what I want to celebrate within each of these recipes is the "in-between." In 2016, I embarked on a journey to explore who I am through food. I left my job in retail, and teaching violin and piano on the side and started a small street-food stall in Glasgow on a very limited budget. My first one was extremely hawker like, it was down an alley in the center of Glasgow. It would be here that I would feel the warmth and welcoming nature of Glasgow's hospitality industry. Supported by so many, and I was only 25, I felt like I was on the right path. Reflective of my love of night markets in Malaysia, I cooked some classic dishes like ayam goreng (fried chicken), sate ayam (chicken satay), nasi goreng (fried rice), or with a twist like sesame shrimp toast using a local delicacy—Scottish, thick-cut Mothers Pride bread. (It works perfectly, by the way, as the slightly burned crust goes so well with the sweet, eggy shrimp.) The stall became an instant hit and we were soon being asked to cater events, festivals and even cook at weddings. Who knew there would be an appetite for Malaysian food in my hometown? It would also be here that I would meet some of the best friends I could have asked for, they ran the roast chicken stall right beside me. Ilona and Dave, in this little life I lead it turns out they'll support me for ten years following that point. Going on trips together, trying all of my dishes, coming to all of my pop ups and we have since grown our little group of friends. It felt like in hindsight, that year was one of the most important of my life.

The truth is, it took me at least six years to finalize the concept for my first book. The initial idea was to create a traditional Malaysian cookbook, brimming with recipes for pastes made from scratch and classic Nyonya dishes. Perhaps that will come one day. But as time passed, I grew. When I first thought about writing a book, I was 26, but now, in my 30s, my understanding of who I am has evolved. The acceptance of being "sama sama"—the same-same from two different places—brings me immense comfort, and this book reflects that identity.

One thing that won't change is that this will always be book number one (and hopefully the first of many) and there's something significant about the first book. For someone who wasn't particularly academically strong at school, this is a substantial task, so it really did take a few years to carefully conceptualize exactly what I want to put out into the world. I know I'm never going to win the masses by trying to sound like a worldly, trained intellect, but I do know exactly how to explain food from the heart.

When I picture how I want people use this book, I want it to be a book that you share with your friends to make Friday night girl-dinners, one stained with rings of red wine from a memorable dinner party. I want my mom and dad to pick it up and recognize bits of themselves in it. I want it to reach someone who wants to cook to look after themselves. Or for it to be in Malaysia and respectfully show a different take on food I admire and love, from the bonny banks of Scotland.

I've poured love into the words, laughed at memories, and felt pure joy knowing I have been my authentic self, even including some silliness every few pages. I've shed happy tears while exploring these memories and essays, and I've lovingly tested these recipes time and again in my rented kitchen, with its mismatched plates, pots and pans (this is the stage I'm at, documented for future me, who might one day have matching pots and pans—one can dream). I want you to feel as comfortable as I do with adjusting the quantities to suit your own taste, as if you're sitting in the kitchen with me, sipping a cup of tea or a glass of wine while I explain the dish. You might taste it and add a bit more salt or sugar to your liking. In my heart, I know this is the most authentic book I could create.

In writing this book, I've realized I'm fully committed to the idea that my knowledge will never be perfect, but I'm entirely willing to learn and share the wisdom I've gained so far. I rather enjoy the feeling of being a novice; it's not my style to be a big fish in a small pond, but rather a small fish in a big pond, always with more to explore.

One thing I will certainly not do is gatekeep. I do not believe in withholding knowledge; I think it's detrimental to society to hoard valuable teachings. I'll never pretend to be an expert because I'm not. What I am certain of, however, is that with this book, I want to share the generational joy that my ancestors found in food.

This book shares recipes and tells the stories of moments that have strengthened my sense of self through food. I believe that in this modern era of constant movement and travel, this notion will resonate with many. I want to broaden your ideas of "authenticity," to encourage you to cook in a way that nourishes both your body and soul, and to embrace sustainability. This book acknowledges that to accept ourselves, we must continually expand our boundaries in learning and knowledge about food and culture. So I'll start this book by showing my gratitude for embracing the "Sama Sama," or "same-same" identity.

Terima Kasih—*Thank you*
Sama Sama—*You're welcome/same-same*

In the Middle

authentically in-between
every dish you make

it's in there—
a pinch of matriarchal know-how

a dash of ancestral connection
when you chop the greens
flip the wok
circle the spurtle in the bubbling pot

there it is—
centuries of experience

generations of trial and error
when you serve the dish
you tell the stories of those who came before
great great granny who stoked the fires
great baa baa who kept soil from home in his pockets
each recipe is a seed from your family
tree—a message on a plate

SEAN WAI KEUNG

My thoughts on what it's like to be mixed will forever change because times and opinions change. It's important to continually reassess how you feel about things as the world redraws the boundaries of society... and that's a good thing. With the world in a ceaseless bout of change, my understanding of what it means to be a mixed-race person will transform alongside it. These days, I think of my identity with a sense of assuredness, but it's not always been that way. Moments of uncertainty have shaped me, but I've learned to view life through a lens of abundance, not scarcity, constantly evaluating and appreciating the value of my dual heritage.

Opening my first restaurant was a significant moment when I realized that I didn't want to be categorized, in the sense of whether the dishes I served were "authentic" or "inauthentic." My dishes were unabashedly Asian in parts, steeped in the authentic aromas of pungent shrimp paste and the comfort of store-bought, white bread kaya toast, while other dishes were simply things my mom and I had made up along the years, such as sambal halloumi and char siu sausage rolls. Certain dishes get tarred with the description "fusion," a term that became a dirty word at some point in the noughties, so let's call them "authentically in-between."

I was challenged on the inclusion of certain dishes on my menu, but I regarded them as opportunities to share the profound story of Malaysia's complex and colonial past and educate diners on its enduring impact on our food culture to this day. When a white customer questioned the quintessential ingredient in our char kuay teow, asking if we made our own noodles, I said no as we were lacking the space and equipment needed to make fresh, thick kuay teow (rice noodles). He was appalled and walked out of the restaurant in a dramatic fashion for all of my team and other customers to see. I remember putting on a jovial smile and trying to giggle it off. It would soon be followed by a negative one-star review of the restaurant explaining how we weren't authentic. "If pasta restaurants can do it, why can't you?" he exclaimed as he walked out of the door. Then there was the customer who hated our kung pao (stir-fried chicken) because we used Sichuan peppercorns, which is authentic to the dish, but it wasn't the version of the dish that they knew from British-Chinese takeout places. The frustrations of managing customers' expectations while serving food from a culture unfamiliar to them is difficult to explain. Swapping elements in certain traditional dishes to adapt to the place you inhabit, while maintaining the dish's original silhouette, speaks of the shared histories that flavor our identity and reflect the tapestry of migration. I've had some difficult times with this concept, with complex arguments forming in my mind. Why does Western culture expect us to cook with the exact ingredients from our homelands, thousands of miles away, in order to be deemed "authentic"?

These vignettes of my restaurant life are not kept as scars but as reminders of the power of perception and resilience. Nowadays, the culinary landscape has shifted to be more inclusive and appreciative of global cuisines, yet there remains room to gently correct the missteps—the misuse of the term "jerk" to describe rice dishes, and the mislabeling of supermarket sandwiches as "laksa." My motto is to shrug it off and choose to engage rather than cancel, to educate rather than dismiss, to find strength in patience and understanding.

My identity is often questioned with the well-meaning but tired inquiry, "But where are you *really* from?" In Malaysia, I stand out with my Western features, while in Scotland, my Asian heritage comes into focus. These questions have become a part of my narrative, one that I now embrace with confidence. I often think that the hybrid language, Manglish, a delightful blend of Malaysian and English, has become a linguistic sanctuary that bridges my two worlds with affectionate ease. Despite the occasional sense of diaspora and displacement, I have arrived at a profound truth: I am whole precisely because I embody halves of two worlds equally. There is empowerment in being the observer, in constantly learning and growing from the side lines. My mixed-race friends and

I share this unique journey, our appearance prompting curious glances as we defy easy categorization. I've learned to embrace each quizzical look and each attempt to place me in a box with the knowledge that I represent so much more, along with so many of us in the world. If we trace back our bloodline roots, which many are starting to do with online DNA kits, people find themselves connected to a plethora of places. We are all mixed.

My story is not easily read from my appearance; I am a living, breathing anthology of experiences that defies simple understanding. And I continually reassess. Whether I'm walking the streets of Glasgow or navigating the hawker stalls in Melaka, I am both. When I am cooking a mix of two cultures, I am both.

The phrase "Don't Yuck My Yum," coined by @doobydobap, a brilliant TikToker from Korea, is a rallying cry for culinary inclusivity, to never grimace at someone else's inner food identity. It resonates deeply with me. Every dish has a unique story, and this phrase acts as a reminder of the emotional connections food can forge. "Don't Yuck My Yum" should be taught from school age, with parents, caregivers and teachers encouraging kids not to grimace at each other's lunch boxes.

In confronting prejudice, I've found my voice, using it to challenge misconceptions. Being mixed-race is not a static state, but rather a dynamic one, filled with the power to educate, to advocate and to connect. It has given me the fortitude to stand up for minority communities, to champion equality and to pass on a legacy of openness and strength to future generations. This is the charge I carry, the mission that fuels my passion, and the story I will continue to tell with unwavering conviction and a welcoming heart. The gateway to all of these conversations is food, and how the acceptance of many different cultures can create something beautifully harmonizing.

With embracing being mixed-race, I've allowed for substitutions in my recipes, and see pages 21 for how to further adapt my recipes with ingredients that may be more available to you. Substitutions are a necessity at times but can also be the stroke of serendipity that leads to new creations. When respectfully thought of and carried through, they can be equivalent of a stranger's smile in an unfamiliar land; a gesture of understanding, a sign that we are learning, adapting and embracing the diversity that surrounds us.

In my own journey as a mixed-race person, I've found that the meals I create and cherish are much like my identity: a blend of flavors, traditions and stories that refuse to be boxed into a single category—but respectfully they honor culture. The global movement across our plates is a mirror to the movement within our bloodlines. Here's to the dishes that speak gracefully of our past and go forth in the future with the understanding of immigration, people and culture.

Here

mine says I am here
and with me are my ancestors
who themselves are from
the snowiest mountains
the most tropical forests
the greenest fields
and the most industrial cities
please sit down
and eat with us

SEAN WAI KEUNG

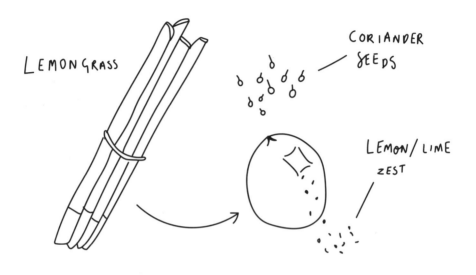
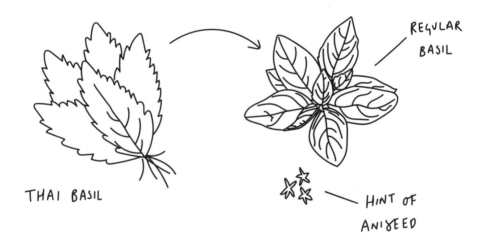

Substitutes

For me, the simple act of food shopping can be a source of endless delight. My local grocery store is a treasure trove where the thrill of the hunt is very much alive. It's where I've stumbled upon exotic hot sauces and, much to my delight, Maggi chile sauce—a taste of Malaysia right there in its aisles. In Malaysia, Maggi chile sauce proudly replaces barbecue sauce at McDonald's. It's these little finds that make my day.

In my hometown of Glasgow, nestled close to the university, the streets are lined with a vibrant population of Asian supermarkets, thanks to the influx of students from across the continent. Stepping into the local Thai market is like teleporting to Malaysia, with its fragrant incense, pungent durian and that iconic beaded doorway. It offers cute embroidered purses, kaftans and even traditional mortar and pestles that have been imported. The food shelves are a celebration of ingredients like homemade curry pastes and good-quality coconut milks, stocked with everything from fresh herbs to frozen banana leaves. The convenience of enjoying an array of Asian delights—yum cha, xiao long bao, Korean barbecue, ma la hot pot and Korean sushi—just a stone's throw away fills me with gratitude. It's awe-inspiring to reside in a neighborhood where cultural diversity doesn't just survive; it thrives. The courage of local shopkeepers has paved the way for eateries to flourish, providing us with a gateway to the whole world through dishes served on melamine plates and food that comes in rectangular boxes.

Away from these areas of cultural richness in the city, there are the mainstream supermarkets with their "world food" aisles. The primary issue with these aisles is the implicit othering it represents. By segregating items from various cultures into one condensed section, there's an unintended suggestion that these foods are somehow exotic or outside the norm of mainstream cuisine. This division can perpetuate the idea of a culinary hierarchy, where foods from non-Western cultures are seen as novelties, rather than integral parts of the global food landscape. Moreover, the selection within these aisles can sometimes lack depth and authenticity. The limited shelf space means only a handful of items from each culture can be represented, often leading to a superficial portrayal of complex cuisines. The choice of products can feel tokenistic, catering more to Western palates and perceptions of what these cuisines should entail rather than offering a genuine reflection of traditional ingredients.

Despite these challenges, the presence of "world food" aisles in supermarkets is a testament to the growing interest in and appreciation of global cuisines. The solution might not be to eliminate these sections but to rethink how we categorise and present foods from different cultures. Integrating these ingredients throughout the store, alongside their more familiar counterparts, could encourage a more inclusive and exploratory approach to cooking and eating. It could foster a deeper understanding and appreciation of the diversity that enriches the global culinary landscape.

In essence, while these aisles attempt to bring the world's pantry to our doorstep, they also open up a conversation about how we value, represent and engage with the myriad cultures that make up our community. It's a reminder that food is a powerful medium for connection and understanding, deserving of thoughtful representation and accessibility. These aisles provide an easy, accessible way for us to obtain certain ingredients, which is sometimes a joy, but the stock is scattered and limited. As a mixed person who often seeks comfort in food, thousands of miles away from Malaysia, while facing the realities of import politics and the critical issue of food miles on our climate, I'm conscious that I can't always indulge in the luxury of authentic Malaysian ingredients and at times will have to hunt for items. Demand for exotic ingredients throughout the year is unsustainable, but this doesn't mean we must sacrifice our culinary heritage.

As I've noted on page 14, authenticity in cooking is often debated, with some chefs insisting on traditional ingredients as the only path to "real" cuisine. But what's truly authentic about importing fresh durians regularly at the expense of our planet? My mother's ingenuity in substituting ingredients when she first arrived in the UK led to a new, equally delectable range of mish-mash cuisine. These dishes may not mirror Malaysia's flavors exactly, but they carry the essence and adaptability of our culture. Innovation is born from necessity, and some of the finest dishes have been conceived through substitution. What's more authentic than making the most of what's available to us?

We live in an ever-changing world—the winds shift in Glasgow, the heat intensifies in Malaysia—and our culinary practices must evolve in tandem. To remain unyielding in our methods is to risk losing the very essence of our cooking. Adaptability is the key to sustainability and the preservation of our skills. No matter how traditional the recipe, we can celebrate its origins by adapting the recipe to our climate, our ingredients, our unique cultural landscape. It's not about authenticity (or certainly not in the gatekeeping way we often use that word); it's about the homage we pay to traditional flavors while embracing the ingredients that are available to us.

Embracing this philosophy in our kitchens doesn't diminish the value of traditional dishes; it enriches them. It allows us to honor our roots while being mindful stewards of the world we inhabit. This mindset is more than a cooking lesson; it's a life lesson. It encourages us to cherish the past and innovate for the future, ensuring that our culinary heritage continues to evolve, just as we do.

I've listed some simple swaps opposite. These ingredients are not an exact replacement, they will not taste precisely the same as the missing ingredients, but they will respectfully point the dish in the right direction.

Some Useful Substitutes

INGREDIENT	HOW TO SUBSTITUTE
1 lemongrass stalk	Zest of ½ lemon or lime + 1 tsp coriander seeds
2 tbsp hoisin sauce	1 tbsp barbecue sauce + 1 tsp dark soy sauce + 1 tbsp light soy sauce + 1 tsp honey
2 tbsp fish sauce	1 tsp light soy sauce + 1 tsp Worcestershire sauce + salt (or roasted canned anchovies with added water)
1 tbsp belacan	1¾ oz (50 g) canned anchovies roasted until dry and blended to a paste
1 tbsp candlenuts	1 tbsp macadamia nuts
2 tbsp Malaysian curry powder	1 tbsp medium curry powder + 5 green cardamom pods + 1 tsp fennel seeds + 1 tsp chile powder + 1 tsp ground cinnamon
Thai basil	Regular basil + a hint of aniseed (either star anise, fennel seeds or cloves)
Soy cooking caramel	1 tsp cornstarch + 2 tbsp hot water + 2 tbsp dark soy sauce + a pinch of salt + a pinch of MSG
Rice wine vinegar	White wine vinegar or apple cider vinegar + a pinch of sugar

A Glossary of Food Terms

PHRASE	MEANING	NOTES
Apam balik	Peanut pancakes	Originated in Malaysia and Indonesia
Ayam *"i-am"*	Chicken	Malaysian/Indonesian term for chicken (ayam goreng/fried chicken)
Baba (male) Nyonya (female)	Malaysian-Chinese man or woman	Malaysian Singapore Peranakans trace their origins to fifteenth-century Melaka, where their ancestors were thought to be Chinese traders who married local women. Peranakan men are known as Baba, while the women are known as Nonya (or Nyonya). Nyonya cooking embodies different ingredients, cooking techniques and spices that are seen throughout many cuisines in Malaysia—Portuguese, Indian and Chinese.
Babi/ Daging babi	Pork	Malaysian term
Bakwan jagung	Sweetcorn fritters	Delicious street food snack, best eaten with a sauce with heat
Bee/Mee hoon	Thin rice noodles	Used in noodle salads (usually gluten free)
Belacan *"bell-achan"*	Dried shrimp paste	Fermented and dried shrimp paste, commonly used in curry pastes, sambals and stir fries. It has a salty umami flavor (not usually gluten free).

Candlenuts	A waxy nut frequently used in curry paste	Called candlenuts due to their high fat content—they can light like a waxy candle. Macadamia nuts are a great substitute here.
Char kuay teow	Smoky fried flat noodle dish	One of Malaysia's best-known noodle dishes. It is usually made with shrimp, Chinese sausage and beansprouts.
Chinkiang vinegar	Black soy and malt vinegar (aka black vinegar)	Frequently used in dumpling vinegar (not usually gluten free)
Fish sauce	—	Fermented anchovies turned into a pungent-smelling sauce full of flavor
Goreng	Fried	Malaysian/Indonesian term for "fried" (nasi goreng/fried rice and mee goreng/fried noodles)
Gula melaka	Palm sugar from Melaka	A treacly palm sugar originating from Melaka (please note: palm sugar has nothing to do with palm oil and doesn't have the same detrimental impact on the environment)
Ho fun *"ho fan"*	Wide, flat rice noodles	Used in the famous Malaysian dish char kuay teow (usually gluten free)
Kari	Curry	Malaysian/Indonesian term
Kecap manis *"ketchap man-ease"*	Sweetened, thickened soy sauce	Excellent for wok frying and adds a treacly, sweet and salty flavor

Kerabu	Salad flavored with chiles and garlic	Malaysian term. This can be made in many different ways, but usually it consists of cucumber and pineapple.
Kopi	Coffee	General term for black coffee (there are lots of different types of coffee)
Laksa	Malaysian and Singaporean dish of spicy fragrant soup with noodles	There are so many different types here, but generally we are looking at a fragrant noodle soup with different protein and vegetable toppings
Limau *"lee-m-ow"*	Lime	Malaysian/Indonesian term
Makan, Makan	"Eat, Eat"	Malaysian/Singaporian/Indonesian way of instructing everyone to start eating at the beginning of a meal. The equivalent of "bon appetit!"
Mee	Noodles	Malaysian/Indonesian general term for egg and wheat noodles
MSG	Monosodium glutamate	Naturally occurring in Parmesan, tomatoes, etc. MSG powder is a manufactured flavoring that was developed in Japan.
Nasi	Rice	Malaysian/Indonesian term
Nyonya	—	*see* "Baba"
Rempah	Spice paste	Malaysian/Indonesian term. Used in curries, usually consists of shallots, garlic, chiles, lemongrass, galangal and more.

Sambal	Chile paste or condiment	Malaysian/Indonesian term. Chile paste that comes in various forms and can be cooked in a dish or served as an accompaniment. Primarily made of shallots, garlic and chiles, then flavored with different ingredients such as dried shrimp, sugar, anchovies, etc.
Sate/Satay	Barbecued meat or veggies on a skewer	Not to be confused with peanut sauce, satay refers to the skewer
Sichuan/ Szechuan	A province of China famous for a peppercorn that is numbing in flavor	Both spellings are correct. Sichuan peppercorns are spicy and a very unique flavor to that province of China.
Sotong	Squid	Malaysian/Indonesian term
Soy sauce (light and dark)	—	Light soy sauce should be used for flavorings, dips and cooking. Dark soy sauce should be used in smaller amounts for deeper color and a saltier flavor. It's richer than light soy and very dark brown in color. Neither are usually gluten free as the soy beans are fermented with wheat, therefore not suitable for coeliacs or gluten-free diets unless GF is specified on the bottle.
Tamari	A type of Japanese soy sauce similar to light soy	Please note, it is not always gluten free, the bottle must specify that it is GF for it to be suitable for coeliacs or gluten-free diets
Udang *"ooo-dang"*	Shrimp	Malaysian/Indonesian term

Before You Begin...

RICE

Rice often intimidates people when they're cooking it at home. I see people opting for microwaveable rice bags from the supermarket, which are fine in moments of desperation but cooking your own simply tastes better. There are many different types of rice—jasmine, brown, basmati, sticky and a host of others—and it's important to know the different methods for each type. I usually go for a good-quality triple "A" jasmine rice—it makes the world of difference—from my local Asian grocery store as it's usually cheaper when bought in bulk.

Regardless of the variety, the most important (and often overlooked) part of the rice-cooking process is that the grains must be rinsed before being cooked. This is essential for achieving a fluffy finish. I use the "claw" method. Hold your hand in a rigid claw shape, keeping it really strong and sturdy. Place the rice in a large bowl, cover with cold water and use your claw to stir through the rice—this will ensure that the grains don't break. Scrunching or squeezing the rice is a common mistake which can lead to breakages—as a result, some parts of the rice will cook quicker than others, leaving you with an unwelcome sludge. Drain the rinsed rice.

RICE TYPE	RATIO OF RICE TO WATER (CUPS)
Jasmine rice	1:1½
Basmati rice	1:1½
Sushi rice	1:1⅓
Brown/Long grain rice	1:1¾

Microwave method

When she moved here in the 1970's, my mom used to make rice from raw in the microwave. It's still one of my favorite ways to cook rice. Begin by thoroughly rinsing the rice using the claw method, repeating a few times until the water is no longer cloudy, then drain. Add the correct ratio of cold water to rice using the table above. For one cup of rice, microwave on full power for about 15 minutes in a microwave-safe bowl; for every additional cup add 5 minutes. Once all of the water has been absorbed, put a microwave-safe plate on top of the bowl to cover completely, then pop it back in and microwave for another 2–3 minutes. This will result in perfect fluffy rice. The microwave is quite forgiving, so if you find it's not cooked, return to the microwave for a few more minutes.

Rice cooker method
Transfer the rinsed, drained rice to your rice cooker. Add the correct ratio of cold water to rice using the table opposite. Gently stir the rice and turn the cooker on. Once the timer has finished, allow the rice to sit and steam inside the cooker for 5–10 minutes. A good indication that your rice is ready is when the grains on top are sticking up. When ready, use a large fork to gently fluff the rice from the bottom up. Make sure the grains are separated and serve immediately.

Stovetop method
Transfer the rinsed, drained rice to a medium pot with a lid. Add the correct ratio of cold water to rice using the table opposite. Gently stir the rice and bring to a boil. Stir again, reduce the heat to the lowest setting and cover with a lid. Simmer for about 15 minutes, depending on how much rice you're cooking. Do not lift the lid during this period as it will cause the rice to cook unevenly. There should be no water left at the end of the cooking time and the grains should be slightly tender. Take the pot off the heat and let the rice sit, uncovered, for a few minutes to cool slightly. Using a large fork, gently fluff the rice from the bottom up. Make sure the grains are separated and serve immediately.

If you have rice left over, allow it to cool completely to room temperature (try and do this within one hour or as quickly as you can). Transfer the rice to a container, cover and store in the fridge. Cooked rice must only be reheated once and until piping hot.

WOK HEI

Wok hei is achieved in restaurants and at hawker stalls by the use of a wok burner. The edges of the wok hit the flames of the burner, which sets any of the fats or liquids alight to create a distinct, smoky flavor within the dish. Such an effect is difficult to achieve in a domestic setting as gas burners tend to be flat, making it harder for the flame to reach the top of the wok. And not everyone has a wok burner in their kitchen.

However, through years of experimentation and determination, I've found a way to get that same flavor, even with an induction stovetop. In the absence of a flame, it's all about creating caramelization at the bottom of the pot to get the flavor we're after. Simply by leaving the ingredients in your pan for a couple of seconds longer than usual will give its contents a charred, smoky flavor. It's all about having the confidence to over-fry when using a wok. Using a wooden spatula, you can also carefully scrape the caramelized bits of char that remain into the dish. This will make some of the simplest dishes extremely flavorful. Alternatively, a blowtorch could be used to set any of the fats or alcoholic liquids within the wok ablaze. Extreme caution should be used if you go down this route, but it's a sure-fire way to achieve that elusive, smoky flavor.

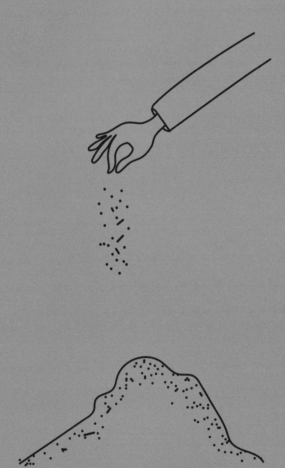

AGAK-AGAK

Your Agak

I've always said there are two types of cooks in this world. Cook Number One will open up a recipe book and meticulously follow every single instruction to the letter: painstakingly measuring out each ingredient by the teaspoon and gram, methodically working through every technique in order, reading out and executing each line as though it is the instruction pamphlet for a complex piece of flatpack furniture. Cook Number Two will open up a recipe book, quickly glance over the ingredients, scan the method, close the book, and then follow an interpretation of the recipe that they have held in their head. Depending on which camp you fall into, you'll likely agree or disagree with one or the other approaches, and there are positives and negatives to both.

Cook Number One provides an excellent demonstration of restraint, taking clear guidance and committing to the act of learning from someone else's expertise. They will turn out a beautiful dish by following the recipe. However, they may not fully learn the extent of their own palate in terms of seasoning; if everything is followed to a tee, you're cooking a dish how someone else wants it to be cooked. Your creative flare may be kept at bay, and you're only as good as your teacher. On the flip side, Cook Number Two fosters confidence in their own ability and shows creative flare, gets to know the flavors and ingredients on the page, doesn't need to measure things but is guided by their own senses… and perhaps will create something entirely new. This method also has its downfalls; it could lead to a dish being badly executed and is not a true reflection of a culture's dish.

Most recipe books will give you definitive instructions for how to do things perfectly. For baking recipes which rely on science, such as sponge cakes and pastries, they must be followed precisely. In my early years of making pastry, I made some truly unrecognizable choux buns by following my own instincts. However, some of the best dishes I've ever made have come from following my mother's sturdy guidance alongside independent knowledge. Growing up, I watched my mom whizz around the kitchen with an artistry that had exactness in the outcome, but was open to deviation in the moment. She taught me that cooking is about following a method with concentration just as much as it is about experiencing the process with your senses. She would say, 'Look at the red oils that split at the top of the kari ayam (chicken curry), smell the cardamom being toasted, feel the heat from the wok at different points of making char kuey teow (stir-fried rice noodles).' Above all, *tasting* the dish was paramount to understanding whether we had achieved that state of utopia when you make something that is perfect for you. Recipes were fluid, guided by instinct—what we call "agak-agak"—rather than by strict measurements. That's not to say we take recipes and change them into something completely different, but rather we follow the guidance of our own senses as well as our intuition.

Me and Mom, 1997

My mother is a maestro at adjusting flavors, adding a few dashes of fish sauce here, a sprinkling of sugar there, or spicing up a curry with sambal belacan (see page 47) that we had brought home from Malaysia, in order to capture the essence of tradition while embracing the inevitable changes in ingredient quality. We never shied away from tweaking a recipe to recreate the cherished flavors of her youth in Melaka.

This journey has imparted a vital ethos: to be bold and, most importantly, *adaptable* in the kitchen. To understand that cooking is an intimate voyage and, to truly relish food, it's important to adapt to your surroundings. Every day, we are learning so much about our impact on the environment, including our diet. And with the climate changing due to global warming, I'm sure we'll see a huge change in the produce available to us over the coming decades, and so we will have to adapt. I want this cookbook to stand the test of time and so, if certain ingredients are no longer available, with a new-found culinary confidence, you'll be able to use your cook's instincts to substitute something that you think is suitable, or something that you love.

On top of everyone having different palates, our own tastes also change over the course of our lifetime. The biology of our taste buds can vary, and it's a change that profoundly affects our relationship with food. We're born with about 10,000 taste buds, which are replaced every two weeks or so. However, as we progress through our adult years, the rate of regeneration slows down and the total number of taste buds can decrease. I often think of my dad at this point—he was so incredibly open to all foods when I was a youngster, and my mom would cook the most potent of foods. With years gone by, he now has a deep-seated hatred of cumin and anything too potent or rich. Nevertheless, as a clever man and a former science teacher, he can understand his adverse reaction to these foods. The sensitivity of our taste buds also diminishes over time. This means that flavors may become less intense, and we might start to crave more strongly flavored foods, as subtler tastes become harder to detect. Our sense of smell, which is closely linked to our sense of taste, also declines with age. Since much of what we perceive as flavor comes from smell, this can significantly change the way we experience food. As a result of all these changes, over time we might find that we prefer different foods than when we were younger.

This poses so many varying factors when writing a cookbook. My initial thought was how will I teach everyone if I'm not physically in the room with them, showing how to adequately season a dish? And then came the brainwave: every single person holds the power to learn exactly the way they want it for themselves. Sensory cooking is how these recipes should be executed. And I have just as much confidence in you as I did in myself when I first started cooking. I made some pasta in tomato sauce and... Boom! I thought I was a chef because I added just the right amount of Parmesan. You, too, should feel this chef's kiss reaction when you get something spot on.

This book's purpose is to serve as your guide and to foster your palate's growth, which may change over time. The intent isn't to replicate dishes with exactitude, but to embolden you to learn as I was taught, with a degree of independence and a confidence in your taste. So, if you sense a need for more salt or less chile, trust your judgment—your "agak"—and adjust as needed. And it's wise to postpone the final seasoning until the end, especially with ingredients like soy sauce, belacan, lime juice and sugar, which develop over time. I advocate keeping a seasoning station (see page 36) at arm's reach throughout your cooking. While mastering techniques like sautéing, emulsifying, chopping and searing takes time, everyone possesses a unique palate. Begin by earmarking your favored recipes and refining them until they meet your ideal. This book is an invitation to share with me the myriad ways you've interpreted these recipes to craft your very own "agak-agak."

Incorporating sensory cooking into our repertoire enriches the entire experience. It's about more than just taste—it's about the aroma of herbs crisping in the pan, the vibrant colors of fresh produce and the tactile joy of kneading dough. It's the warmth that fills the kitchen as a loaf of bread bakes, the sizzle as spices hit hot oil, the comforting steam from a boiling pot. Cooking is a concert for the senses, where every dish is a symphony and you, the conductor, bring it to life. Let this book be your score, guiding you to create dishes that not only nourish but also delight every sense.

The Flavor Map

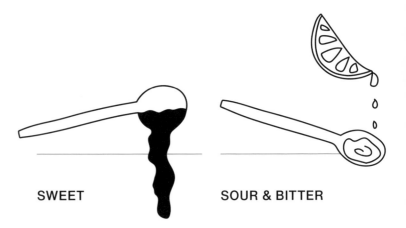

SWEET **SOUR & BITTER**

A cookbook isn't well used unless it is covered with food stains and your own scribbles. The philosophy of agak-agak means that you season until you feel it's right, and these recipes are a supportive guide to finding the flavors that best suit your tastebuds.

Use this flavor map to help you understand the different directions you can take dishes with their flavor profiles. It's all about making each recipe your own, see this as an open scrapbook to learn what you like to taste.

Palm sugar
Honey
Hoisin sauce
Kecap manis
Sweet veg:
Carrots
Peas
Fruits, etc.
Caramelization
Maillard reaction

Lime juice
Lemon juice
Vinegars:
Rice wine vinegar
White vinegar
Black vinegar
Kimchi
Salted plum
Citrus rinds
Kimchi juice
Cherries

 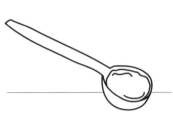 

SALTY	FATTY	UMAMI & FERMENTS
Dark soy sauce		
Light soy sauce		
Fish sauce		
Belacan		
Salt		MSG
Miso paste		Seaweed
Salted plum		Miso paste
Belacan		Kimchi
Dried anchovies	Sesame oil	Kombucha
Capers	Olive oil	Fish sauce
Bacon	Lard	Belacan
Cheese	Butter	Dried anchovies
Stock	Rendered fats	Dried mushrooms
MSG	Nuts	Roasted tomatoes
Caramelization	Ghee	Parmesan

Condiment Corner

At the heart of every kitchen where the principle of "agak-agak" is followed, there stands a seasoning sanctuary. More than a mere section of the counter, it's a treasure trove of ingredients to balance the salty, sweet, acid, heat and umami notes of a dish, all available at your fingertips. Let's call it the seasoning station, if you will. This seasoning station is the bedrock of culinary customization, the place where a dish truly becomes your own. It's more than just a collection of condiments. It's a testament to the belief that cooking should be an intimate dialogue between cook and ingredient, a conversation in which a whisper of salt or a smack of chile can transform the narrative of a meal. It's here that we find the freedom to express our culinary identity, to adjust, to experiment, to truly "agak" our way to gastronomic delight. Although I'll never be able to fully know your palate, I'll always be able to teach you how I found mine. And hopefully this will lead you on a confident path when cooking recipes from not just this book, but any recipe book you choose to learn from.

In my own restaurant, the meticulous arrangement of this seasoning station is a ritual. It's the most time-consuming aspect of our prep work, and rightly so. It's here that we lay out an array of condiments, salts and spices, each component awaiting its call to the stage. It's a place of reverence, where we pay homage to the heritage of "agak-agak." It's where you'll find bottles of fish sauce, soy sauce and hoisin sauce alongside jars of sambal, pinches of salt and dashes of sugar. The tang of rice vinegar, the nuttiness of sesame oil and the rich depth of oyster sauce stand ready to elevate a dish from the mundane to the sublime. And let's not forget the spicy kick of gochujang or the earthy punch of miso paste, or the stinky but blissful belacan (shrimp paste). So, let's delve into this section with the understanding that while recipes provide a road map for the direction of the dish, the seasoning station is your compass—an instrument of personal precision in your own kitchen.

In some recipes in this book, I've included guidance on what you might reach for from your seasoning station to enhance the dish, hoping to eventually encourage you to follow your instincts and individual palate when cooking.

BASIC SAUCE RECIPES IN THIS SECTION ARE:

Salad Dressing (page 39)
Base Curry Paste (page 42)
Master Wok Sauce (page 43)
Sweet Dim Sum Dipping Sauce (page 44)
Simple Sambal (page 45)
Sambal Oelek (page 46)
Sambal Belacan (page 47)
Green Chile Chutney (page 48)
Sweet Chile Sauce (page 49)
Julie's Kopitiam Chile Oil (page 50)
Peanut Sauce (page 52)
Black Tahini Dressing (page 53)

SEASON THE DISH UNTIL THE GHOST OF OUR ANCESTORS TELLS YOU TO STOP

KEVIN TAN

SALAD DRESSING
TUNING INTO YOUR AGAK AGAK

Let's kick things off with something simple: a salad dressing. But first, I'm going to talk to you about ice cream. That's right. You know when you've sat with an ice cream for slightly too long and it's turned a bit liquidy? Well, you may have noticed there's a stark difference in flavor between the first bite of the frozen ice cream and the last spoonful when it's melted. That's because in its original frozen form, the ice cream tastes less sweet, but when it's slightly warmer, the sugar becomes more apparent to our taste buds. It's the easiest analogy to understand because we've all been there and it gives an indication of how we taste—it's something we can bear in mind when cooking.

This recipe isn't just about combining ingredients to make a dressing; it's where you start to get a feel for your own "agak-agak" approach, it's your first step in learning about what tastes good to you. I've given a basic recipe below, but that's just a starting point. Use this dressing to identify your own preferences. Do you like your dressing to taste saltier, sweeter, or with more of a kick? This point leads me to the chiles themselves; look at the inside to see how many seeds are there, the more seeds, the hotter the chile will be. That's why putting an exact quantity on chiles in recipes can cause a bit of variance in the outcome of the recipe. Take each recipe to the heat you like it, but look at each of the chiles you buy to get more of a control on the heat. As you mix in the different elements, taste the dressing and think about how each addition changes the overall flavor. And, of course, observe the difference in taste when the dressing is hot versus when it's cold. It's all about finding what works for you, and this recipe is a tool for doing just that. It's more than the first recipe of a cookbook—it's your hands-on introduction to figuring out what you love in the food you make.

MAKES 1 BOTTLE

1 cup (90 g) white sugar
scant ½ cup (100 ml) boiling water
about ½ cup (135 ml) fish sauce
2 tsp salt
1½ tsp MSG (optional)
Juice of 6 limes
3–6 fresh long red chiles, deseeded (depending on how hot you like it, and how many seeds are inside the chiles) and very finely chopped

Place the sugar in a large heatproof bowl. Pour in the boiling water and stir briskly until all the sugar crystals have completely dissolved. This creates a base sugar syrup and ensures there are no gritty bits in the dressing.

Stir the fish sauce, salt, MSG and lime juice into the sugar syrup. The boiling water tempers the strong aroma and taste of the fish sauce, making it more palatable.

Add the finely chopped chiles to the bowl, stirring continuously to let the heat distribute evenly throughout.

SALTY

Light soy sauce
Fish sauce
Tamari

FATTY

Sesame oil
Canola oil
Coconut oil

SWEET

Palm sugar
Regular sugar
Honey
Maple syrup

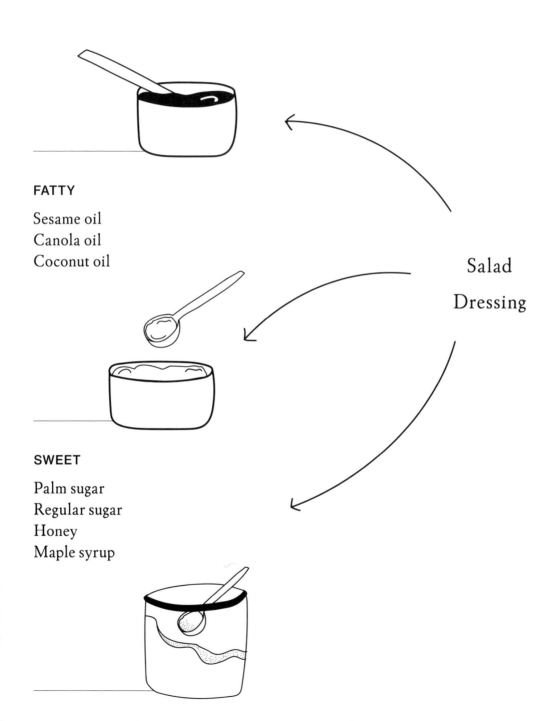

Salad Dressing

HEAT

Fresh red chile
Dried chile
Ginger

SOUR

Lime juice
Vinegar
Kimchi juice (ferment)

This is where you figure out your own palate. Balance out the dressing to your taste using something from each section.

TEMPERATURE

How were the flavors when the liquid was hot?

How were the flavors when the liquid was cold?

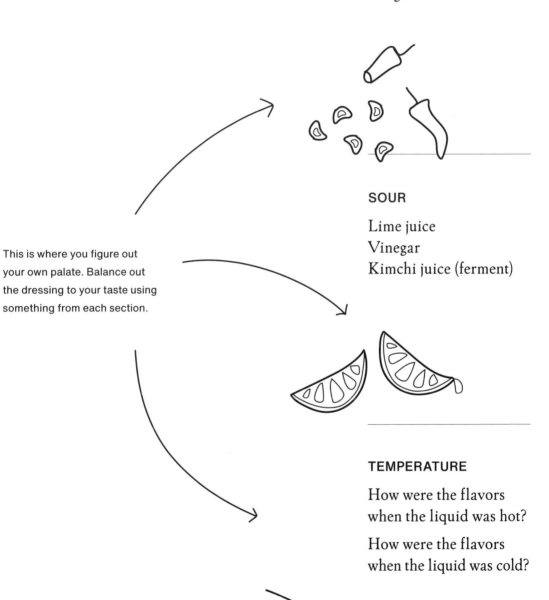

BASE CURRY PASTE

Making curry paste is famously labor-intensive, but it isn't difficult—there's a difference between difficult recipes and time-consuming recipes. I've tried to keep things simple here; I haven't suggested grinding the paste by hand, because most people I know don't have the time, so you can use a blender instead. This recipe intentionally makes a large quantity to avoid having to prepare it every time. When making curry paste, I like to prepare a large batch and freeze it divided into small portions, similar in size to ice cubes, to use as and when needed. This recipe should make a batch of about 20 cubes. Use the basic rule of one curry paste cube per person when cooking a dish.

In my restaurants, we spend most Mondays making curry paste. We peel shallots, ginger, galangal and garlic, play some great songs, enjoy lots of tea. It can be a fun activity if you approach it with the right mindset. The song I listen to most while making curry paste is Angie Stone's "Wish I Didn't Miss You." I suggest adding it to your cooking playlist to turn your kitchen into a noughties' curry disco, and I promise you a feeling of smugness with the knowledge that you'll have enough curry paste to see you through lots of meals.

MAKES 1 JAR

1 tbsp belacan (for a vegan version, replace with 1 tsp white miso paste mixed with 1 tsp Lao Gan Ma black bean chile sauce)
12 oz (350 g) shallots, peeled
1¾ oz (50 g) fresh turmeric
4–5 lemongrass stalks, cleaned and trimmed
1¾ oz (50 g) galangal, peeled
1¾ oz (50 g) ginger, peeled
1 head garlic, cloves peeled
1 fresh long red chile, deseeded
20 dried red chiles, soaked in warm water for 20 minutes, drained and deseeded
scant ½ cup (100 ml) vegetable oil, plus extra if needed

Begin by heating a dry pan over medium heat. Add the belacan and toast it until it's very bronzed on all sides. (The toastier the better in this situation as it enhances the flavor of the paste.)

Roughly chop all of the ingredients (except the oil) into small chunks—they need to be small enough to go through your blender. Add the toasted belacan to the blender, too. Blend the curry paste to a super-fine texture—if it helps, work in batches and add a little water to assist the blender. If the curry paste isn't completely smooth at this stage, don't worry—it can be blended again in the curry using a handheld immersion blender.

Once everything has been finely ground, put the vegetable oil in a wide, nonstick pan that won't discolor from the turmeric. (Using a wider pan gives a greater surface area for frying off the paste and allows it to caramelize a lot more quickly.) Allow the oil to reach medium-low heat.

Once the oil is hot enough, add the curry paste to the pan. Continuously moving it around, fry until fragrant. Add a little more vegetable oil whenever necessary—this needs to be a super-oily paste. Once fried, cool the paste, put it into ice-cube trays, freeze, then transfer to a freezer-proof container to use as needed (defrost before using).

MASTER WOK SAUCE

I may be about to give away one of the industry secrets, but in most Asian restaurants (including my own), we have a secret weapon that ensures every wok dish served is bursting with flavor: our homemade master wok sauce. Define wok sauce, you say. It's a base sauce that balances sugar, soy, sesame and saltiness, which is used to stir-fry noodles, rice and veggies. It simplifies the cooking process without sacrificing depth of flavor… and it's adaptable, too. That base sauce can be built upon with different flavors—chile, garlic, Sichuan pepper, etc.—depending on what dish you're making. It's a fundamental recipe that captures the essence of wok cooking and is the backbone of our stir-fry dishes, a reliable base that guarantees a delicious result every time.

This wok sauce is an indispensable kitchen ally. It's what I reach for to ensure my food carries that signature taste. And now, you can bring that same assurance into your home cooking. This recipe makes a big batch and the sauce lasts for up to a month. Keep any old squeezy sriracha bottles to store some of this wok sauce by your stove—it's like having a cooking safety net that will give you ultimate smugness every time. It means that no matter what you're stir-frying—vegetables, meat or noodles—you're just a skoosh away from a perfectly balanced dish.

MAKES 1 BOTTLE

⅓ cup (75 g) white sugar
3 tsp MSG
5 tbsp rice wine vinegar
1¼ cups (300 ml) light soy sauce
scant ½ cup (100 ml) dark soy sauce
3½ tbsp sesame oil

Begin by combining the sugar, MSG and vinegar in a bowl, whisking until all the sugar crystals have completely dissolved.

Next, add both the light and dark soy sauces to the bowl and stir until everything has mingled.

Once it's all well blended, stir in the sesame oil.

Transfer the sauce to a sealed sterilized jar or squeezy bottle and give it a shake. This will keep for up to a month at room temperature.

SWEET DIM SUM DIPPING SAUCE

This dipping sauce is usually served with cheung fun (rice noodle rolls) at dim sum restaurants, but I think it's the perfect accompaniment for any grilled vegetables, meat or seafood. If you have spring rolls in the freezer and want a fresh sauce to go with them, this is your go-to dipping sauce.

MAKES 1 JAR

⅓ cup (75 g) white sugar
¾ cup (180 ml) boiling water
6 tbsp light soy sauce
3 tbsp dark soy sauce
¼ cup (60 ml) oyster sauce
2 tbsp sesame oil

Place the sugar in a large heatproof bowl. Pour in the boiling water and stir briskly until all the sugar crystals have completely dissolved. (This creates a base sugar syrup and ensures there are no gritty bits in the sauce.)

Add all the remaining ingredients to the bowl with the sugar syrup and stir together to ensure everything is well combined. Serve.

SIMPLE SAMBAL

I pretty much always have this sambal in my fridge. I eat it with nasi goreng, meat, seafood, clams and even scrambled eggs in the morning. For some people, a hot sauce is essential, which I completely understand. This is my version of that. To make a vegan version for a friend, I substitute the belacan for miso paste and black bean chile sauce, or miso paste with a few dashes of vegan "fish" sauce. You can season this sambal to suit your own taste. And it keeps really well, so batch-cook away.

MAKES 1 JAR

1¾ oz (50 g) dried red chiles
1 thumb-sized piece of belacan (for a vegan version, replace with 1 tsp miso paste mixed with 1 tsp Lao Gan Ma black bean chile sauce)
½ onion, peeled and chopped
4 garlic cloves, peeled and chopped
1 in (3 cm) piece of ginger, peeled and chopped
Vegetable oil, for frying
1 tbsp lemon juice, or to taste
3 tbsp coconut sugar (or any white sugar), or to taste
1 tsp salt, or to taste

Begin by soaking the dried red chiles in warm water until they soften, which usually takes 20–30 minutes. Once softened, drain the chiles and remove the seeds. (This reduces the heat level to make the sambal more palatable.) Toast the belacan in a dry pan over medium-high heat until it is fragrant.

In a blender or food processor, combine the soaked red chiles, the onion, garlic, ginger, toasted belacan and 1 cup (250 ml) of water. Blend to a fine paste. If needed, add a splash more water to assist the blender.

Heat enough vegetable oil to cover the base of a wok over medium heat. Once the oil is hot enough, carefully add the chile paste to the wok. It might splatter, so be cautious and consider using a splash guard. Cook the mixture, stirring occasionally, until it thickens and becomes fragrant, which usually takes 15–20 minutes.

Taste the sambal and adjust the seasoning with the lemon juice, sugar and salt, as needed, but be mindful that it will become sweeter once it cools down. Mix well, then continue to cook for a further 1–2 minutes.

Remove the sambal from the heat and allow it to cool to room temperature. Once cooled, transfer to an airtight container. The sambal can be stored in the fridge for up to 5 days. Alternatively, it can be frozen in portions and stored in the freezer for up to 6 months (defrost before using).

SAMBAL OELEK
THE OG CHILE PASTE

If you're a condiment queen, like me, then you need this recipe to develop a love of sambal. In the realm of Malaysian cuisine, sambal stands out as the cornerstone of flavor, and sambal oelek is where it all begins. Containing chiles and just a few other key ingredients, this straightforward chile paste is the base-level condiment from which an array of other, more complex sambals can be born.

Having a jar of sambal oelek in your kitchen is always a good idea. It's a basic building block that gives you an insight into the world of sambals. With its pure chile heat, it allows you to appreciate the depth and balance of a sambal, which make it such an indispensable part of Malaysian food culture. Whether you're using it to add a kick to your dishes or as a foundation for a more elaborate sambal, sambal oelek is, without a doubt, a quintessential element of Malaysian cooking. Hot sauces regularly take center stage on the dinner table, so it's about time sambal was a table condiment contender.

MAKES 1 JAR

3½ oz (100 g) fresh long red chiles
2 tbsp rice wine vinegar or lime juice
1 tsp salt, or to taste

Remove the stems from the chiles and roughly chop them so they fit in your blender. Blend the chiles to a coarse paste. If you're using a mortar and pestle, pound them until they are paste-like.

Add the vinegar or lime juice and salt to the chiles and blend again until combined. Transfer the paste to a sealed sterilized jar or airtight container.

If you have time, let the sambal sit for at least 24 hours before using to allow the flavors to develop. (I find that the sambal massively intensifies in flavor.) Store in the fridge and consume within a couple of days.

SAMBAL BELACAN

This is one of the best sambal recipes I've come up with to date, and trust me, I've done a lot of testing. The large quantity of garlic is necessary here, so keep patient when peeling the cloves as "jarlic" and pre-peeled garlic give a slightly acrid flavor. This sambal will help you make so many of the recipes that follow in this book, so it's well worth making a batch as it keeps for such a long time due to the high fat and sugar content.

MAKES 1 JAR

10½ oz (300 g) dried red chiles
1 tbsp belacan (for a vegan version, replace with 1 tsp white miso paste mixed with 1 tsp Lao Gan Ma black bean chile sauce)
1 fresh long red chile, deseeded and finely chopped
30 garlic cloves, peeled and chopped
3 lemongrass stalks, cleaned and trimmed
⅔ cup (150 ml) neutral oil (use an oil with a high burning temperature, such as rice bran or canola)
¼ cup (60 ml) coconut oil
⅔ cup (120 g) white sugar, or to taste
1 tsp salt, or to taste

Begin by soaking the dried red chiles in warm water until they soften, which usually takes 20–30 minutes. Once softened, drain the chiles and remove the seeds. (This reduces the heat level to make the sambal more palatable.)

Meanwhile, heat a dry pan over low heat. Add the belacan and toast until it becomes fragrant. Be cautious as it can have a strong smell. Set aside.

In a blender or food processor, combine the soaked red chiles, chopped fresh chile and garlic cloves. Finely chop the lower, softer parts of the lemongrass stalks and add those too. Blend to a fine paste. If needed, add a splash of water to assist the blender.

Heat both oils in a wok or large pan over medium heat. Once the oil is hot enough, carefully add the chile paste to the pan. It might splatter, so be cautious and consider using a splash guard. Stir in the toasted belacan and cook the mixture, stirring frequently, for about 10–15 minutes, or until the paste darkens to a ruby red color and the oil begins to separate from the mixture.

Add the sugar and salt to the paste, then continue to cook while stirring for a further 5–10 minutes. The sambal should thicken and become fragrant.

Taste the sambal and adjust the seasoning with more salt or sugar, as needed, but be mindful that the sambal will become sweeter once it cools down.

Remove the sambal from the heat and allow it to cool to room temperature. Once cooled, transfer the sambal to a sealed sterilized jar or airtight container. The sambal can be stored in the fridge for up to a month.

GREEN CHILE CHUTNEY
UNSUNG HERO OF LEFTOVERS AND VERSATILITY

This green chile chutney strikes a vibrant chord. It's a celebration of flavors, where the sharpness of the chile and the robustness of the herbs meet in a perfect green harmony. It's an unsung hero when it comes to utilising those leftover herbs that linger in the fridge, transforming them into something that zings with freshness and spice. The beauty of this green chile chutney lies in its simplicity and adaptability. This recipe is a canvas for creativity, allowing you to tweak the flavors to your heart's content. Fancy a hint of garlic? Go ahead—throw a clove into the mix to add another layer of flavor. If you prefer this chutney to be a little milder, deseed all of the chiles or at least some of them. Whether you're looking to use up those sprigs of cilantro or are simply in need of a condiment that packs a punch, this green chile chutney is sure to become a staple. This chutney isn't just a condiment; it's a multipurpose legend. For a burst of herbaceous heat, spread it generously on a sandwich, dollop it on top of crispy pakoras or stir it into creamy mayo for a dip.

MAKES 1 JAR

2 fresh long green chiles
1 fresh green bird's eye chile
1 garlic clove, peeled
A large bunch of fresh cilantro (about 3½ oz/100 g)
1 tsp cumin seeds
1 tsp coriander seeds
1 tbsp salt
2 tbsp white sugar
1 tbsp malt vinegar
2 tbsp canola oil

Roughly chop the chiles, garlic and cilantro—they need to be small enough to go through your blender.

Add all of the ingredients (except the canola oil) to the blender with 1¼ cups (300 ml) of water and blend until smooth.

Once blended, stir the canola oil into the chutney with a metal spoon. Store in an airtight jar in the fridge and consume within a few days.

SWEET CHILE SAUCE

There's something deeply satisfying about crafting your own condiments from scratch, and homemade sweet chile sauce is a testament to that. I find the store-bought ones a bit too sweet, so I've reduced the sugar in this recipe. It's another exercise in self-expression through flavor. You hold the power to dictate the sweetness and sourness, tailoring the sauce to your precise taste. It's a chance to play with the balance of sugar and vinegar until you hit that sweet spot. Not only will this sweet chile sauce become a staple in your own kitchen for its versatility and ease of creation, it will also double as a much-appreciated gift. Imagine bottling up this vibrant, glossy sauce and sharing it with friends and family. Its homemade charm and the ability to customize the flavor profile make this a must-have. So, let's dive into the world of sauce-making, where the magic of a little sweetness and a little heat come together in a personalized bottle.

MAKES 1 JAR

2/3 cup (150ml) fresh lime juice
3½ tbsp fish sauce (or light soy sauce for a vegan version)
9 oz (250 g) palm sugar, grated (or 1¼ cups light brown sugar)
6 garlic cloves, peeled and minced
4 fresh long red chiles, finely chopped
1 fresh red bird's eye chile, finely chopped
1 tbsp cornstarch, mixed with 4 tbsp water to make a paste
A handful of fresh cilantro, finely chopped

Begin by combining the lime juice, fish sauce and grated palm sugar in a saucepan with a scant 1 cup of (200 ml) water, then place over medium heat until all the sugar crystals have dissolved.

Next, add the minced garlic and chopped chiles to the pan, bring the heat right down to a low simmer and simmer for a further 5 minutes, or until the garlic isn't quite as pungent.

Gradually pour the cornstarch paste into the pan, slowly whisking it into the chile sauce until it thickens.

Let the chile sauce cool completely, then add the chopped cilantro and mix through before transferring to a sealed sterilized jar or airtight container. This can be kept in the fridge for up to a month.

JULIE'S KOPITIAM CHILE OIL

Lao Gan Ma, the queen of chile oils, whose jars grace kitchen shelves across the globe, this recipe is for you. Your iconic stare is a familiar comfort, a promise that any dish graced by the fiery touch of your hot sauce will be transformed, elevated to new heights of dizzying spice. Lao Gan Ma translates as "Old Grandmother." Tao Huabi is the woman, the titan behind that iconic stare. She began her remarkable ascent in a modest noodle shop. It was in that small eatery that Tao's culinary prowess shone, where noodles were expertly tossed in her famous chile oil. (If ever I am asked what my dream restaurant would be, that is it. And I haven't even eaten there.) Encouraged by her customers' adoration for her noodles and chile oil combinations, Tao rose from humble cook to business titan. In the 1980s, she began bottling her signature chile oil, and so Lao Gan Ma was born. It's a name that echoed her apparently loving and nurturing presence. By 1996, the Lao Gan Ma brand had established itself as a successful business with Tao at its helm. How bold and brilliant it was to have Guizhou cuisine break through as a globally recognized food product, finding its way into people's pantries internationally. I find Tao Huabi's success absolutely breathtaking, yet her story is not generally known by the shoppers I see giggling at her face on the label. When it comes to food heroes who inspire me, Tao demonstrates the power of starting something small and communicating a love language via food. Her image, which graces every bottle of Lao Gan Ma, is more than a hallmark of her stupendous cooking quality; it's a symbol of one woman's journey from a simple noodle shop to becoming a global food icon.

While researching Tao, I was led down a bit of an internet wormhole, so I began researching other well-known brand mascots, like Aunt Bessie, Captain Birdseye, Betty Crocker and Ronald McDonald. Unlike Tao, all of these characters are fictional. They were made up by corporations to lure consumers into buying their products, sometimes with sinister intentions—to promote unhealthy foods, to foster cultural homogenization and even to distract from poor product quality or ethical concerns.

It's a culinary certainty that there will always be one or two jars of Tao's brilliant, bright red chile oil in my pantry. However, even as a Lao Gan Ma devotee, I take inspiration from Tao's fiery legacy and on those tranquil Sundays, when the world slows down and the kitchen beckons, I find myself crafting my own homemade chile oils. A recipe born out of the bustling kitchen of my first little restaurant, Julie's Kopitiam, this chile oil was a hit and sold out every time. We made batch after batch, but could barely keep up with the fervent demand in the tiny space that I called my professional kitchen. Now, I'm lifting the veil on this coveted recipe, sharing its secrets for all to enjoy. I've always been a believer in the open exchange of culinary wisdom, so I've never been one to gatekeep recipes. Sharing, after all, is at the very heart of cooking. This chile oil, with its punchy, salty and sweet notes, is a knockout, a champion in the world of condiments, enhancing any and every dish it encounters.

This chile oil makes a large quantity to ensure you're never without it. Store it, treasure it, let it be your secret culinary weapon, and gift it to your loved ones. Make it uniquely yours—add belacan, add more Sichuan peppercorns, add whatever you feel you need from a chile oil. Here's to the shared love of a good chile oil. May our fridges never be without it, and may our dishes always sing with its spicy, soulful notes.

MAKES ROUGHLY 6 JARS

3½ oz (100 g) dried red chiles
½ oz (10 g) dried round red chiles
4¼ cups (1 liter) vegetable oil
10 oz (285 g) shallots, peeled and sliced into thin rounds
8 oz (225 g) garlic, peeled and finely diced
1 cup (150 g) salted roasted peanuts
Salt, to taste

FOR THE SPICE BLEND

3 star anise
2 black cardamom pods
1 green cardamom pod
1 tsp Sichuan peppercorns
4 whole cloves
1 tbsp ground white pepper
1 tbsp ground cinnamon
2 tsp ground cumin
2 tsp Chinese five-spice powder
2 tbsp mushroom bouillon powder
1 tbsp white sugar
3 tbap salt
1 tsp MSG

Begin by making the spice blend. In a coffee grinder, grind all of the whole spices to a fine powder. Combine the ground spice powder with the white pepper, cinnamon, cumin and Chinese five-spice. Stir in the bouillon powder, sugar, salt and MSG, then set aside.

Deseed half of each type of dried red chiles; do this by slicing the tops off the chiles and shaking the seeds out, this will tone down the heat intensity, so if you are particularly sensitive, then remove all of the seeds from the chiles. Once this is done, pulse all the dried chiles until they are down to the size of chile flakes.

Heat the oil in a large, heavy-based pot over medium heat. Meanwhile, line a tray with paper towels and keep a spider strainer or slotted spoon and fine sieve on hand.

Pat dry the sliced shallots with paper towels. Working in batches, carefully lower the shallots into the hot oil and fry until golden and crispy. Transfer them to the lined tray, season immediately with salt and leave to cool on the paper towels and any excess oil to drain. (You need to salt the shallots straightaway, otherwise they will not hold the grains of salt once completely cool.)

Next, fry the diced garlic in the hot oil until golden and crispy. Use a fine sieve to catch the pieces, then transfer them to the lined tray with the shallots.

Place the peanuts in a food processor or blender, then pulse until the nuts are finely chopped. Fry the chopped peanuts in the hot oil for just a few seconds.

Add the spice blend to the pan with the peanuts. Once fragrant, return the crispy shallots and garlic to the oil in the pan along with the chile flakes. Take the pan off the heat and allow the chile oil to cool.

Once completely cool, transfer the chile oil to sterilized jars or airtight containers. When stored in the fridge, this chile oil will keep for up to 3 months.

PEANUT SAUCE

This is the peanut sauce I remember from childhood, full of rich nuttiness from the peanuts and citrus fragrance from the lemongrass. There are quicker ways to make peanut sauce, and I have no judgment for using peanut butter as a shortcut. We live in a fast-paced world, and peanut butter makes a speedy yet delicious sauce. If you have the time, however, please do try making this sauce from scratch. There is also a method of deep-frying the peanuts to make the same recipe ten times more delicious. If you can spare the time and effort, heat up some oil in a saucepan and deep-fry the peanuts (skin on) until darkened and fragrant. Remove them from the oil and use these instead of dry roasted peanuts. It is laborious but delicious. I make this peanut sauce in large batches and store it in jars, so feel free to double this if you want to have a bit more on hand.

MAKES 1 JAR

1 cup (150 g) dry roasted peanuts
3½ tbsp vegetable oil
1 tbsp tamarind concentrate (or paste)
3 tbsp gula melaka palm sugar (or dark brown sugar)
1 tsp salt
1 tsp ground coriander
1 tbsp kecap manis (sweet soy sauce)

FOR THE SPICE PASTE

8 dried red chiles, soaked in warm water for 20 minutes, drained, deseeded and roughly chopped
3 garlic cloves, peeled and roughly chopped
4 shallots, peeled and roughly chopped
1 lemongrass stalk, cleaned, trimmed and roughly chopped
½ in (1.5 cm) piece of galangal, peeled and roughly chopped

SEASONING STATION (OPTIONAL)
Lime juice, chile flakes, salt, brown sugar

Begin by pulsing the dry roasted peanuts in a food processor until they are fine but still have a bit of texture, then set aside and clean the food processor.

Place all of the ingredients for the spice paste in the food processor and blend until smooth. If needed, add a few tablespoons of water to help it blend together.

Heat the vegetable oil in a nonstick saucepan over medium heat. Add the spice paste and fry it until fragrant.

Add the ground peanuts, the tamarind concentrate (or paste), sugar, salt, coriander and kecap manis to the pan along with a scant 1 cup (200 ml) of water. Stir to combine well and then adjust the balance of the sauce to your taste with the seasoning station ingredients.

Keeping the pan over medium-low heat, stir continuously so the sauce doesn't catch on the base of the pan. The oil should separate from the sauce once it is ready—this should take around 15 minutes.

Let the sauce cool completely before transferring to a sealed sterilized jar or airtight container. Stored in the fridge, this can be kept for up to 2 weeks.

BLACK TAHINI DRESSING

Among the many treasures to find a home in my fridge, black tahini dressing holds a special place. It's a versatile concoction that has become an indispensable ally for simple dishes. Similar in richness to white sesame dressing, this black tahini dressing is far nuttier and takes on a gorgeous black-gray color. It's my go-to drizzle for dumplings, but it's equally at home over a pan-fried fillet of meaty white fish, like hake, lending a rich, creamy texture and earthy flavor that complement the flaky flesh. Black tahini dressing can transform a salad, threading through the greens, and roasted veggies in the winter months too. Whenever you're looking to enhance the natural flavors of ingredients, this black tahini dressing is sure to become a cherished staple in your kitchen.

MAKES ENOUGH FOR 2 PEOPLE

3 tbsp black sesame seeds
¼ cup (60 ml) sesame oil
White sugar, to taste
Salt, to taste

Combine all the ingredients in a food processor or blender and blend to a smooth paste. Taste and adjust the flavor with sugar and salt, as preferred. Transfer the dressing to a sealed sterilized jar or airtight container. This can be stored in the fridge for up to a week.

Agak–Agak

AUTHENTICALLY
IN-BETWEEN

Authentically In-Between

There are certain dishes I've grown fond of despite being technically "incorrect." Take the Yorkshire pudding, a popover-like pastry annd quintessential item on the British roast dinner plate. My mom would make Yorkshire puddings from scratch, but occasionally they wouldn't rise, instead turning into spongy, blini-style pancakes with a crispy edge. Soaked in gravy and with an added slice of beef with horseradish sauce and a lightly charred roasted parsnip, these Yorkshires-gone-wrong are now one of my favorite Sunday treats. Some people might take offence at what I'm about to say, but I prefer them to proper Yorkshire puddings. I find it fascinating the mistakes we make in cooking that lead to the discovery of delicious morsels, or the moments of joy we take from not following the rules. This is largely how we learn cooking from different cultures. There's often mistakes and botched dishes.

For a fine-dining example of this, my brain goes to Massimo Bottura. A wizard of his craft, he is as passionate about his food as a famous conductor during the finest concerto piece. Every dish he serves is plated with intense precision. In an episode of *Chef's Table* on Netflix, one of his team drops the dessert—it's the last one of the service at his booked-out-for-months restaurant. There it is on the plate, completely smashed. Shards of glossy white meringue and tangy lemon curd are everywhere; the masterpiece has been made imperfect. Massimo stops the team with a great halt and looks down at the shattered dessert and declares that this is the way it will be served to every customer now. In the same way, I think of carbonara with cream as an imperfect classic. Yes, the original made with golden egg yolks and rich guanciale oil is delicious, but many of us have a fondness for that combination of back bacon, cream and hard cheese. Then there is the head-spinning example of banana on pizza. Bananas weren't available in Sweden until the 1990s, so when this exciting exotic fruit arrived, which hadn't been seen before, nobody quite knew what to do with it. So, what did they create? A pizza with banana, mushrooms, peanuts and curry powder. There is power in keeping an open mind and embracing the old saying, "try everything once."

    This process of learning how we get to a dish is integral when considering immigration and food. I think fondly of my mom, along with others who emigrated and learned how to make Western dishes. Even if cooked incorrectly, to me, those dishes are full of determination and bravery. The way that dishes develop is often determined by history, politics and the movement of peoples.

    When I opened my first restaurant, I overheard many misplaced comments and read several misguided reviews. The attacks varied, but a typical example is "That place only serves Asian food for white people." This is something I often hear from non-Asian chefs and foodies. There is a naivety in the desire to eat "authentically," as though eating something will magically transport you back to a country you once visited on vacation, or your birthplace or where your family are from. Perhaps you do really want to learn about a particular cuisine and culture, but I find there can be another side to this desire. The notion that we *must* have the most "authentic" food on our doorstep, miles away from the birthplace of a dish, is a viewpoint that feels quite colonial and capitalistic.

There are so many Asians who have bravely migrated from their country of birth to the West. A large number of my Asian friends have mothers, fathers, aunts and uncles who came here and opened up takeout places—there is a sizeable demographic of people who ended up in the UK following this path. It's a proven way to earn a living here, but one that requires lots of hard work to figure out the local taste in order to keep your business running. There's an entire menu of dishes in Chinese restaurants that were born out of the industriousness and determination of migrants catering to Western palates—perfectly breaded, flattened chicken breasts coated in a tangy, citrusy sauce and golden globes of deep-fried chicken coated in a delicious blend of salt and chile spices with green and red peppers, all served with a thick curry sauce, for example. I have good friends who grew up in takeout places as second-generation Asians. From a young age, they would help with tasks like prepping for service, taking orders and bagging up somebody's Friday-night order. More often than not, they tell unique stories of the struggles, triumphs and courage behind these takeout dishes. Angela Hui's book *Takeaway* covers this beautifully; her writing shares the emotions of growing up in a one such establishment.

The concept behind both of my restaurants was to serve food that was authentically inauthentic—the food my mother would cook to communicate with others as English wasn't her first language. The ingredients available to her weren't always an exact replica of what she could access in Malaysia, but she built a hybrid cuisine that glowed with integrity and love. For so many others like me, that "in-between" cuisine has such soul. The notion that authenticity in food can only be applied to a limited concept inhibits our ability to embrace the cultures of diverse ethnicities. Incredibly moving and authentic stories lie within the experiences of immigrants, and food is an added bonus of their bravery.

There is a plethora of British-Chinese dishes. Consider the humble shrimp toast, for example: shrimp mashed with ginger, Shaoxing rice wine, nutty sesame seeds, ground white pepper and a sprinkling of MSG or chicken powder, then sandwiched in-between two pieces of processed white bread and fried to golden brown perfection. An early example of fusion cuisine, shrimp toast is believed to have originated in Hong Kong and yet I'm often told that, by serving it in my restaurants, I'm creating inauthentic food. For me, this simple dish tells a story of bravery, strength and determination, how someone had the boldness to create it, then opened and ran a business without English as their first language, selling their creation to the public to make a living. If we broaden our ideas of authenticity, we widen our acceptance of all cultures.

When I opened my first street-food stand, I boldly cooked a mix of dishes that people knew, including a version of satay chicken, the Malaysian classic. I would marinate halal chicken from the local South Asian butcher in lemongrass, cumin, cilantro and chiles that I would then roast and stew down with peanut sauce. It was served in a small takeout box with steamed jasmine rice, pickled shallots and chile-dressed cucumber. That dish was in no way reflective of satay chicken's authentic roots, but it was absolutely delicious and is still a recipe I'm extremely proud of. It was a riff on the pork and chicken skewers that I have enjoyed from smoky outdoor hawker stalls in Kuala Lumpur since I was a child, but it also reflected the fact that I was cooking on a small budget, could only afford a domestic slow cooker and the local food safety councillors refused us permission to have an open barbecue flaming on a narrow alleyway in Glasgow...

In the dance of cooking, sometimes it's the missteps that lead to the creation of the most memorable of dishes. Just as flat Yorkshire puddings are the apple of my eye, when a traditional dish is not slavishly reproduced, we may benefit from a happy accident. Many of the world's favorite dishes have been serendipitously crafted from "mistakes." The flavors we enjoy in these "incorrect" or "inauthentic" dishes are a celebration of the human ability to adapt, to accept new innovations while honoring old traditions. They remind us that authenticity isn't a rigid adherence to original recipes, but rather the spirit in which food is prepared and the stories it tells. The recipes that follow are the story I like to tell through the food that I've learned rightly or wrongly through my mentors, my mom, other cookbooks, friends and restaurants. They are reflective of wonderful mistakes and a celebration of a lack of rules, reflected in the flavors you can tweak in each recipe to suit you.

Dad, Mom, me and Uncle Kenny at Uncle Kenny's wedding, 1994

CHAAT MASALA POTATO FRITTER
IN A MORNING ROLL

What you're about to read really leans into the Scottish stereotype that our makeup is 90% battered, deep-fried foods washed down with a glug of Irn Bru soda. When it comes to potato fritters, this is joyfully very true for me. A minute's walk from my school was a row of shops, including an Auld's Bakery—an old-school Scottish bakery with rows of sausage rolls, Scotch pies, empire biscuits (classic Scottish iced cookies) and bright red strawberry tarts; Casa Blanca—a glorious takeout place with pizza by the slice, chicken pakoras or potato wedges with garlic mayo; and the local "chippy," the fish and chip shop where we'd go for snacks during our morning break.

At the chippy, the classics sat, golden and crisp, under the heat lamp: battered cod and haddock, battered haggis, smoked or battered sausage, pizza crunch (pre-made thick-crust pizza dipped in batter and deep-fried, which I later found out is a take on a genuine Italian street food) and the much-coveted potato fritter. You had to be fast if you wanted a fritter as they frequently sold out. As soon as the bell sounded at the end of class, we bolted out of the door for the chippy. If you were quick, the reward was great: a thickly battered potato disc, soft and fluffy on the inside, deliciously oily and crunchy on the outside. The potato fritter was placed in a generously buttered Mortons roll, a morning roll that comes in two forms—soft or crispy. These rolls have a very short shelf life, so they must be ordered in every day. It's one of Glasgow's most stupendous food products, and paired with the fritter, it was a combination to die for. The butter melted into the roll, encasing the potato fritter, which was doused in malt vinegar and sprinkled with salt… a match made in heaven. This snack is now rarely found in Scottish chippies, but to me, it remains one of the most delicious treats. Perhaps you need to have grown up with the roll and fritter to love it? I'm on a mission to restore its popularity as it should not be forgotten.

Once, after a busy shift in the restaurant, when I hadn't eaten all day and had been on my feet for hours, all I wanted was a roll and fritter. It was one of those cravings that hits maybe once or twice a year, which you just have to satisfy immediately. So, I went to the convenience store to retrieve a Mortons roll (crispy for me). At that time of night, the roll wasn't quite as fresh, but beggars can't be choosers. I found some potatoes and began peeling. I fried the potato slices in a quickly mixed batter and watched the discs turn into crispy flying saucers in the oil. In my pantry, I had some chaat masala, a seasoning often used to add saltiness and a punch of flavor. I buttered the roll thickly to sandwich the fritter. Craving chile heat, I added some Green Chile Chutney (page 48) mixed with mayo, and some sweet tamarind sauce, similar to traditional British brown sauce but sweeter and tangier. I savored this delightful creation with sheer joy.

Now, I feel compelled to share this irresistibly delicious snack with the world. The original chippy roll and fritter is divine in itself, but would I even be a Malaysian-Glaswegian girl if I didn't add some chile flare? Absolutely not.

MAKES 4

FOR THE FRITTERS

4 large potatoes, peeled
2 cups (250 g) all-purpose flour, plus extra for dusting
1 tsp baking powder
1 tsp salt
½ tsp freshly ground black pepper
1 egg, beaten
1 cup (250 ml) milk
Vegetable oil, for deep-frying
2 tbsp chaat masala
Malt vinegar, to taste

TO SERVE

4 crispy bread rolls (ideally Scottish morning rolls), split and generously buttered
Tamarind sauce
Green Chile Chutney (page 48) mixed with a few dollops of mayo

SEASONING STATION (OPTIONAL)

Lime juice, salt, pepper, tamarind sauce for sweetness

Slice the potatoes lengthwise into ¼ in (5 mm) thick slices. You can adjust the thickness of the potato slices to suit your preference, but I like mine on the chunky side so they have a bit of bite. Submerge the potato slices in a bowl of cold water to prevent them from browning and to remove any excess starch. I leave them in the water for at least an hour before cooking, but they can also be prepared the day before and left overnight.

In a large mixing bowl, combine the flour, baking powder, salt and pepper. Whisk in the beaten egg, then gradually add the milk, little by little, to form a smooth batter. The consistency should be similar to pancake batter; not too thick but should coat the back of a spoon.

Make a dusting and dipping station by putting some extra flour in a wide, shallow bowl and the batter in a second bowl right beside it.

Fill a deep-fryer or large, heavy-based pot no more than two-thirds full with oil. Heat the oil to 350°F (180°C). Meanwhile, line a tray or plate with paper towels and keep a spider strainer or slotted spoon on hand.

Drain the potato slices and pat them dry with paper towels. Lightly dust each slice with some flour by dropping it into the bowl. (The flour will ensure that the batter sticks to the potato.)

Working in batches so that you don't overcrowd the pan, dip the potato slices into the batter until they are well coated and then carefully lower them into the hot oil. (If there are too many potato slices in the fryer at once, the oil temperature will drop and they won't go crispy.)

Deep-fry the potatoes for 2–3 minutes on each side or until they are golden and crispy. Transfer the fritters to the lined tray or plate to drain any excess oil. While the potato fritters are hot, dust them with chaat masala and sprinkle over some malt vinegar. (Don't forget to remove any crispy nubbins left in the pan—sprinkle them with the chaat masala and enjoy as a snack.)

When ready to serve, fill each morning roll with the warm potato fritters and squeeze on some tamarind sauce. Spread some of the green chile chutney mayo on the top half of the bun for added spice and add whichever seasoning station ingredients you feel like today, to taste.

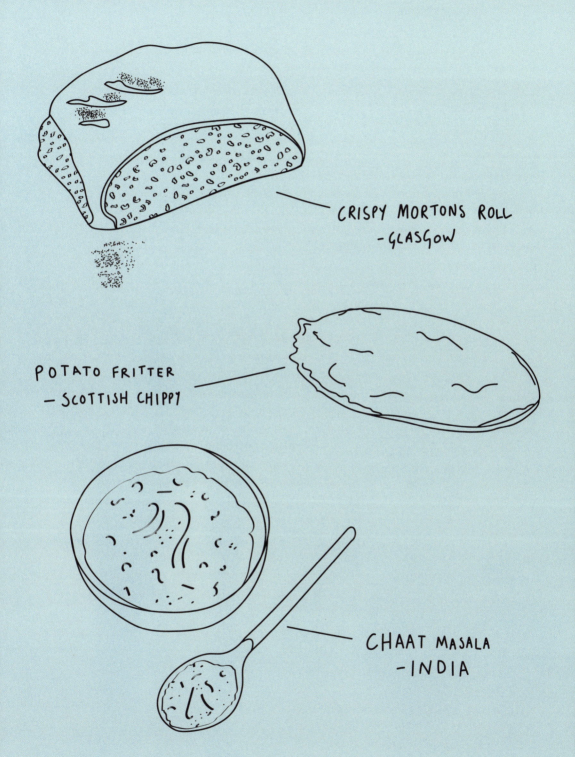

CHILE CRISP PUTTANESCA

This dish entered my regular repertoire of easy dinners on a blustery evening at the start of fall. I could see the leaves blowing around from my apartment window, so I decided it was not the night for leaving the house and I couldn't face going grocery shopping. I was all out of noodles and there were just a few scraps of food in the fridge—a stalk of celery, a bit of ginger, some wilting cilantro, a package of Irish butter I'd been gifted by a friend. I opened the pantry to find some bucatini, a can of crab meat and my essential jar of anchovy chile crisp oil. I figured that this was going to be the start of something beautiful. I snapped the bucatini into short lengths for this dish (Italians, look away) because I wanted a short pasta. I find a shorter length of noodle makes it simpler to wok-fry the rest of the ingredients and the oils seem to infuse far more easily. This dish is the perfect mash up of the best exported ingredients from Italy and some traditional Chinese wok-frying. It's my Asian-inspired version of spaghetti alla puttanesca. So wrong, it's right.

SERVES 1

3½ oz (100 g) bucatini (or spaghetti), snapped into short lengths
1 tsp vegetable oil
1 tbsp butter
1 celery stalk, finely sliced on an angle
1 tsp finely chopped garlic
3½ oz (100 g) mixed white and brown crab meat (you can use canned when fresh is not available)
1 tbsp capers
1½ tsp chile crisp oil (both regular and anchovy chile crisp oil work)
1 tbsp light soy sauce
2 fresh cilantro sprigs, chopped, to toss

SEASONING STATION (OPTIONAL)
Chile crisp oil, salt, fish sauce, a bit of extra pasta cooking water to tone down the flavors

Begin by boiling the bucatini in a large pan of salted water according to the package instructions.

Meanwhile, heat the vegetable oil and butter in a nonstick wok over medium-low heat. Once hot, add the celery and garlic and fry until fragrant.

Add the crab meat, capers and chile crisp oil to the wok and fry over high heat until fragrant.

Once cooked, drain the bucatini, reserving a scant ½ cup (90 ml) of the cooking water. Add the pasta to the wok with the reserved cooking water and the soy sauce. Keep stirring the bucatini into the crab mixture until everything is thoroughly combined and coated in a thick glossy sauce.

When ready to serve, toss in the chopped cilantro. Add whichever seasoning station ingredients you feel like today, to taste, and eat with chopsticks for the full noodle experience.

Authentically In-Between

GARLIC UDON IN SESAME AND CHILE OIL

Whenever I'm in London, I try to visit one of the Koya restaurants for their udon, which are just so warming—I adore them. This is a quick version to satisfy that craving even when I'm in a rush. Sesame paste can be easily found in Asian supermarkets now. It's a brilliant pantry ingredient, which makes vegan broths nicely rich without being overpowering. If I'm feeling extra indulgent, I'll eat this with Kangkung Belacan (see page 232) on the side. This is one of my go-to meals for when I'm eating alone as it's such a quick recipe.

SERVES 1

7 oz (200 g) fresh udon noodles
2 tbsp Asian sesame paste
1 tbsp light soy sauce
1 tsp dark soy sauce
1 tsp rice wine vinegar
1 tsp white sugar
2 tsp Sichuan-based chile oil, or to your taste, plus extra to garnish
3 garlic cloves, peeled and minced
1 in (3 cm) piece of ginger, peeled and minced
2 scallions, finely sliced
1 tbsp toasted sesame seeds
Kangkung Belacan (see page 232), to serve (optional)

SEASONING STATION (OPTIONAL)
Black vinegar, salt, light soy sauce

Blanch the fresh udon noodles by plunging them into boiling water for 2 minutes. To stop the cooking process, submerge the noodles in ice-cold water, then drain and rinse under cold running water. Set aside.

To make the dressing, whisk together the sesame paste, both soy sauces, the rice wine vinegar, sugar, chile oil and the minced garlic and ginger in a bowl until well combined. Add a splash of water until you get a creamy consistency. Adjust the seasoning to your taste.

Toss the cold noodles in the dressing, ensuring that each strand is evenly coated. Taste and add whichever seasoning station ingredients you feel like.

Pile the noodles into a deep bowl, scatter over the scallions, then sprinkle on the toasted sesame seeds and a drizzle of the chile oil. Serve with Kangkung Belacan, if you like.

CHOP SUEY EGGPLANT WITH THAI BASIL

Whisky often takes a back seat in Asian cuisine, yet I find a certain alchemy unfolds when the smoky notes of a good Scotch meet the robust flavors of my heritage. This dish is a testament to that splendid friendship. When cooked just right, the rich, earthy depth of the eggplants holds its own against the bold smokiness of whisky.

The secret to this dish's success lies in its preparation: the eggplants must be fried to perfection. This step transforms them, softening their flesh to a velvety texture and enriching their natural flavors, so they become almost buttery. It's about coaxing out that creamy smoothness, a counterpoint to the fiery dram, creating a balance where each enhances the other. I adore the striking purple color and long, snaky shape of Chinese eggplants, but you could use regular ones too. Pair with steamed rice and a good whisky.

SERVES 2–3

3 baby eggplants aka Chinese eggplants (or regular eggplants), weighing about 1 lb 5 oz (600 g)
Oil (use a neutral oil, such as rice bran or vegetable), for frying
1 red pepper, deseeded and sliced into strips
9 garlic cloves, peeled and finely diced
1 fresh red bird's eye chile, sliced

FOR THE WOK SAUCE
2 tsp sugar
1 tbsp light soy sauce
1 tbsp oyster sauce
1 tbsp white wine vinegar

SEASONING STATION (OPTIONAL)
Sugar, light soy sauce, black vinegar, MSG

TO SERVE
3 fresh Thai basil sprigs (or regular basil), leaves picked
Crispy fried shallots (or onions)
Dram of whisky

Begin by slicing the eggplants lengthwise down the center and then into 1½ in (4 cm) chunks. Salt the eggplant pieces generously and leave for 5 minutes. Rinse the salt off the eggplant, drain away any excess water and pat dry with paper towels.

Add the oil to a large wok until it rises about ½ in (1 cm) up the sides and heat over medium heat. Add the eggplant pieces and fry until smooth and buttery. Transfer to a plate lined with paper towels to drain any excess oil.

Return to the wok. You'll need to keep enough oil to cover the base of the wok and can dispose of the rest. Add the red pepper strips and stir-fry over high heat for 1–2 minutes or until softened. Now add in the garlic and chile and fry until fragrant. Return the fried eggplants to the wok and mix all the ingredients together.

To make the wok sauce, combine all the ingredients in a small bowl. Add whichever seasoning station ingredients you feel like today, to taste. Pour the wok sauce into the wok and stir-fry everything for 1 minute. Try to achieve "wok hei" (see page 27).

When ready to serve, garnish the eggplants with the Thai basil leaves and scatter over some crispy fried shallots. Enjoy with a glass of whisky.

Authentically In-Between

GOODBYE BUTTERMILK CHICKEN,
HELLO TEA-BRINED CRISPY FRIED CHICKEN

I once spent an entire summer testing fried chicken recipes, and it was glorious. In 2020, I opened a street-food stall called Ga Ga Chicken, which became so popular that I later turned the concept and name into a restaurant and bar in Glasgow. Over those months, I tested various different methods of making fried chicken, including the classic technique of brining it in buttermilk. In doing so, I developed a severe issue with the amount of buttermilk being discarded. It's such a special ingredient that works so well to tenderize chicken, but I grew to resent the amount of wastage. By using buttermilk merely as a brine, I felt like I was underusing this precious dairy product. Instead, I wanted to find a way of tenderizing chicken that really infuses the meat with flavor but without relying on an ingredient as special as buttermilk.

Enter the concept of tea brining. Trust me, put down the buttermilk—when it comes to infusing chicken with robust flavors and ensuring a juicy interior, brining it in sweet tea is a revelation. The beauty of this technique lies in its versatility. Imagine steeping your chicken in a concoction where the traditional sweet tea is enlivened with star anise, peppercorns, coriander seeds and makrut lime leaves for a deliciously fragrant version. As teas vary in flavor profiles—from robust black teas to delicate greens—it was a natural progression for cooks to use it as a brining liquid, lending the chicken a subtle tannic depth alongside the traditional sweet and salty notes of the brine. Additionally, the tannins found in tea interact with the proteins in chicken, helping to gently break them down and resulting in a more tender texture when it is cooked.

Now, let's talk dredging. Specifically, the wonders of dredging with potato starch. This humble ingredient is a game-changer in the world of fried chicken. When used as a dredge, potato starch contributes to a crust that's incomparably crispy, almost glass-like. It withstands high temperatures without burning, ensuring your chicken is perfectly golden every time. As I've spoken about many times in this book, I adore cooking for friends—in fact, so much so that I changed the dredge recipe used in my restaurant to contain no wheat flour, as one of my nearest and dearest is gluten free. I wanted her to always be able to visit without ever worrying about gluten contact in the fryer. And do you know what, I don't miss the wheat flour! I've found potato starch is far superior to using wheat flour as a batter. What's more, as long as the temperature is right, it's less prone to oil absorption, resulting in a much lighter and less greasy bite.

The recipe overleaf is for a great basic fried chicken, but it can be altered with seasonings depending on what you're cooking. For example, if you want to make it a

TEA-BRINING

DREDGING

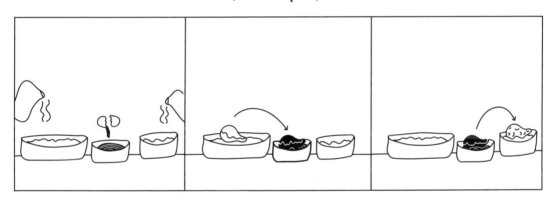

FRYING

bit more colorful, add a pinch of ground turmeric and paprika to the mix. Be liberal with the spices in your dredge mixtures because deep-frying takes away a lot of the flavor. I find thicker fried chicken batters to be a bit gummy, so instead add little drops of water into the dry dredge mix to encourage bits to stick on. The recipe below will make a big batch of the dredge, so keep it on hand to use as and when you need.

Tea-brined chicken paired with the supremely crunchy potato starch batter results in the juiciest fried chicken you could ask for. What follows is a blueprint for both the brine and the batter that can be used for so many different sauces and techniques. I've included a couple of recipes on pages 74–9 to get you started, and to inspire you to adapt with other flavors. I worked hard to perfect this dish in the restaurant and I, for one, am not a gatekeeper—this is one recipe I'm extremely proud to share with you. Consider this your fried chicken manual…

MAKES ENOUGH TO BRINE 1 LB 2 OZ (500 G) CHICKEN PIECES

FOR THE BRINE
8 black tea bags
4¼ cups (1 liter) boiling water
Generous 2 cups (500 ml) pineapple juice
3 onions, peeled and sliced
10 garlic cloves, peeled and sliced
1¾ cups (350 g) light brown sugar
⅓ cup (100 g) salt
¾ cup (100 g) black peppercorns
3 tbsp cloves
3 limes, thinly sliced
10 fresh or dried makrut lime leaves

FOR THE BATTER
Scant 1 cup (100 g) cornstarch
3 eggs
1½ cups (240 g) potato starch
Salt and freshly ground black pepper

Step One: Tea-Brine the Chicken

Place the tea bags in a large heatproof bowl and pour over the boiling water. Add in all the other brine ingredients and stir well. After 15 minutes, remove the tea bags.

Allow the liquid to cool down completely before using it to brine any chicken. If you need to speed up the cooling process, add some ice cubes to the bowl. The brine must be cold before adding in any chicken.

To brine any chicken, submerge the pieces in the brine, place the bowl in the fridge and leave it to tenderize for at least 4 hours but preferably up to 24 hours. Once it's ready, drain the chicken and discard the brine.

Step Two: Dredge the Chicken

Place the cornstarch into a wide, shallow bowl. Whisk the eggs in a second bowl and lightly season with salt and pepper. Put the potato starch into a third bowl and season with 1 tablespoon of salt and 2 tablespoons of pepper.

First, toss the chicken pieces in the cornstarch to coat them. Next, dunk the chicken pieces in the beaten egg. Add a few drops of water to the potato starch dredge mix until small pieces form (this will make the chicken extra crispy) then transfer the chicken pieces to the dredge-mix bowl, making sure each piece is evenly coated.

Step Three: Deep-Frying the Chicken

Fill a deep-fryer or deep, heavy-based pan no more than two-thirds full with oil—you can use any that reaches a high temperature, such as vegetable. Heat the oil to 350°F (180°C). Use a digital thermometer to check the temperature of the oil—I always find it's better to be safe rather than sorry, especially when it comes to deep-frying chicken, and only start cooking the chicken once the oil is at 350°F (180°C).

Working in batches if necessary, carefully lower the dredged chicken pieces into the hot oil and deep-fry for roughly 10–15 minutes. Check the internal temperature of the chicken with the thermometer—it must be 170°F (75°C) or above for at least a few minutes before you remove it from the oil. Do not overcrowd the fryer or pan, otherwise you won't achieve a crispy exterior. When frying any chicken pieces with a bone in them, probe the chicken close to any joints in the bone as this is where it will be coolest and will give you the best indication of whether it's ready or not.

Once cooked through and crispy, remove the chicken pieces from the fryer or pan and place them on a wire rack to drain for 5 minutes. If you don't have a wire rack, paper towels will do, however a wire rack is much better as the oil drips away from the crispy batter.

Top tip: Double-frying is a great plan if you're having people over for dinner. On the first fry, cook the chicken for a few minutes less than usual, but use a thermometer to make sure the internal temperature of the meat is at least 170°F (75°C). Cool the chicken pieces on a wire rack and store in the fridge, covered, with the pieces laid flat and not touching, up to a day ahead. When ready to serve your guests, heat up the oil again and perform the second fry. It won't take nearly as long the second time, which means you can relax a bit more during the deep-frying process.

ORANGE AND CASHEW CHICKEN

Orange chicken is a beautiful dish… there, I've said it. I've grown up loving the food of immigrants, and often that includes dishes that aren't exactly traditional to the culture, but I find they tell a story of courage and adaptation.

We've all had an ex's mom who we adored. Mine was Karen. She was full of joy and welcomed me in with open arms. She was incredibly encouraging of my cooking. As a 20-year-old, I would go to her house to eat takeout Chinese food and drink gin together on the weekends. One of Karen's favorite dishes was lemon chicken—again not a truly traditional dish, but it features a lot on Chinese takeout menus in Britain and, for me, it's steeped in happy memories of enjoying takeaways and my first days of adoring cooking. I've adapted this to be orange chicken because I prefer the flavor. And I adore how gorgeous the chicken looks when you place a few citrus slices on top.

SERVES 2

FOR THE CHICKEN
2 skinless, boneless chicken breasts
A handful of roasted cashews

FOR THE ORANGE SAUCE
$2/_3$ cup (150ml) orange juice (freshly squeezed from 3–4 oranges)
Zest of 1 orange
2 tbsp light soy sauce
1 tbsp rice vinegar
2 tbsp brown soft sugar
2 garlic cloves, peeled and minced
1 in (2.5 cm) piece of ginger, peeled and finely grated
1 tbsp cornstarch, dissolved in 2 tbsp water
½ tsp chile flakes (optional, for heat)

TO SERVE
Steamed or egg-fried rice (optional)
1 scallion, sliced
1 orange, sliced
Shichimi togarashi powder (optional)

To prepare the chicken, first place it between two sheets of parchment paper and flatten it with a rolling pin, then brine, dredge and deep-fry the chicken following the instructions on pages 72–3. Set the fried chicken on a wire rack to drain.

While the chicken is draining, make the orange sauce. Combine the orange juice, orange zest, soy sauce, rice vinegar, brown sugar, minced garlic and finely grated ginger in a pot. Bring to a simmer over medium heat. Add the cornstarch mixture to thicken the sauce. Stir continuously until the sauce reaches your desired consistency. If you like some heat, add the chile flakes.

Add the fried chicken breasts and roasted cashews to the pan with the orange sauce. Turn until the chicken breasts are well coated in the sauce.

Serve the orange chicken with steamed or egg-fried rice, if you like. Garnish the chicken with the scallion and orange slices, and a pinch of shichimi togarashi, if you like.

Authentically In-Between

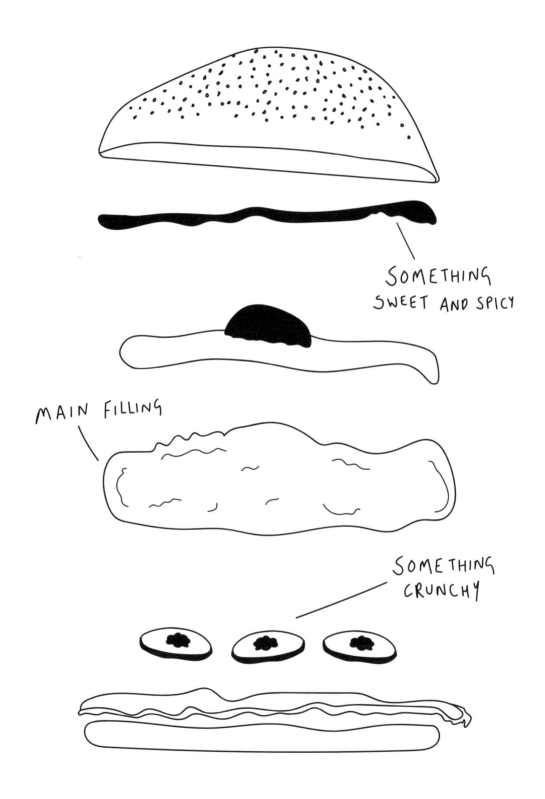

CRISPY CHICKEN BURGER
THE ONE WITH SAMBAL, MAYO, CUCUMBER AND A FRIED EGG

During one trip to Malaysia, I visited a certain fast-food chain that had a nasi lemak burger on special—crispy fried chicken with sambal, mayo, cucumber and a fried egg. It was a flavor combination that I simply couldn't resist and, to this day, I still think it's the best thing I've ever purchased from beneath those golden arches. I made my own version of that particular fried chicken burger, using my trusted brining and dredging methods, which I served at a pop-up in a local burger restaurant in Glasgow.

MAKES 1 BURGER

1 skinless, boneless chicken thigh
Vegetable oil, for frying
1 egg
1 sesame brioche bun
Kewpie mayonnaise
3 cucumber slices
2 tbsp Sambal Belacan (see page 47)
Salt and freshly ground black pepper

To prepare the chicken, brine, dredge and deep-fry following the instructions on pages 72–3, but heating the oil to 325°F (160°C) and cooking the chicken for roughly 10–15 minutes. Check the internal temperature of the chicken with a meat thermometer to test if it is ready—it must be 170°F (75°C) or above for at least a few minutes before you remove it from the oil. (Because thighs are thicker/denser than chicken breast, they're best cooked at the slightly lower temperature of 320°F/160°C and for longer to ensure they cook through on the inside without overcooking on the outside.) Set the fried chicken on a wire rack to drain.

While the chicken is draining, fry the egg. Heat enough oil to cover the base of a frying pan over medium heat. Once the oil is very hot, crack the egg into the pan. Fry until the white of the egg is golden and crispy, and the yolk is as runny as you like it. Season the yolk with some salt and pepper.

Split open the bun and toast it until golden. Smear a generous amount of mayo over the bottom half of the bun, then layer over the cucumber slices. Spread the sambal liberally over the top half of the bun.

Once the chicken and fried egg are ready, assemble the burger. Place the crispy chicken thigh on the base of the bun and sit the fried egg on top. Place the bun lid on top of the stack and give it a good squish down before digging in.

CRISPY CHICKEN BURGER
THE ONE WITH FISH SAUCE CARAMEL

Forever inspired by my team—Sascha, our chef, shared the idea for this burger inspired by one she had in a Vietnamese-Thai diner in the US. We recreated it and put it on the menu. It's wonderful, and an ode to my many brilliant restaurant staff over the years.

MAKES 1 BURGER

1 skinless, boneless chicken thigh

FOR THE FISH SAUCE CARAMEL
½ cup (100 g) sugar
1½–2 tbsp fish sauce (or to taste)
Juice of ½ lime
¼ tsp chile flakes (optional, for a spicy kick)
½ garlic clove, peeled and finely minced (optional, for extra flavor)

TO SERVE
1 sesame brioche bun
Shredded cabbage and grated carrots, pickled in 1 quantity Pickling liquid (see page 158), then drained

To make the caramel, place the sugar in a heavy-based pot and add 2 tablespoons of cold water. Stir over low heat until the sugar dissolves. Increase the heat to medium. Without stirring, continue warming the sugar solution until it turns golden.

Once it's a deep amber color, carefully add 2 tablespoons of warm water to the caramel to adjust the consistency—the caramel will bubble vigorously as soon as the water is added. Stir gently until the caramel is smooth.

Reduce the heat to low, then add the fish sauce and lime juice along with the chile flakes and minced garlic, if using. Stir well and simmer for 2–3 minutes, or until the caramel thickens slightly.

Remove the pan from the heat and leave the caramel to cool. It will thicken further as it cools. Once completely cool, transfer the caramel to a sealed sterilized jar or bottle. When stored in the fridge, this caramel will keep for up to a week.

To prepare the chicken, brine, dredge and deep-fry following the instructions on pages 72–3, but heating the oil to 325°F (160°C) and cooking the chicken for roughly 10–15 minutes. Check the internal temperature of the chicken with a meat thermometer to test if it is ready—it must be 170°F (75°C) or above for at least a few minutes before you remove it from the oil. (Because thighs are thicker/denser than chicken breast, they're best cooked at the slightly lower temperature of 320°F/160°C and for longer to ensure they cook through on the inside without overcooking on the outside.) Set the fried chicken burger on a wire rack to drain.

While the chicken is draining, split open the bun and toast it until golden. Place the crispy chicken thigh on the base of the bun, drizzle over some caramel and place the pickled veg on top. Place the bun lid on top.

Authentically In-Between

SICHUAN BROWN BUTTER EGGPLANTS

If I've said it once, I'll say it twice—eggplants require a lot of fat during cooking. They soak it up perfectly and the result is a buttery, creamy texture that absorbs punchy flavors. The nuttiness of the brown butter here goes so well with the earthy eggplants. Personally, I love Sichuan peppercorns and their numbing spiciness, but if Sichuan isn't your bag then you can use some chipotle or ancho chile flakes for smokiness. You can make a vegan version of this using coconut oil instead of butter.

SERVES 2–4

2 medium eggplants
7 tbsp (100 g) unsalted butter (or coconut oil if you require this to be vegan)
2 tsp Sichuan peppercorns
Vegetable oil, for frying
10 garlic cloves, peeled and minced
1 tbsp minced ginger
2½ tbsp light soy sauce
1½ tbsp rice vinegar
2 tsp sugar
Salt, to sprinkle
Fresh cilantro leaves, to serve
Toasted sesame seeds, to serve

SEASONING STATION (OPTIONAL)
Chile crisp oil, lime juice

Slice each eggplant lengthwise into two halves. Sprinkle the cut sides with a little salt and set aside for 10 minutes. Gently pat the eggplants dry to remove any excess moisture.

Melt the butter in a small saucepan over medium heat. Once the butter starts to melt, add the Sichuan peppercorns and continue to cook the butter, stirring occasionally, until it turns golden brown and gives off a nutty aroma. Try not to blacken the butter at this point and ensure the peppercorns are popping. Strain the butter to remove the peppercorns, then set aside.

Heat a generous amount of vegetable oil in a frying pan over medium-high heat. Carefully lower the eggplant halves into the hot oil, cut-side down, and fry until they are golden and tender. (Essentially, the easiest way to get the eggplants soft and tender is to deep-fry them.) Flip over the eggplants to lightly brown the skin side as well. Remove and drain on paper towels.

Drain any excess oil from the frying pan and then reduce the heat to medium. Add the minced garlic and ginger, then fry for about 30 seconds or until fragrant. Add the soy sauce, rice vinegar and sugar, then stir to combine. Pour in the Sichuan brown butter and bring the mixture to a gentle simmer.

Return the fried eggplants to the pan, cut-side up, and spoon the brown butter sauce over them, ensuring they are well coated. Cook for a further 1 minute, allowing the eggplants to absorb some of the sauce.

When ready to serve, carefully transfer the eggplants to a serving dish and garnish them with the cilantro leaves and sesame seeds, as well as whichever seasoning station ingredients you feel like today.

CLAMS WITH CHINESE SAUSAGE AND SAMPHIRE

We had tangerine orange dining tables in Julie's Kopitiam. It was the only vibrant color in the restaurant and it made the plates of food look really delicious. I remember how the tables used to really suit the clams—if that's a sentence you're allowed to say. The creamy color of the clam shells and the pinky hues of the caramelized Chinese sausages (lap cheong) always made this dish so visually appealing.

When I think of clams, I think of the ocean's bounty. Pairing them with Chinese sausages is like bringing together two different stories from the same ancestral book. The lap cheong, with its rich fat and distinct umami, wraps around the tender brininess of the clams in a culinary embrace. And all this is brought together by the Shaoxing wine, which I fondly consider the golden thread in Chinese cooking. Its subtle, nutty sweetness is the perfect medium to marry the diverse flavors in the pan. And when you're tossing everything around, listen out for the clink of the clams in the wok. It's something to marvel at; it's almost like playing a percussion instrument as you turn them around in the pan.

Creating this dish is as much about building layers of taste as it is about reviving memories and paying tribute to the past through every savory mouthful. It's a dish best enjoyed shared, surrounded by the clamor of good company (pardon the pun).

SERVES 4

2 lb 4 oz (1 kg) fresh clams in shell
1 tbsp vegetable oil
4 Chinese sausages (lap cheong, weighing about 7 oz/200 g), thinly sliced (if you can't find lap cheong, chorizo is a different, but nicely smoky alternative)
3½ oz (100 g) samphire/sea beans (or green beans or choi sum)
10 garlic cloves, peeled and minced
1 fresh red bird's eye chile, finely diced
3 tbsp Shaoxing rice wine (or you can use sherry or white wine with a splash of vinegar)
1½ tbsp light soy sauce
1 tbsp oyster sauce
1 tsp chicken bouillon powder
1 tsp sugar

First, prepare the clams. Soak the clams in a large bowl of salted water for at least 1 hour to purge them of any sand or grit. Rinse the soaked clams under cold running water several times until the water runs clear, then leave them to drain. Discard any that are open or don't close with a sharp tap.

Heat the oil in a large frying pan or wok over medium heat. Add the sliced sausages and fry until the oils have been released and the slices are lightly caramelized and crispy. Transfer the sausages to a plate with a slotted spoon, leaving the oil in the pan, and set aside.

In the same pan, fry the samphire, garlic and chile over medium heat until fragrant, adding a bit more oil if needed and being careful not to burn anything.

Pour in the Shaoxing rice wine to deglaze the pan, scraping up any browned bits, then add the clams, soy sauce, oyster sauce, chicken bouillon powder, sugar, salt and ground white pepper. Stir well to coat the clams in the sauce, then cover the pan with a lid and let the clams steam for 5–7 minutes, or until they have opened up.

A pinch of salt
A pinch of ground white pepper
Fresh Thai basil leaves (or regular basil), to garnish
Sesame oil, to serve
Steamed basmati rice, to serve

SEASONING STATION (OPTIONAL)
Fish sauce, salt, lime juice

Discard any clams that do not open.

Add the cooked sausage slices back into the pan with the clams and stir gently to combine. Add whichever seasoning station ingredients you feel like today, to taste. Scatter over the basil leaves and drizzle with a little sesame oil before serving in bowls with some steamed basmati rice on the side. Remember to spoon the delicious clam juices from the pan over the rice.

NASI GORENG WITH SMOKED MACKEREL

Nasi goreng is probably one of the most recognizable dishes in Indonesian and Malaysian cuisines. Nasi means rice and goreng means fried, so it translates simply as fried rice. Full of flavor, this dish can be adapted to use up any ingredients you have in the fridge. I adore adding some mackerel to this; the smokiness of the fish makes it extra punchy and takes it slightly closer to kedgeree in flavor. It's important to cook out the paste (rempah) here so that all of the roundness of the flavors can coat the rice. All of the day-old rice grains should absorb maximum flavor. Remember, nasi goreng is a simple dish to cook, but it's all about making sure it's not still wet at the end of the frying process.

SERVES 2

Vegetable oil, for frying
2 scallions, chopped into
 1½ in (4 cm) chunks
5½ oz (150 g) string beans, trimmed
1¾ oz (50 g) smoked mackerel, flaked
2 cups (300 g) cooked and cooled
 jasmine rice (preferably a day old)
1½ tsp kecap manis (sweet soy sauce)
1½ tbsp fish sauce, or to taste
4 eggs
5½ oz (150 g) beansprouts

FOR THE REMPAH
1 long shallot, peeled and
 roughly chopped
5 garlic cloves, peeled and
 roughly chopped
2 fresh long red chiles, deseeded
 and roughly chopped
4 dried red chiles, soaked in warm
 water for 20 minutes, drained,
 deseeded
2 tbsp dried anchovies (ikan billis)

SEASONING STATION (OPTIONAL)
Sambal Belacan (page 47),
 chile crisp oil, fish sauce,
 light soy sauce, lime juice, salt

First, make the rempah. Place all the ingredients in a food processor or blender and blend to a paste.

Heat plenty of oil in a wok over medium-high heat. (You need lots of oil to make the paste oily enough that it coats the rice.) Once the wok is hot, add the rempah, scallion chunks, trimmed green beans and flaked mackerel. Fry everything for 1–2 minutes, stirring continuously so that the paste doesn't catch and burn.

Turn the heat down, then add the cooled rice to the wok with a few tablespoons of water. Add the kecap manis and fish sauce, stirring furiously until everything is mixed together.

Create a well in the center of the rice. Keeping the heat on medium-low, crack two of the eggs into the center of the well and allow them to scramble. Once fully cooked through, mix the scrambled egg through the rice with the beansprouts.

Heat enough oil to cover the base in a separate pan over a very high heat. Once the oil is very hot, crack the remaining two eggs into the pan. Fry until the whites of the eggs are golden and crispy.

When ready to serve, spoon the rice into two bowls and top with the crispy fried eggs. Add whichever of the ingredients you fancy from the seasoning station.

GRILLED CHEESE SANDWICH WITH TAMARIND ONIONS

Picture this: a bustling "cheese toastie" festival where golden, melted cheese is the star of the show. We were asked to join just such a festival in Glasgow. Now, I love a challenge, but it turns out that in order to churn out around 60 cheese toasties every hour, you really need to have miles of griddle space. Alas, we did not. Luckily, you'll be making this snack in modest quantities.

Combining the classic comfort of salty Cheddar with the tangy kick of tamarind onions and the fiery punch of Green Chile Chutney turns the humble grilled cheese into a flavor bomb. Rich and sweet, the caramelized onions are transformed by tamarind's sweet and sour depth, giving each bite a complex layer of flavors. It's become more than just festival fare for me now. This grilled cheese is the epitome of a perfect lazy Saturday afternoon snack, enjoyed with a cup of tea when it's raining outside. Simple pleasures.

MAKES 1 SANDWICH

Neutral oil, for frying
½ red onion, peeled and thinly sliced
2 tbsp tamarind sauce
1 tbsp butter, softened,
    plus extra for griddling
2 thick slices of white bread
2½ oz (70 g) vintage or mature
    Cheddar, grated
2 tbsp Green Chile Chutney
    (see page 48)

Heat a glug of oil in a frying pan over medium heat. Add the red onion slices and fry them until they begin to color. After 5 minutes, stir in the tamarind sauce and continue to fry the onion until caramelized—this should take about 10 minutes.

Butter both sides of each slice of bread, then assemble the grilled cheese by sandwiching the grated cheese, tamarind caramelized onions and Green Chile Chutney between the bread.

Warm a grill pan over medium-low heat. Grill the sandwich on both sides with an extra pat of butter until the bread is golden brown and the cheese has melted.

Authentically In-Between

MUSHROOM AND POTATO POT STICKERS

Every so often, I dabble with being vegan. Whenever I do, I always think about how much I'm going to miss the fattiness of meat-filled dumplings. It can be difficult to get that same feeling of ingredients binding in a dumpling without using any natural fats, however, I've discovered that the natural starchiness of potato to bind salty mushroom flavors is a perfect way to marry everything together.

Crescent-shaped, pleated dumplings that are first pan-fried, then steamed, pot stickers are a little trickier than simply boiled or steamed dumplings. I have a strong dislike for deep-fried dumplings—I'm not sure why, but I feel like it's a bit of a cheat. Also, deep-fried dumplings are a bit too oily for my liking; personally, I prefer a silky exterior rather than a purely crunchy one. These dumplings are perfect pot stickers. Intensely mushroomy, they are delicious with my Black Vinegar Dipping Sauce.

MAKES AROUND 40

Flour, for dusting
40 dumpling wrappers (to make your own, see page 126)
3 tbsp vegetable oil, for frying

FOR THE FILLING
7 oz (200 g) large flat mushrooms
9 oz (250 g) cremini or oyster mushrooms
1¾ oz (50 g) button mushrooms
3 tbsp vegetable oil
2½ tbsp grated ginger (I use a regular cheese grater for this)
3½ oz (100 g) potato, peeled, grated
½ cup (120 ml) Shaoxing rice wine (or sherry)
3 tbsp dark soy sauce
1 tsp black vinegar
½ tsp MSG
1 tsp ground white pepper (optional)
Salt, to taste (optional)

FOR THE DIPPING SAUCE
3 tbsp dark soy sauce
1 tsp black vinegar (or malt vinegar)
2 tsp good chile oil (optional)

First, make the filling. Preheat the oven to 400°F (200°C). Place the large flat mushrooms on a baking pan and roast in the hot oven for 15 minutes to enhance their umami flavor. Once the flat mushrooms have cooled, remove the stalks and slice them into tiny ¼ in (5 mm) chunks. Do the same with the flat mushroom heads. Repeat all this for the chestnut or oyster and button mushrooms.

Heat the vegetable oil for the filling in a nonstick wok over medium heat, then add the grated ginger and fry until fragrant. Add in all of the chopped mushrooms and fry them, stirring frequently, for 10 minutes.

After 10 minutes, add the grated potato, Shaoxing rice wine, soy sauce, vinegar and MSG to the wok. Fry everything for a further 10–15 minutes, or until the mixture is thick, glossy and dark in color. It needs to be a sticky consistency at this point to allow you to spoon the mixture into the dumpling wrappers. Once the filling is ready, taste a teaspoonful and adjust the seasoning with the white pepper and salt, if you feel it is needed. Leave the filling to cool completely.

Prepare your dumpling-making station. Dust a clean surface or board with flour, set a bowl of water to the side and have the dumpling wrappers in easy reach.

Continued →

← *Pot Stickers continued*

If you're right-handed, lay a dumpling wrapper in the palm of your left hand (and vice versa if you're left-handed). Place one heaped teaspoon of the filling right in the center of the dumpling wrapper, dab a little water on one side to help it stick, then fold and—if you can—pleat the dumplings. There are many different ways to do this. I find the easiest method is to fold the dumpling over and firmly pinch the wrapper in the middle on one side. Now use both hands to create small pleats, working from the center of the semicircle towards the outer edges to seal the dumplings. Make three pleats on one side and four on the other for a total of seven pleats—and good luck! This does take a bit of practice, so try simply folding the wrappers over the filling and tightly sealing the dumplings first, then work your way up to making seven pleats. Keep the finished dumplings on the dusted board covered with a clean tea towel while you make the rest to ensure they don't dry out.

Heat the vegetable oil for frying in a nonstick frying pan with a lid over high heat and add as many dumplings as fit the pan (see Tip), placed in a circular formation. Fry for a minute or two until they have a crispy bottom, then fill the pan with water so it comes about ¾ in (2 cm) up the side of the dumplings. Put the lid on. Once it has started to bubble, remove the lid and allow all of the water to evaporate. When you hear the bottoms sizzling, check the dumplings are golden and crispy.

Meanwhile, make the dipping sauce by combining the ingredients in a small bowl with 1 tablespoon of water.

Serve the pot stickers immediately, straight from the pan, with the dipping sauce alongside.

Top tip: Dumplings are best cooked from fresh or frozen; they don't keep well in the fridge. Any dumplings left over before cooking can be frozen—lay them out on a tray so they're not touching (otherwise they'll stick together) and put them in the freezer for a few hours. Once they're frozen, you can transfer them to a freezer bag or airtight container and they will last for a month or two. You can cook them from frozen; just add a few minutes to the cooking time.

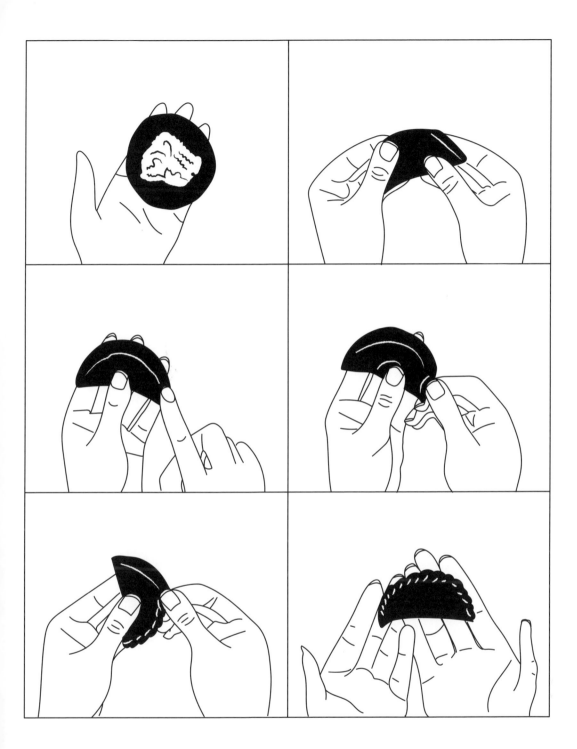

CURRY LEAF CHICKEN LEGS
with SALTED EGG YOLK SAUCE

I became obsessed with salted egg yolk sauce after trying it at a restaurant in Singapore. It has an incredible, full-bodied flavor, a rich and velvety texture. There's something so satisfying about salting your own egg yolks. The transformation of the yolk, as it solidifies, reminds me of an orange gummy candy. Combined with evaporated milk—an ingredient used a lot in Malaysia due to the lack of fresh dairy farms—the richness is irresistible.

SERVES 4

2 tsp ground turmeric
1 tsp chile powder
4 chicken legs, skin on
Vegetable oil, for frying
Salt and freshly ground black pepper

FOR THE SALTED EGG YOLK SAUCE
2 tbsp butter
2 garlic cloves, peeled and minced
1–1½ in (3–4 cm) piece of ginger, peeled and minced
4 baked salted egg yolks (see Note)
10 fresh curry leaves, plus extra (optional) to garnish
2 fresh red or green bird's eye chiles, chopped (optional)
3 tbsp evaporated milk
1 tsp white sugar
¼ tsp ground white pepper

Combine the turmeric and chile powder in a small bowl, then season with salt and black pepper. Rub this spice mixture into the chicken legs and let them marinate in the fridge for at least 30 minutes, or ideally overnight.

Heat a generous amount of vegetable oil in a heavy-based pot over medium heat. Carefully lower the chicken legs into the hot oil and fry until golden and fully cooked. This should take about 10–15 minutes on each side, depending on their size. Once cooked, set the chicken aside on paper towels to drain any excess oil.

Melt the butter in a sauté pan over medium heat. Add the garlic and ginger, then fry until fragrant. Add the salted egg yolks and cook, stirring continuously, until it becomes a creamy, emulsified sauce. Add the curry leaves and chiles (if using), then stir for a further 1 minute. Pour in the evaporated milk, then mix in the sugar and white pepper. Stir until the sauce becomes thick and creamy.

Once the sauce is ready, add the fried chicken and toss in the sauce until each piece is well coated. Serve hot, garnished with additional curry leaves, if desired.

Note: To salt egg yolks, cover the base of a shallow plastic container with fine salt, ¾–1 in (2–3 cm) deep. Use a spoon to make dents, then add a yolk to each. Cover them with more salt, then refrigerate for 8 hours or overnight. The yolks should now have a sticky, gummy texture, perfect for layering on rice. They keep for 3 days in an airtight container in the fridge, or bake them to use in sauces or sprinkle like Parmesan on top of dishes. Preheat the oven to its lowest setting (about 140°F/60°C), place the yolks on an oiled wire rack and bake for 3 hours until dry and hard. Store in an airtight container in the fridge for up to 3 months.

SAMBAL HALLOUMI MORNING BUNS

This was the brainchild of my mom. She created it when my adopted sister Susan, who has always been vegetarian, came over for dinner. I absolutely adore this dish: it's bizarre and brilliant and has to be tried. The halloumi is marinated in sambal until it soaks up all of that chile flavor. The squeakiness of the cheese sings brilliantly with sambal and the runny yolk of the fried egg melds with all of the fiery flavors. I adore making this because it's so simple, especially if you have that big batch of sambal on hand (see page 47). If you haven't managed to make your own sambal yet, there are great sambals to be found in Asian grocery stores.

SERVES 2

1 x 9 oz (250 g) block of halloumi
2 tbsp regular or vegan Sambal Belacan (see page 47), plus a little extra to serve
½ tsp lime juice
Vegetable oil, for frying
2 eggs
2 sesame brioche buns
Kewpie mayo
1 ripe avocado, peeled, stoned and sliced
Salt and freshly ground black pepper (optional)

Slice the halloumi into ½ in (1.5 cm) thick pieces, coat them in the sambal and lime juice and leave to marinate at room temperature for at least 30 minutes.

Heat some vegetable oil in a pan over medium heat, then fry the halloumi slices in batches until golden on both sides.

Heat enough oil to cover the base in a separate pan over medium heat. Once the oil is very hot, crack the eggs into the pan. Fry until the whites of the eggs are golden and crispy, then season the still-runny yolks with some salt and pepper, if you like.

When ready to serve, split and toast the buns. Smear one side of the buns with mayo and the other side with a little extra sambal. Fill the buns with the avocado slices, fried sambal halloumi and crispy fried eggs.

COME OVER
FOR DINNER

Come Over for Dinner

Throwing dinner parties is my equivalent of an Olympic sport, minus the physical exertion and with way more eating. My mom would throw together a dinner for a dozen faster than I could say "Can we just order pizza?" Those nights weren't about racking up an eye-popping check in a swanky restaurant, they were about our house buzzing with friends and family, accompanied by the clatter of silverware as guests dug into home-cooked goodness. Recently I've been carrying on this tradition. Introducing Will Christie, my best friend and the ultimate partner-in-crime when hosting dinner parties. With a budget of about £4.50 ($6.00), he'll turn your average IKEA table into an interior-design masterclass. He has a sixth sense for style—I swear he can make a garbage bag look like a chic tablecloth by draping it right. With me manning the stove and Will working his magic on the ambience, we're pretty much the Bonnie and Clyde of dinner parties. But instead of robbing banks, we're stealing hearts—or so we let ourselves believe—in our charmingly romantic, "delulu" dinner-party world. With his flair for hosting and my knack for cooking up food in abundance, we've got all the bases covered. But it's about more than just food and decor for us; it's a performance, because quite honestly, we like to show off. And sometimes that's just what dinner parties are about.

For your own dinner parties, ditch the idea of the formal three-course meal in favor of the more relaxed communal meal. Be less conformist, think ease and comfort. Pick dishes you can nail with your eyes closed, so you can spend less time sweating over the stove and more time having fun with your guests. This is where the Nyonya style of eating comes into play, showcasing the best of communal dining. Born out of the Peranakan culture, which blends Chinese and Southeast Asian culinary traditions, Nyonya cuisine is a feast of multiple dishes (usually 8–9) served up in a vibrant, communal setting. Picture a table groaning with colorful, aromatic dishes—spicy curries, shrimp, vegetables and perfectly cooked char siu—all waiting to be shared. As well as being a social way of eating, it's honestly much easier to serve up large bowls and platters of food for everyone to serve themselves, rather than having to execute a row of expertly garnished plates. Opting for the sharing approach not only simplifies hosting but also enriches the eating experience. You set out the bowls and platters, then sit down with everyone and enjoy an evening celebrating the diversity of flavors and joy of discovery. Drinks? Keep it simple, too. Nobody expects a full-on cocktail menu from their friend's kitchen bar. A couple of crowd-pleasers will do the trick.

Bringing people together to eat is what I live for. It's the laughs, the mess, the last-minute saves. So here's to hoping these recipes make you the dinner-party champ you aspire to be. Just remember: the simpler, the better. And always save the dish washing for the morning after.

Me and my sisters, Gillian and Susan, with our first love of Caterpillar Cake, Glasgow, 1993

How to Look After Yourself
When Hosting a Dinner Party

1. Ask everyone what their dietary requirements are ahead of the dinner party. Okay, you're not running a restaurant, but it's far less stressful to avoid a surprise request on the night when you're trying your hardest to be cool, calm and collected.
2. As I've already mentioned, ditch the idea of an appetizer, main and dessert. This may be a radical move for those who are wedded to that formula, but a few big platters of shared dishes look far more impressive. Plus you avoid the hassle of having to find five appetizer plates, five main plates, five dessert bowls, etc. and it saves on the dish washing.
3. Begin the dinner party before anyone arrives. While you're cooking and getting everything prepared, light some candles for yourself, maybe stick on a favorite playlist or listen to a few podcasts. I always make a non-alcoholic spritzer to hydrate me while I'm cooking away. Create an atmosphere that truly reflects the vibe of your home, rather than an ambience that feels forced, by taking yourself on a solo date before everyone else arrives.
4. Set out a few snacks for yourself to enjoy during the cooking. Some olives or achar pickle to nibble on during prep is an act of appreciation for you, the chef.
5. Use a nice apron. It doesn't have to be expensive, just one that you like. The act of putting on an apron and getting stage-ready for your prepping of dinner-party dishes puts you mentally right where you need to be.
6. Factor in enough time to have a shower after you've finished your meal prep and before everyone turns up. Pamper yourself with lush lotions and potions. Having done most of the cooking, showering will give you a mental refresh and make you feel dinner-host ready.
7. On the evening, put all of the dirty dishes in buckets of soapy water and then forget about them. Deal with them in the morning.

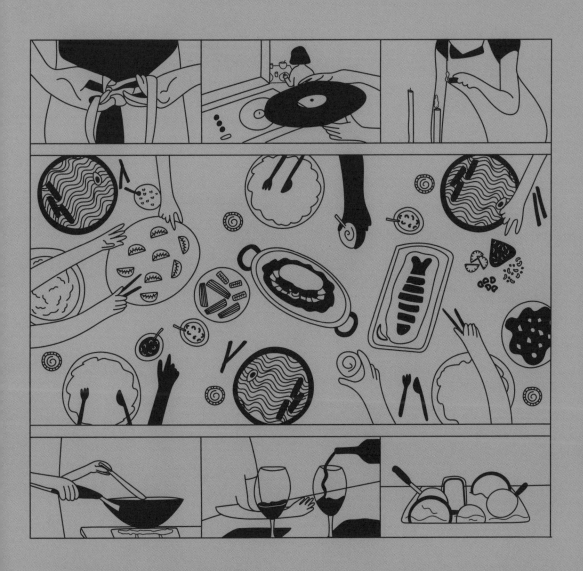

GARLIC DHAL

This is my take on a recipe I learned from Glaswegian-Indian chef, Rachna Dheer, who taught me how to make the most delicious dhals. She taught me always to use far more water than you'd expect, since dried lentils are thirsty and soak up a lot of moisture. This has become my go-to healthy lunch. Rich in fiber, it's filling without feeling like you're missing out on any flavor. When I'm whipping up dishes like this for lunch, I often don't have the time for lots of chopping and so I adore the fact that the garlic can be processed rather than chopped. There's a little work involved in dicing the onion garnish, but this is optional, of course. Remember to season with lime juice and salt until your taste buds are satisfied.

SERVES 2

1 cup (200 g) dried brown lentils
1 black cardamom pod, lightly crushed
Vegetable oil, for frying
8–10 garlic cloves, or to taste, peeled and minced or blended to a paste
2 tsp garam masala
2 tbsp tomato paste
Juice of 1 lime
Salt, to taste

SEASONING STATION (OPTIONAL)
Salt, lime juice, sliced fresh green chiles

TO SERVE
½ small red onion, peeled and finely diced
Pickled green chiles, sliced
A handful of fresh cilantro, finely chopped
Steamed rice or toasted chapatis

Rinse the brown lentils under cold running water until the water runs clear. This removes any debris from the lentils and stops quite as much of that foamy stuff from rising to the top during cooking. This is an extra step, but if you don't have time then just go ahead with cooking the lentils and scoop off the foam during the cooking process.

Place the rinsed lentils in a large pot with the black cardamom pod, then pour over 3 cups (700 ml) of water. Bring to a boil over high heat. Reduce the heat to a simmer and cover the pot with a lid. Cook the lentils for 20–25 minutes, or until tender, skimming off any foam. If it becomes too thick, add a little more water.

While the lentils are cooking, heat a good amount of vegetable oil in a separate pan over medium heat. Add the minced garlic to the pan and fry until fragrant, but not burned. Stir in the garam masala and tomato paste. Cook for a further 2 minutes, stirring frequently.

Once the lentils are cooked, add the garlic, garam masala and tomato paste mixture to the pot and stir well to combine. Season with salt to taste. Let the dhal simmer for a further 5–10 minutes, allowing all the flavors to meld together. Remove the dhal from the heat and stir in the fresh lime juice, along with whichever seasoning station ingredients you feel like today, to taste.

Serve the dhal hot, ladled into bowls and garnished with a generous amount of red onion, pickled green chiles and chopped cilantro on top. Serve with steamed rice or toasted chapatis.

GADO-GADO

This is one of those dishes that show off how excellent salads can be. Gado-gado is a mixture of raw and cooked vegetables, sometimes with boiled egg, tossed in a rich peanut sauce. You could add shrimp or chicken if you like, but I find the fatty brilliance of the peanut sauce carries raw veggies through with a lot of joy. I love the bitterness of cold Brussels sprouts in this salad in place of cabbage, so I make this dish over the festive season to break up the monotonous month of rich dinners, but do adapt this basic recipe to use up anything lurking in the fridge. Last night's leftover roasted cauliflower? Throw that in. Half a can of spare chickpeas from making hummus? Throw those in too.

SERVES 4, AS A SIDE

7 oz (200 g) white cabbage, shredded
3½ oz (100 g) Tenderstem broccoli, steamed and cooled
3½ oz (100 g) green beans, trimmed, steamed and cooled
1 carrot, peeled and cut into long matchsticks
½ cucumber, cut into bite-sized chunks
3½ oz (100 g) beansprouts
2 medium potatoes or a handful of new potatoes, boiled, cooled and cut into bite-sized cubes
1 small pineapple, peeled, cored and cut into bite-sized chunks
2 eggs, hard-boiled, peeled, cooled and quartered
9 oz (250 g) store-bought tofu, dry-fried, cooled and cut into bite-size cubes
3½ oz (100 g) tempeh, fried, cooled and sliced
Crispy fried shallots, to serve
7 oz (200 g) Peanut Sauce (page 52), loosened with water and lime juice, salt and sugar to taste, to serve

On a large serving platter, arrange the cabbage, broccoli, green beans, carrot matchsticks, cucumber chunks and beansprouts.

Scatter the potato, pineapple chunks, hard-boiled egg quarters, tofu cubes and tempeh slices over the vegetables.

Serve the gado-gado with crispy fried shallots sprinkled over the top for added crunch and flavor.

Typically, gado-gado is served with a peanut sauce dressing. If you have made the Peanut Sauce in advance, it might need to be loosened with a splash of water, then season it to taste. Either drizzle the Peanut Sauce over the gado-gado as a dressing or serve it on the side as a dipping sauce.

FRAGRANT SOY ROAST CHICKEN

I made this once for a friend who was having a rough time. I invited her over for a glass of wine, something to eat and a vent. In this kind of crisis situation, I feel chicken noodle soup is not the right dish. This dish gives that same hug-in-a-bowl feeling that you get from noodle soup, but it's slightly easier to eat while chatting. It's also simple enough that you can listen intently at the same time. Hearty and delcious, it's one of my favorite dishes. Cook this as an act of love for yourself or that pal who is having a rough one.

SERVES 4–6

3 lb 5 oz (1.5 kg) chicken legs, skin on
1 tbsp vegetable oil
scant ½ cup (100 ml) dark soy sauce mixed with 4 tbsp honey and 1 tsp cornstarch, to glaze

FOR THE POACHING LIQUID
Scant 1 cup (200 ml) Shaoxing rice wine
⅔ cup (150ml) light soy sauce
5 tbsp dark soy sauce, plus extra to taste
¾ cup (150 g) gula melaka palm sugar (or dark brown sugar)
2 tbsp sea salt flakes
1 tsp MSG
15 cloves
10 slices of ginger, ¼ in (5 mm) thick
8 scallions, cut into about 3 in (7 cm) pieces and smashed flat
5 star anise

SEASONING STATION (OPTIONAL)
Light soy sauce, lime juice, black vinegar, MSG

TO SERVE (OPTIONAL)
Fresh cilantro leaves
Fresh Thai basil leaves
Steamed rice
Steamed green vegetables

In a large, deep pot, combine the Shaoxing rice wine, both soy sauces, the sugar, sea salt, MSG and 10½ cups (2.5 liters) of water. Stir until all the sugar crystals dissolve. Add the cloves, ginger slices, scallions and star anise to the pot, then bring the mixture to a gentle simmer over low heat, ensuring the sugar has fully dissolved.

Carefully lower the chicken legs into the pot, making sure they're fully submerged in the poaching liquid. If you need to add more water to cover the chicken, that's fine at this stage as the liquid will be reduced later to create a sauce. Simmer over the lowest heat until the chicken is fully cooked through—use a digital meat thermometer to check the chicken has reached at least 170°F (75°C) inside. This usually takes 40–60 minutes over low heat, but the cooking time will vary depending on the size of the chicken legs.

Preheat the oven to 425°F (220°C).

Remove the chicken legs from the poaching liquid and lay flat on a baking pan. Gently pat dry with paper towels and place in the hot oven for 10–15 minutes, or until the skin has gone crispy and golden.

Meanwhile, simmer the poaching liquid until it has reduced by half. Taste this sauce and adjust the seasoning with whichever seasoning station ingredients you feel like today.

Once cooked, brush the chicken with the vegetable oil and soy-honey glaze, making sure it's well coated.

Serve the chicken with the herbs scattered over, alongside some steamed rice and green veggies, if you like, and a bowl of the reduced poaching liquid (any left over is excellent as a fragrant noodle broth the next day; just strain to remove the flavorings before storing).

Come Over for Dinner

GREEN APPLE AND GREEN BEAN KERABU

In Malaysia, kerabu can take many different forms. It's essentially a salad, but what goes into it differs. It usually has a vibrant dressing of lime juice, sugar, chile and seasoning tossed over raw and cooked vegetables. I just love kerabu for the simple fact it is so versatile. Here, I adore how the green apple has the crunchy texture of water chestnuts and the tangy sharp flavor that keeps everything fresh, and how the toasted coconut binds everything together. If you want to make this salad into an even more substantial meal, toss through some cooked rice vermicelli noodles.

SERVES 1–2, AS A SIDE

2 tbsp desiccated coconut
2 tbsp dried shrimp, soaked and roughly chopped (optional)
⅓ cup (50 g) roasted salted peanuts, crushed
3 fresh red or green bird's eye chiles, finely chopped (adjust to taste)
3½ oz (100 g) green beans, trimmed
1 green eating apple, cored
3½ oz (100 g) carrots, shredded
3½ oz (100 g) cucumber, deseeded and cut into matchsticks
1¾ oz (50 g) red onion, peeled and thinly sliced
A handful of fresh mint leaves, roughly torn
A handful of fresh cilantro leaves, roughly chopped

FOR THE DRESSING

1 garlic clove, peeled and finely minced
Juice of 1 lime
2 tbsp fish sauce
1 tbsp sesame oil
2½ tbsp palm sugar (or dark brown sugar)
A pinch of salt

First, toast the desiccated coconut in a dry pan over medium heat, stirring continuously, until golden. Take care not to burn the coconut. Set aside to cool.

Using a mortar and pestle, pound the dried shrimp, roasted salted peanuts and 2 of the chiles until they are ground down into a rough paste. In a small bowl, whisk together all the ingredients for the dressing, then whisk in the chile paste. Taste and adjust the balance of flavors as needed—it should be a harmonious blend of sour, sweet, salty and spicy. Set aside.

Next, prepare the green beans. Blanch the beans in boiling water for 1 minute, then drain and immediately plunge into iced water to stop the cooking process and retain their crunch. Drain again and set aside.

Cut the green apple into thin matchsticks, then place them in salted water to prevent browning. Set aside.

When ready to serve, drain the apple matchsticks and place them in a large salad bowl. Add the blanched green beans, the shredded carrot, cucumber matchsticks, sliced red onion, the remaining chopped chile, torn mint leaves, chopped cilantro leaves and toasted coconut.

Pour the dressing over the salad, then toss gently to coat all the ingredients in the dressing.

Pictured on page 110

CUCUMBER AND CRYSTALLIZED GINGER SALAD

In the world of side dishes, this one really stands out. It's unpretentious yet bold, the kind of dish that could easily wear the title of "palate cleanser," if one were inclined to be a bit fancy. My mom used to serve this at the start of dinner parties; it's perfect for awakening the taste buds, even if, like us, you're not an intricate hors d'oeuvres kind of household. My mom has a knack for using deliciously sweet ingredients in savory salads. This is a knockout combination, with the sweet pepperiness of the crystallized ginger contrasting with the cooling cucumber. It's fabulous during hot summers, too.

SERVES 2, AS A SIDE

1 large cucumber
1 small red onion, peeled and thinly sliced
2 tbsp crystallized ginger, finely chopped
2 tbsp rice vinegar
1 tsp honey
A bunch of fresh mint, roughly torn
A bunch of fresh cilantro, roughly chopped

SEASONING STATION (OPTIONAL)
Sea salt flakes, freshly ground black pepper, palm sugar, lime juice, chile crisp oil

Peel the cucumber and slice it in half lengthwise. Using a teaspoon, scoop out the seeds from the center. (Rather than discard the cucumber peel, you can toss them into noodle salads or wok fries.) Cut the deseeded cucumber halves at an angle into thin slices, then place them in a salad bowl.

Add the red onion and crystallized ginger to the bowl with the cucumber slices.

In a small bowl, whisk together the rice vinegar and honey until well combined. Season with whichever of your seasoning station ingredients you fancy today.

Pour the dressing over the cucumber salad and toss gently to ensure all the ingredients are well coated. Let the salad sit for 10 minutes to allow the flavors to develop.

Just before serving, sprinkle the torn mint and chopped cilantro over the salad, then toss to evenly distribute the herbs. Taste and adjust the seasoning.

Pictured on page 111

PINEAPPLE CURRY WITH LIME LEAVES

Many people wince at the thought of sweet pineapple infiltrating the savory space on their plate. Of course, the age-old argument is against pineapple on pizza. Culturally, I know pineapple on pizza upsets many Italians, but I have a level of acceptance for this garishly delicious combination. Recently, at Errol's Hot Pizza Shop in Glasgow, I had an exceptional pizza with pepperoni, pineapple and hot honey—the pepperoni provided salty goodness to counter the sweet pineapple, while the hot honey brought a delicious intensity. Granted Errol's serves my favorite pizza in this universe, but wherever you are, if it's a good pizza base with salty pepperoni and caramelized pineapple on top, then it'll taste good. Simple. If it's a bad-quality pizza with drab ham and canned pineapple on it, it won't taste great.

Here, in this curry, the pineapple isn't merely a quirky addition; it's the soul of the dish, lending a bright, tangy chunk that simmers in the fatty coconut milk, laden with all of the spices to make it fragrant.

If you like, you can add some pork to this—wok-fry some sliced pork loin in garlic, soy sauce and salt—but if you want to keep it vegetarian, leave it as it is. It's phenomenal either way. Epitomizing those warm, laughter-filled, family dinners, this dish is a celebration of pineapple's versatility and a nod to my mom's ingenuity in the kitchen. The way she wields her spices over the pineapple's juicy flesh to create a tangy, savory flavor will convert even the staunchest sceptics. It's a dish that offers respite from the mundane, a sweet and savory escape that I hold dear to my heart.

SERVES 2–3

FOR THE RENDANG PASTE
2 tbsp vegetable oil
7 oz (200 g) Base Curry Paste (page 42)
1 tbsp coriander seeds
1 tsp cumin seeds
2 tsp fennel seeds
6 candlenuts or macadamia nuts

FOR THE CURRY
14 oz (400 ml) can of coconut milk
1 lemongrass stalk, bruised
2 fresh makrut lime leaves
1 tbsp tamarind paste

Heat the vegetable oil in a large pot or wok over medium heat. Add the Base Curry Paste and cook, stirring frequently, for 10 minutes, or until fragrant and the oil is beginning to separate from the paste.

Meanwhile, add the whole spices to a dry frying pan. Toast over low-medium heat for 3–4 minutes until starting to brown—watch them carefully or they will burn.

Place the nuts and whole spices in a spic grinder and blend to a paste. Add this nutty paste to the pan and stir into the Base Curry Paste.

Add the coconut milk, bruised lemongrass and lime leaves to the pan and bring to a simmer. Add the tamarind paste, palm sugar and salt, stirring until all the sugar crystals have dissolved. Reduce the heat and simmer over low heat for 5–10 minutes.

2 tbsp palm sugar (or dark brown soft sugar)
1 tsp sea salt flakes (adjust to taste)
1 large pineapple, peeled, cored and cut into bite-sized pieces (save the peel to make Pineapple Peel Iced Tea, see page 272)
½ cup (50 g) toasted desiccated coconut

SEASONING STATION (OPTIONAL)
Lime juice, sugar, salt, fish sauce, light soy sauce

TO SERVE
Fresh makrut lime leaves, very finely shredded
Fresh cilantro sprigs
Steamed rice

Drop the pineapple pieces into the sauce and let the curry gently simmer for about 15 minutes, or until the pineapple is tender but not mushy. Towards the end of the cooking time, stir in most of the toasted coconut for a nutty flavor and to thicken the sauce slightly.

When ready to serve, taste the curry and adjust with your seasoning station ingredients, whatever your taste buds need. Garnish the curry with fresh lime leaves, cilantro sprigs and the remaining nutty toasted coconut just before serving. Serve with steamed rice.

Pictured on page 111

Come Over for Dinner

SINGAPORE BUTTER SHRIMP

This recipe is famous in Singapore. It uses a brand of cereal that is unavailable in the US, Nestle Nestum. It's quite unique, but since my taste buds won't let me sit on an idea, I decided to test out some sweetened oats in this recipe… and they worked marvelously. The sweetness of the oats, which coat the shrimp, marries so well with the seafood. It's unbelievably tasty.

SERVES 2-3

1 lb 5 oz (600 g) raw jumbo shrimp, deveined (you can leave the shells on; frying softens them so they're edible)
1 tsp salt
1 tsp sugar
2½ tbsp all-purpose flour
2½ tbsp cornstarch
1 egg, beaten
Vegetable oil, for frying
¼ cup (30 g) maple brown sugar oats (I use Quaker Oat So Simple)
3½ tbsp butter
15 fresh curry leaves
2 fresh red bird's eye chiles, sliced
1½ tbsp chicken bouillon powder (you can also use a crumbled chicken stock cube and a pinch of MSG)
Steamed jasmine rice, to serve

SEASONING STATION (OPTIONAL)
Chile crisp oil, lime juice, salt

Toss the shrimp with the salt and sugar in a shallow bowl. Let them sit for a few minutes to marinate.

Combine the all-purpose flour and cornstarch in a separate shallow bowl and put the beaten egg in another.

Heat enough vegetable oil for shallow frying in a frying pan over medium-low heat.

Dip the shrimp first in the beaten egg and then into the flour mixture until fully coated. Carefully lower the shrimp into the hot oil and fry until golden and crispy. Transfer the shrimp to a plate lined with paper towels to drain any excess oil.

In a separate pan, heat 1½ tablespoons of vegetable oil over medium heat. Add the oats to the pan and fry until golden. Transfer to a bowl and set aside.

In the same pan, melt the butter with a splash of vegetable oil so the butter doesn't burn. Add the curry leaves and sliced chiles, then fry until fragrant.

Add the fried shrimp to the pan with the aromatic butter. Sprinkle the chicken bouillon powder over the shrimp and toss to coat evenly. Finally, return the crisped oats to the pan, and toss again to coat the shrimp. Add whichever seasoning station ingredients you feel like today, to taste.

Serve the shrimp immediately, alongside some steamed jasmine rice.

GRILLED LEMONGRASS CHICKEN THIGHS
with PEANUT SAUCE

When I opened my modest street-food stall in Glasgow, this dish was our first offering. During those early days, my mom was so encouraging and helpful that she would help me prepare umpteen batches of this chicken in her kitchen. She then used to drive into the city center with my dad, transporting large trays of prepped chicken on the back seat of the car. I truly couldn't have done it without her, or my father. It swiftly became a crowd favorite, a beloved classic that still holds a special place in my heart.

It's my homage to the traditional Malaysian satay chicken skewers, albeit with a personal twist borne out of necessity due to the resources I had at my disposal. Originally, I had named this Roasted Satay Chicken—alas, that's not the correct name as there's not a skewer in sight. "Sate" or "sati" implies skewered, which I was always aware of, but over the years I've grown and realized it's important not to mislabel food. Hence a new name, celebrating the succulent chicken thighs in their own right. The accompanying Peanut Sauce is the pièce de résistance, elevating the already sublime grilled chicken.

SERVES 4–6

2 lb 4 oz (1 kg) boneless chicken thighs, skin on
2 tbsp kecap manis (sweet soy sauce)
Peanut Sauce (see page 52), to serve
Steamed rice, to serve

FOR THE SPICE PASTE
3 lemongrass stalks
10 garlic cloves, peeled
3 tbsp ground coriander
2 tbsp ground cumin
1 tbsp Kashmiri chile powder
1 tsp sea salt flakes
Vegetable oil, for blending

First, make the spice paste. Trim the top and base from the lemongrass stalks, remove the tough outer leaves and roughly chop the tender middle part. Place the chopped lemongrass into a blender along with the garlic, ground coriander, ground cumin, Kashmiri chile powder, sea salt and a little vegetable oil to help with blending. Blend to a smooth paste.

Spread the spice paste evenly over the chicken thighs. Place them in a bowl, then drizzle over the kecap manis and rub it all into the chicken skin to ensure everywhere is well coated. Cover the bowl and leave the chicken thighs to marinate in the fridge for at least 1 hour, or for up to 24 hours.

When ready to cook, preheat your broiler and place a broiler pan on the middle rack of the oven to heat. Remove the chicken thighs from the marinade, setting any excess aside. Place the chicken, skin-side down, on the hot broiler pan and cook for 10 minutes, or until the skin is crisp and golden. Turn the thighs over and continue to cook for a further 15–20 minutes, or until completely cooked through.

FOR THE SALAD

⅓ *pineapple, peeled, cored and cut into bite-sized chunks*
½ *cucumber, deseeded and sliced*
Juice of 1 lime
A pinch of chile flakes
Salt and freshly ground black pepper

Meanwhile, make the salad. Combine the pineapple chunks and cucumber slices in a salad bowl. Season generously with some of the lime juice, the chile flakes and a pinch of both salt and black pepper. Just before serving, drizzle the salad with more fresh lime juice and toss gently.

Serve the grilled chicken thighs hot with the Peanut Sauce alongside, accompanied by the pineapple and chile cucumber salad and steamed rice.

STICKY TAMARIND SHRIMP

For the small number of ingredients that goes into this, these tamarind shrimp are stupidly tasty. I've adapted my initial recipe which simply had tamarind, sugar and salt to add a bit more flavor for my own preferences. Lemongrass isn't "authentic" to the classic recipe, but I adore the fragrance it brings here; it's my addition that I love. If you don't have any, don't worry, this recipe is delicious without. Keeping the shell on the shrimp adds a huge amount of flavor, they're full of juice from the shrimp and mixed with the distinctly sharp, sweet tamarind sauce they are just perfect. These would be excellent on the grill with a bit of char on them too. I crunch right through the shells with this one, I know that might not be for everyone, but I urge you to give it a try—it's so ridiculously delicious and adds even more joy to eating them. At the very least eat this with your hands; no silverware is allowed here. Get your fingers sticky, mop up the juices with steamed rice and enjoy this all in an extremely animalistic fashion.

SERVES 2–4

1½ tbsp tamarind concentrate
2 tbsp vegetable oil
1 lemongrass stalk, cleaned, trimmed and finely sliced (optional)
2 tbsp dark soy sauce
2 tsp light soy sauce
Lime juice, to taste
2½ tbsp palm sugar (or dark brown soft sugar)
A pinch of salt, or to taste
16 extra-large raw jumbo shrimp, deveined, with shells left on
Toasted desiccated coconut, to garnish

First, marinate the shrimp. In a bowl, combine the tamarind concentrate, vegetable oil, sliced lemongrass, if using, both soy sauces and lime juice, to taste. Add the sugar and a pinch of salt, or to taste, and mix well until the sugar crystals have dissolved. Add the shrimp to the marinade, making sure they are well coated, and leave in the fridge for at least 30 minutes, or overnight.

If cooking the shrimp on the grill, preheat the barbecue to medium-high heat. Once the shrimp have marinated, thread them onto metal skewers (if using bamboo skewers, soak them for at least an hour first). Grill the shrimp, turning occasionally and basting with the marinade, for 2–3 minutes on each side, or until pink and lightly charred.

If cooking the shrimp on a stove, heat a nonstick wok or large frying pan over medium heat. Add the marinated shrimp, along with all of the marinade and a scant ½ cup (100 ml) of water. Cook, stirring occasionally, for 6–8 minutes, or until the shrimp are pink and cooked through and the sauce has thickened.

Once the shrimp are cooked, transfer them to a serving dish, scatter over the toasted desiccated coconut and serve while hot.

BEEF SHANK RENDANG

Rendang is a slow-cooked dry curry that is so rich in flavor. There are two key factors in a good rendang. As all of the spice paste ingredients cook at different rates, frying them individually is the key to a good paste. The second factor is the double-cook. The coconut milk splits and reduces to a paste-like consistency, at which point your meat releases its fats and the fats released draw out the flavor for the rendang.

SERVES 6

7 oz (200 g) can of coconut cream
8¾ lb (4 kg) boneless beef shank, cut into 1½–2 in (4–5 cm) chunks
2 x 14 oz (400 ml) cans of coconut milk
8 fresh makrut lime leaves
3 star anise
2 cinnamon sticks
4 green cardamom pods, lightly crushed
2 cups (150 g) toasted coconut flakes
Palm sugar (or dark brown sugar)

FOR THE SPICE PASTE

1½ tsp belacan
10 banana shallots, roughly chopped
6 lemongrass stalks, trimmed and hard outer layer peeled off
2 in (5 cm) piece of fresh turmeric, peeled and roughly chopped (or ½ tsp ground turmeric)
2 in (5 cm) piece of ginger, peeled and roughly chopped
2 in (5 cm) piece of galangal, peeled and roughly chopped (optional)
1 head garlic, cloves roughly chopped
20 fresh dried red chiles, soaked in warm water for 20 minutes, roughly chopped, deseeded
2 long red chiles, roughly chopped (deseeded for less heat)
15 candlenuts (or macadamia nuts)

To make the spice paste, first toast the belacan in a dry pan over medium heat for about 3–4 minutes until fragrant and browned on the outside. Set aside. Thoroughly blend each of the remaining ingredients separately in a food processor or blender.

Heat a generous amount of vegetable oil in a large, heavy-based pot over medium heat. Start by adding the blended shallots and, stirring continuously to keep everything moving, fry them until they have spluttered and cooked a little. Next, add the blended lemongrass to the pan and fry for 1 minute or so.

Now add in the turmeric, ginger and galangal, if using, and continue to fry for a further 1 minute. Finally, add the garlic, chiles, candlenuts and the belacan, then reduce the heat as these ingredients can burn a lot quicker than the others. Keep the spice paste moving so that it doesn't catch on the base of the pot; it needs to brown a little and eventually turn a deep orange color.

Place the coconut cream in the pot with the spice paste and allow it to melt. (I prefer to add it now in order to give the coconut cream ample time to split once boiled.)

Add the beef shank to the pot along with the coconut milk. Turn up the heat to medium-high and allow the milk to come to a boil, then add a little water.

Add the makrut lime leaves and whole spices (star anise, cinnamon sticks and cardamom pods), reduce the heat to the lowest setting, then simmer slowly, stirring occasionally, for 6–8 hours until it has reduced down, the meat is tender and falling apart. You could add this to a slow cooker at this point and cook on the low setting for 6–8 hours (or overnight).

Continued →

← Rendang continued

Using a mortar and pestle, pound the toasted coconut flakes so they begin to release their oil and become even nuttier in flavor. Once the curry has reduced, add the toasted coconut to the pot and stir. The curry will immediately thicken at this stage and the sauce should be darker in color. The beef should still be in whole chunks but tender, the curry paste around it should cling to each piece and not be saucy.

Taste and adjust the balance of the curry with sugar and salt to suit your taste. Serve with rice and pickles.

BLEND THE SPICES

COOK THE INGREDIENTS

GIVE IT TIME

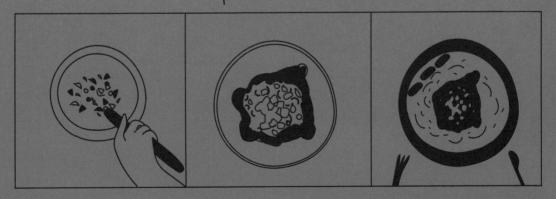

SALT AND PEPPER OYSTER MUSHROOMS

I adore mushrooms so much, especially oyster mushrooms. They can give me ten times the satisfaction that fried chicken does. Be careful not to confuse oyster mushrooms with king oyster mushrooms, though, which are more cartoon-like in appearance with a white base and a brown top. Oyster mushrooms are brownish-gray in color, tearable and incredibly meaty in flavor. They're probably the vegetable I buy the most often from the supermarket. Gently shallow frying these mushrooms gives them the flavor needed for this dish.

SERVES 4, AS AN APPETIZER OR SNACK

10½ oz (300 g) oyster mushrooms
3 tbsp cornstarch
3 tsp freshly ground black pepper
1 tsp salt, or to taste
½ tsp garlic powder
½ tsp onion powder
½ tsp Chinese five-spice powder
A pinch of MSG
Vegetable oil, for frying
2 scallions, finely chopped
A handful of fresh cilantro, chopped
1 fresh red chile, thinly sliced
Store-bought tamarind dip, to serve

Carefully clean the mushrooms and then gently tear them into strips.

In a bowl, combine the cornstarch, black pepper, salt, garlic powder, onion powder, Chinese five-spice powder and MSG. Toss the mushrooms in this mixture until well coated.

Heat a generous amount of vegetable oil in a frying pan over medium-high heat.

Working in batches, add the mushroom strips to the hot oil and fry until golden and crispy. Transfer them to a plate lined with paper towels to drain any excess oil.

When ready to serve, arrange the fried mushrooms on a serving platter or dish. Scatter over the chopped scallions, sliced red chile and chopped cilantro. Serve with the tamarind dip alongside.

Come Over for Dinner 125

PORK AND SHRIMP DUMPLINGS

There's a misconception that dumplings are merely a cheap street food, when in fact they're an intricate work of art. The level of skill required is often overlooked in their enthusiastic consumption, but I forgive this as they're wonderfully delicious. The ritual of making dumplings is akin to practicing meditation. In a world that moves at breakneck speed, dumplings slow us down. There's a rhythm and precision to the act of pleating the delicate wrappers that requires a focus and attentiveness to rival the crafting of French pâtisserie. I've often noted that homemade tortellini are marvelled at for the technique required, with society willing to pay a premium for an otherwise humble dish made from scratch. Dumplings should command that same respect, with each pleat a testament to the care and concentration poured into them. They're not meant for a quick bite but rather a moment to savor, to appreciate the laborious journey from kitchen counter to dining table.

This is a dish best enjoyed in the company of friends. It's not just about eating, it's about tradition, connection and the celebration of a craft that's as old as time. You could even get your friends involved in shaping the dumplings: it's a shared experience that enriches the soul. I've often held dumpling-making workshops as a means of relaxing people, similar to how a flower-arranging class might make you feel. It's a beautiful experience making these little morsels from scratch.

MAKES 30 DUMPLINGS

FOR THE DUMPLING DOUGH
2 cups (250 g) dumpling flour (high gluten wheat flour), plus extra for dusting
Pinch of salt

FOR THE FILLING
14 oz (400 g) ground pork (40% fat, or the highest fat content available)
1–2 tbsp lard, chilled or frozen (only if using ground pork with 10–20% fat)
7 oz (200 g) raw shrimp, peeled, deveined and roughly chopped
1¾ oz (50 g) ginger, peeled and grated

First, make the infused water. Pour the freshly boiled water into a heatproof bowl and add the ginger, peppercorns, cinnamon sticks and star anise. Leave to cool down and for the aromatics to infuse the water for at least 30 minutes.

Meanwhile, make the dough. Combine the flour and salt in a large mixing bowl. Pour a scant ½ cup (100 ml) of cold water into the bowl and very slowly start to mix the flour and water into a dough. When everything is combined, add a further 1½ tablespoons of cold water and knead to a smooth dough. Once a ball forms and there is no dough clinging to the sides of the bowl or your hands, it's ready. This should take about 20 minutes by hand, but it can also be done in a stand mixer. Cover the bowl with plastic wrap and leave the dough to rest for 30 minutes at room temperature.

While the dumpling dough rests, make the filling. If your ground pork has less than 40% fat, add some lard to increase the fat content (a high fat content is the secret

2 small white onions, peeled and finely diced
2 scallions, finely diced
1 egg, beaten
3 tbsp sesame oil
2 tbsp dark soy sauce
1 tbsp light soy sauce
1 tbsp white sugar
2 tsp salt
½ tsp freshly ground black pepper

FOR THE INFUSED WATER
scant ½ cup (100 ml) boiling water
3 slices of ginger
1 tsp Sichuan peppercorns
4 cinnamon sticks
10 star anise

TO SERVE
1½ tbsp black rice vinegar (chinkiang vinegar)
1 tbsp Lao Gan Ma crispy chile oil
A handful of chopped fresh cilantro leaves

to keeping the filling juicy). If your pork has 20% fat, add 1 tablespoon of lard. If your pork has 10% fat, then add 2 tablespoons of lard. Chop the lard into tiny cubes and scatter them evenly through the ground pork in a large mixing bowl. Add all the other ingredients for the filling to the pork, then strain the scant ½ cup (100 ml) of infused water into the bowl. The mixture will be very liquidy at this point. Bring everything together with your hands until well combined. Leave the pork mixture to sit for at least 20 minutes in the fridge.

Once the dough has rested, knead it again until it reaches the same smooth texture as before. Dust a work surface with flour. You can now either roll the dough out flat (about the thickness of a nickel) and use a circular cutter about the size of your palm to punch out discs of dough, or use the following steps. Divide the dough into 3 equal pieces, then knead each piece into a cylinder. Cut small pieces of dough, each weighing $^1/_3$ oz (10 g), from the edge of the cylinder while turning it 90 degrees after each cut for the next piece—this ensures circular discs. Using a mini rolling pin or dumpling dowel, roll each dough disc into an even circle, continually rotating the dough as you go, to make an even circle. Dust with plenty of extra flour to keep the dough from sticking to the surfaces. Keep the rolled-out wrappers completely covered with plastic wrap while preparing the rest.

Prepare your dumpling-making station. Dust a clean surface or board with flour, set a bowl of water to the side and have the dumpling wrappers in easy reach.

If you're right-handed, lay a dumpling wrapper in the palm of your left hand (and vice versa if you're left-handed). Place one heaped teaspoon of the filling right in the center of the dumpling wrapper (being careful not to overfill it or they will burst during cooking), dab a little water on one side to help it stick, then fold and—if you can—pleat the dumplings. There are many different ways to do this. I find the easiest method is to fold the dumpling over and firmly pinch the wrapper in the middle on one side. Now use both hands to create small pleats, working from the center of the semicircle towards the outer edges to seal the dumpling. Make three pleats on one side and four on the other for a total of seven pleats—and good luck!

Continued →

Come Over for Dinner

← *Dumplings continued*

This does take a bit of practice, so try simply folding the wrappers over the filling and tightly sealing the dumplings first, then work your way up to seven pleats. Keep the finished dumplings on the dusted surface/board covered with a clean tea towel while you make the rest to ensure they don't dry out.

Bring a deep pot of lightly salted water to a boil over high heat. Working in batches so as not to overcrowd the pot, drop in the dumplings, then add 3½ tablespoons of cold water and allow the water to come back up to a boil. Repeat this process three times until the dumplings are floating and cooked through, then remove from the water with a slotted spoon.

When ready to serve, combine the vinegar and chile oil in a small bowl to make a dipping sauce. Serve the dipping sauce alongside the freshly cooked dumplings, scattered with the chopped cilantro.

Come Over for Dinner

PUFFED RICE, PEANUT AND SHRIMP CRACKER BHEL

Bhel puri is a popular Indian street-food snack. It combines puffed rice and sev (small pieces of crunchy noodles made from chickpea flour) with a mixture of diced vegetables, like tomatoes, onions and boiled potatoes, then a tamarind sauce and mint-coriander chutney are drizzled over at the last moment, adding a refreshingly tangy zing. It's finished with a sprinkle of chaat masala. Bhel puri is one of my favorite snacks on the entire planet. When I worked in an Indian café, my then-boss showed me how to make this. Fast-forward to the day I had all of the ingredients and some leftover Thai shrimp crackers, to make a different bhel. I adore fishiness, and the flavors from the crackers add to this amazingly. It's now a snack I regularly make for friends.

SERVES 4, AS A SNACK

3 oz (75 g) puffed rice
2¾ tbsp salted peanuts, crushed
1 oz (25 g) Thai shrimp crackers, lightly crushed
1¾ oz (50 g) sev
½ medium red onion, peeled and finely chopped
1 small fresh long red or green chile, finely chopped (adjust to taste)
A handful of fresh cilantro, chopped
Seeds from ¼ pomegranate (optional)

FOR THE TAMARIND DRESSING

3 tbsp tamarind paste, mixed with scant ½ cup (100 ml) water and 2 tbsp vinegar
1 tbsp lime juice
½ tbsp sugar
1 tsp ground cumin
1 tbsp chaat masala powder
½ tsp chile powder (or to taste)
Salt, to taste

TO SERVE

A few fresh cilantro leaves
Lime wedges
Green Chile Chutney (page 48)

First, make the dressing. Combine the tamarind paste, lime juice, sugar, ground cumin, chaat masala, chile powder and salt in a bowl. Add a little water, as needed, to loosen the mixture to a dressing consistency. Adjust the seasonings according to your taste—it should be spicy, tangy, sweet and a little sour. Set aside.

In a large bowl, mix together the puffed rice, crushed peanuts, Thai shrimp crackers and the sev. Add the red onion, chile and cilantro to the bowl with the pomegranate seeds, if using. Do not dress the bhel mixture until ready to serve.

Immediately before serving, pour the tamarind dressing over the bhel mixture and gently toss everything together to ensure that all the ingredients are evenly coated in the dressing. Scatter the cilantro leaves over the top and serve with lime wedges and Green Chile Chutney.

CLAM-OROUS NOODS

"Hey Alexa. Play Fergie, 'Glamorous.'" In the quiet cocoon of my living room, with the hum of the outside world fading into the background, I find strength in a dish that's as simple as it is comforting: a plate of wok-fried clam and glass noodles. It's the kind of meal that's perfect for those nights when all you want is to curl up on the couch, tv on, with the rest of the world tuned out. I've come to realize that clams, though they may carry a reputation for complexity, are actually quite the opposite. They're my go-to for a fuss-free feast that feels like a treat. Cooking them doesn't have to be a grand production—it's a straightforward affair. A quiet celebration of sorts for evenings spent with friends.

They're simple to prepare, all it takes is bathing them in water for a while to remove the grit, which is perfect for when you're preparing dinner for friends to give you a chance to slip off the apron and put on some eyeliner. They have the added bonus that they don't take long to cook whatsoever, they're quick and easy. The silky glass noodles make this dish even more impressive in its appearance, giving it a wow factor.

This recipe is a nod to the "clam-orous" side in all of us, that inner voice that craves something extraordinary to share with people. It's a dish created for those moments of having the gals over, blasting silly music and drinking beer together. This is also an ode to my friends who out of sheer chance are mostly pescatarian, and they absolutely adore this as a centerpiece.

Recipe overleaf →

SERVES 4   ← *Clam-orous Noods continued*

14 oz (400 g) fresh clams, in shells
7 oz (200 g) dried glass noodles
    (if you can't find glass noodles,
    use dried rice noodles instead)
Vegetable oil, for frying
10 garlic cloves, peeled and minced
2 in (5 cm) piece of ginger,
    peeled and minced
8 scallions, finely sliced
5 tbsp light soy sauce
3 tsp dark soy sauce
3 tsp oyster sauce
2 tsp chicken bouillon powder or MSG
5 tsp sugar
7 oz (200 g) choi sum (or spinach),
    chopped into bite-sized chunks
5 fresh red bird's eye chiles,
    finely sliced
Juice of ½ lime
Salt and freshly ground black pepper
Toasted sesame seeds, to garnish
Sesame oil, to finish

SEASONING STATION (OPTIONAL)
Chile crisp oil, lime juice,
    salt, light soy sauce

First, prepare the clams. Soak the clams in a large bowl of salted water for at least 1 hour to purge them of any sand or grit. Rinse the soaked clams under cold running water several times until the water runs clear, then leave them to drain. Discard any that are open or don't close with a sharp tap.

Meanwhile, put the glass noodles in a heatproof bowl, pour over boiling water and cover with a lid or plate. Leave the noodles to soak until soft. This usually takes 15–20 minutes.

When ready to cook, place a wok over high heat. Once hot, add a generous amount of vegetable oil to coat the bottom of the wok. Add the minced garlic and ginger and half of the sliced scallions to the wok and stir-fry over high heat until fragrant.

Add the clams to the wok and stir-fry for 1 minute. Pour in ⅔ cup (150 ml) of water, cover the wok with a lid and steam the clams for 3–5 minutes or until they open. Discard any clams that do not open.

Once the clams have opened, add both soy sauces, the oyster sauce, chicken bouillon powder or MSG and sugar to the wok, as well as some salt and a pinch of black pepper to taste. Stir well to combine all the flavors.

Drain the glass noodles and add them to the wok, along with the chopped choi sum and sliced red chiles. Toss everything together to ensure the noodles and vegetables are well coated in the sauce. Cook for a further 2–3 minutes, or until the choi sum has wilted and the noodles have absorbed the sauce.

Squeeze the lime juice over everything and give it a final stir. Add whichever seasoning station ingredients you feel like today, to taste. Pile the noodles in a serving dish, scatter over the remaining scallions and the sesame seeds and finish with a drizzle of sesame oil.

MUSHROOM STICKY RICE
with KECAP MANIS OYSTER MUSHROOMS

I am one of those who claims to be flexitarian. I'm conscious of arguments around what we eat and the impact on the environment and I consistently try and do better, but it can be overwhelming. When I'm trying to eat more plant-based, I turn to mushrooms. I am blown away by them, the flexibility of how you can cook them, the textures, the intense flavor from different varieties. Oyster mushrooms are my favorite, as well as the mighty lion's mane, which are a little harder to find. Both offer a meaty depth that I adore. This dish is what I turn to when I'm craving an earthy mushroomy hit.

SERVES 4–6

1½ cups (300 g) sticky (glutinous) rice
3½ oz (100 g) dried shiitake mushrooms
4¼ cups (1 liter) warm water
2 tbsp sesame oil
3 garlic cloves, peeled and minced
1 in (2.5 cm) piece of ginger, peeled and minced
2 cups (500 ml) mushroom stock (made from mushroom bouillon powder)
1 star anise
3 tbsp light soy sauce
4–6 salted egg yolks (see page 137), to serve (optional)

FOR THE CARAMELIZED MUSHROOMS
2 tbsp vegetable oil
14 oz (400 g) oyster mushrooms, cleaned and torn into pieces
3 garlic cloves, peeled and minced
2 tbsp kecap manis (sweet soy sauce)
1 tsp black vinegar (or malt vinegar)
1 tbsp dark soy sauce
½ tsp salt (adjust to taste)
1 tbsp store-bought crispy fried garlic

SEASONING STATION (OPTIONAL)
Light soy sauce, black vinegar

Rinse the rice several times until the water runs clear. Soak it in cold water for at least 2 hours, then drain.

Soak the shiitake mushrooms in the warm water for 30 minutes. Remove the mushrooms, squeeze out excess water, and slice thinly. Reserve the water.

Heat the sesame oil in a large pot over medium heat. Add the garlic and ginger and sauté until fragrant. Add the shiitake mushrooms and cook for a few minutes until starting to soften. Add the drained rice and stir to combine, then add the mushroom stock and some of the reserved mushroom water (if you like, for added flavor) and the star anise. Bring to a boil, then reduce the heat to low, cover and simmer for 20–25 minutes, until the rice is tender and the liquid is absorbed.

Meanwhile, make the caramelized oyster mushrooms. Heat the vegetable oil in a wok over medium-high heat until hot. Add the oyster mushrooms and stir-fry for 5–7 minutes until they start to soften and release their moisture. Add the minced garlic to the wok and stir-fry for about 30 seconds until fragrant, but not burned.

Pour in the kecap manis, black vinegar and dark soy sauce. Stir well to coat the mushrooms evenly. Stir-fry for 3–5 minutes until the mushrooms are caramelized and glossy. Add the salt and adjust seasoning to taste. Cook for another minute to let the flavors meld together.

Return to your rice. Remove the star anise, stir in the light soy sauce and adjust the seasoning to taste. Let the rice sit for a few minutes, then fluff it with a fork. Serve hot, with the oyster mushrooms and crispy fried garlic on top, plus a salted egg yolk each, if you like.

SPICED LEG OF LAMB

This was a staple when my mom had people over for dinner. She'd pick up a leg of lamb from the supermarket and create a really simple marinade. This recipe doesn't involve peeling ginger or blending pastes—it's just mixing, great for when you're hosting a dinner and need something straightforward yet impressive. When Mom served this dish it was the centerpiece, the lamb so tender it fell off the bone. She loved to show off the simplicity of her recipes, much like when someone compliments your outfit and you're keen to explain how cheap it was.

This dish has Indian flavors, similar to the delicious lamb raan. The key is to let the meat marinate in the spicy yogurt and sweet mango chutney to absorb all the flavors. Mom would serve it with pickled onions, parathas, chapati, flatbreads, fluffy rice or sometimes couscous (it works excellently with couscous, by the way, so don't knock it 'til you've tried it). I would also have some curry on the side for added flavor. I hope you find this recipe as effortlessly impressive as I do, and it becomes a way to show off to your friends, just like sharing the deal you got on that fabulous vintage dress.

SERVES 6-8

3 lb 5 oz (1.5 kg) leg of lamb
1 lb 2 oz (500 g) potatoes, cut into 1–1½ in (3–4 cm) chunks

FOR THE MARINADE

1⅓ cups (300 g) full-fat yogurt
½ cup (150 g) mango chutney
10½ oz (300 g) bhuna or balti paste
3 tbsp ground cumin
1 tbsp Kashmiri chile powder
5 black cardamom pods
1 tbsp lime juice
1 tbsp white sugar
1 tsp salt

TO SERVE

Pickled Pink Onions (see page 159)
Steamed rice
Chopped fresh herbs
Parathas, chapatis or other flatbreads

Begin by preparing the marinade. In a mixing bowl, combine the yogurt, mango chutney, bhuna paste, cumin, Kashmiri chile powder, cardamom pods, lime juice, sugar and salt. Stir until well mixed. Place the lamb in a large ovenproof dish, leaving space around it to add the potatoes later. Rub the marinade all over, coating all sides evenly. Cover with foil and let it marinate in the fridge for at least 2 hours, preferably overnight.

When ready to cook, preheat the oven to 325°F (160°C). Cover the dish tightly with foil and roast for 3 hours.

After 3 hours, carefully remove the foil. Turn the leg of lamb over and spoon the sauce from the dish over the meat. Scatter the chopped potatoes around the lamb in the dish, coating them with the sauce as well. Increase the oven temperature to 350°F (180°C) and cook for a further 1 hour, uncovered. Once cooked, the lamb should be tender and falling off the bone. (If it needs extra time in the oven, keep checking every 5 minutes until the meat is ready—the cooking time will vary because of the different fat content of each leg of lamb.)

Transfer the leg of lamb to a serving platter. For a complete meal, serve fresh Pink Pickled Onions, fluffy rice, chopped herbs and flatbreads alongside.

LUNAR NEW YEAR DEEP-FRIED OYSTERS

It took me a while to learn to love oysters. They're a popular Scottish delicacy, which are fairly abundant close to where I live. For the last couple of years, I've been doing cooking demonstrations with oysters at Stranraer Oyster Festival. Rather than swallowing them whole, I prefer chewing oysters (controversial, I know) as I adore the flavor of them and it was actually the slurping that was putting me off. When you chew an oyster, you get much more time to savor its briny, minerally flavor. One Lunar New Year, I tried a deep-fried oyster. It was a whole new experience. So intensely salty, I absolutely loved how deep frying transformed the oyster in flavor. The crispy batter coating is so delicious, especially with a good glug of gochujang ketchup to cut through the hit of the sea. It's a delicious morsel and a great introduction for anyone trying their first oyster.

SERVES 4–6, AS AN APPETIZER

1 lb 2 oz (500 g) shucked fresh oysters
Neutral oil, for deep-frying

FOR THE BATTER
1¼ cups (150 g) all-purpose flour, plus extra for dredging
½ tsp baking powder
½ tsp garlic powder
½ tsp onion powder
½ tsp salt
1 tsp sesame oil
Scant 1 cup (200 ml) sparkling water

FOR THE GOCHUJANG KETCHUP
½ cup (125 ml) ketchup
2 tbsp gochujang (Korean chile paste)
2 garlic cloves, peeled and minced
3 tbsp dark soy sauce
1 tbsp sesame oil
1 tbsp rice vinegar (or you can use white wine vinegar)

SEASONING STATION (OPTIONAL)
Salt, lime juice, vinegar, chile flakes, MSG

First, make the batter. Combine all of the dry ingredients in a large bowl, then whisk in the sesame oil and sparkling water to make a smooth batter.

Gently pat dry the oysters with a piece of paper towel to remove any excess moisture.

Fill a deep-fryer or large, heavy-based pot no more than two-thirds full with oil. Heat the oil to 325°F (160°C). Meanwhile, line a tray or plate with paper towels and keep a spider strainer or slotted spoon on hand. Place some flour in a shallow bowl for dredging.

Working in batches to avoid overcrowding the pot, first dredge an oyster in flour, carefully dip it in the batter, ensuring it's thoroughly coated, then carefully lower it into the hot oil and deep-fry for 2–3 minutes, or until golden, crispy and cooked through. Transfer the deep-fried oysters to the lined tray or plate to drain any excess oil.

While the oysters are frying, make the gochujang ketchup by mixing together all of the ingredients in a small bowl.

Serve the cooked oysters immediately sprinkled with whichever seasoning station ingredients you feel like, and the gochujang ketchup on the side.

ONE PERSON'S TRASH

One Person's Trash

We live in a society where portion sizes can be quite ambiguous. Take a moment to consider our dining options. If we indulge in the all-you-can-eat buffet, a competitive style of dining, then the more you consume, the less you pay per bite. Meanwhile, upscale restaurants serve dishes on eye-wateringly tiny plates, leaving us fearing that we'll actually head home still hungry. It's all part of twenty-first-century consumerism.

During my early years of cooking in restaurants, I was terrible at portioning. Honestly, I wasted so many valuable ingredients. As a young and naive chef, I felt a pang of guilt depositing yet another bag of sludgy spinach in the trash— with better kitchen planning and management, that spinach had the potential to become something quite delicious, rather than meet an unfortunate end. My mother has never been one to waste food, so it never felt right to be throwing away ingredients. I'm not quite sure why I ever came to do it; perhaps it was the society I grew up in, or maybe my own fault for not being more diligent about reducing waste when I was younger, but now is the time for change.

Whenever we discuss cooking—especially professional chefs and cooks— we bear a responsibility to safeguard our environment, our land and our farming processes. Working in food encompasses many challenges, as well as joy, so that's why it feels crucial to include a chapter in this book about the realities of my cooking. I don't mean a fancy chef's mise en place or meticulously measured milligrams of spices, instead it's about actual meals that I've prepared midweek with limited time and a quick glance at what's hanging around in the fridge.

Whenever I watch my friends with children cook, I'm filled with admiration for their innate ability to conjure up the most wholesome family dinners from seemingly nothing. It's a mindset, really. If we label something as a mundane ingredient or leftover, the chances are we won't be excited to eat it, much less cook it. But when we use our creativity to repurpose surplus ingredients or leftovers into something absolutely delicious, there can be a spark of excitement.

Boxing Day, the day after Christmas, is when the word "leftovers" is spoken most often. It's when the conversation turns to the leftover Christmas turkey sandwich. In my corner of the world, this is arguably the most beloved leftover creation. Let's call it the National Dish of Leftovers. The turkey sandwich is regarded as a seasonal highlight, the gold standard of Christmas leftovers. You often hear people saying that they don't like turkey that much, but they love the turkey sandwich. Of course, it's been played out in mainstream television— there's even that iconic scene in *Friends*, with Ross and His Sandwich.

If we take that one dish as a model, it's a template for how we can transform our perception of and enthusiasm for leftovers in general. Consider rice: it can be reborn as Nasi Goreng (see page 85), breathing new life into a simple staple.

Leftover bread: it can form the foundation of a comforting bread pudding or an unusual ice cream (see page 164). Uneaten broth: that can be reduced down to a rich, glossy sauce for spooning over noodles. And leftover chicken: that can be revived as mee siam (wok-fried rice noodles). It's all about your perspective and a little culinary creativity. Leftovers don't have to be the end of the story; they can be the beginning of something even more exciting. Let's embrace the full potential of our ingredients and see where this culinary journey can take us.

Food waste contributes significantly to our carbon emissions. I was born in an era when sell-by dates were aggressively marketed to society, leading to perfectly good food being wantonly discarded. Although science can aid us, we need to break the habit of wasting food in the amounts that we currently do. It's all about baby steps. I believe that the more we just talk about these issues, the less actual action we see. In this chapter, I'm here to demonstrate that there is an open platform for change and how to take practical steps towards reducing our food waste. We must continually think about how to maximize the ingredients we buy and progress on this journey to zero food waste. Having leftovers to work with can result in some of the most delicious dishes. In the recipes that follow I've taken some of the top-wasted food items globally, and also mixed in some I've frequently found nearly going to waste in my own kitchen, to provide a template to inspire and help you to structure your cooking. And of course, you should now have double or triple your initial repertoire of go-to dishes. My mother would never waste a drop, and I aspire to follow in those footsteps. Just remember, always feel free to swap out ingredients to use up what's in your fridge. I often find that I'm more excited about cooking with leftovers; they can be transformed into a dish that's even more delicious than the original.

CASHEW CHICKEN STIR-FRY
made with LEFTOVER CELERY

I adore using celery for its pepperiness, plus the robust, fibrous nature of the stalks means it stands up extremely well in a stir-fry. Nevertheless, it's one of our most wasted food items. I've often wondered if that's because we're not all that aware of how we can use it, so I've been including it a lot more in simple wok fries and zingy kerabu salads (see page 108). When I'm looking for something healthy and simple to make, I often reach for this recipe. Soy-seasoned celery along with steamed rice make me feel so warmed. It's a dish that kids tend to love, too. Chicken thighs are perfect here as the dark meat lends more flavor. Omit the chile sambal if you prefer things more lightly seasoned.

SERVES 3–4

3 tsp light soy sauce
3 tsp cornstarch
2 tsp sugar
½ tsp sea salt
1 lb 2 oz (500 g) skinless, boneless chicken thighs, cut into bite-sized pieces
1 tsp dark soy sauce
4 tbsp Sambal Oelek (page 46)
1 tbsp rice vinegar
½ cup (125 ml) vegetable oil
5 garlic cloves, peeled and minced
2½ in (6 cm) piece of ginger, peeled and finely grated
5 scallions, sliced, white and green parts separated
5 celery stalks, thinly sliced
1 cup (125 g) salted roasted cashews
A bunch of fresh cilantro, leaves picked
Steamed rice, to serve (optional)

SEASONING STATION (OPTIONAL)
Lime juice, sugar, salt

First, marinate the chicken. Combine 2 teaspoons of the light soy sauce, 1½ teaspoons of the cornstarch, 1 teaspoon of the sugar and the sea salt in a shallow bowl. Add the chicken pieces and toss to coat evenly. Let the chicken marinate for at least 15 minutes, or in the fridge overnight.

In a separate bowl, mix the remaining 1 teaspoon of light soy sauce, the dark soy sauce, the remaining 1½ teaspoons of cornstarch and 1 teaspoon of sugar with the Sambal Oelek and rice vinegar. Set aside.

Heat half of the vegetable oil in a wok or large frying pan over medium-high heat. Add the marinated chicken and its marinade and stir-fry for 5–7 minutes until browned and cooked through. Transfer the chicken to a plate and set aside.

Add the remaining vegetable oil to the same wok or pan. Once hot, add the garlic, ginger and scallion whites, then stir-fry until fragrant. Next, add the sliced celery and cook for a few minutes until slightly softened.

Return the cooked chicken to the wok or pan. Pour in the soy sauce-vinegar mixture and cook, stirring continuously, until the sauce thickens and coats the chicken. Stir in the roasted cashews and cook for a final 1 minute. Taste and add whichever seasoning station ingredients you feel like today

Serve hot, garnished with the cilantro leaves and the scallion greens, and with steamed rice alongside, if desired.

HAKE IN GINGER-SOY BROWN BUTTER
made with LEFTOVER CREAM

How many times have you gone to the fridge and discovered that the cream has formed those little lumps because it's been in there for too long? I've taken to turning mine into butter. It's so incredibly satisfying, and a great way to make your own flavored butter that you can then use in all sorts of dishes. For this recipe, which I used to cook in my first restaurant, I've used it to make a ginger butter—it's one of life's greatest joys. The sauce is perfect for soaking into steamed jasmine rice.

SERVES 2

2 hake fillets, skin on
Olive oil, for frying
7 tbsp (100 g) butter (see below)
6 garlic cloves, peeled and minced
2 tbsp finely grated ginger
¾ cup (100 g) peas (fresh or frozen)
2 tbsp light soy sauce
1–2 tbsp honey, to taste (optional)
Squeeze of lemon juice
Salt and freshly ground black pepper
Steamed jasmine rice, to serve

FOR THE BUTTER
Scant 1 cup (200 ml) heavy cream

YOU WILL ALSO NEED
An electric stand mixer
Sieve or colander lined with cheesecloth

SEASONING STATION (OPTIONAL)
Lime juice, sugar, salt

First, make the butter. Ensure the cream is well chilled before you start. Cold cream churns into butter more easily than room-temperature cream. Scoop the cream into the bowl of an electric stand mixer and start whisking at medium speed. As the cream thickens, increase the speed. The cream will go through three stages: first forming soft peaks, then stiff peaks, and finally separating into butter and buttermilk.

Once the cream has separated and butter has formed, tip the contents of the mixer bowl into a cloth-lined sieve/colander to separate the butter from the buttermilk. (You can save the buttermilk for other recipes or for baking.)

Rinse the butter in a sieve under cold running water to remove any remaining buttermilk (which can cause the butter to spoil more quickly), then place it back in the bowl. Pour over some ice-cold water and press the butter with a spatula to release any further buttermilk. Drain the water from the bowl and repeat this process until the water runs clear. Once washed, press the butter into a mold or shape it as desired. Wrap the butter in parchment paper or place it in an airtight container. Store in the refrigerator for up to 2–3 weeks.

To make the hake dish, pat the skin side of the hake fillets with paper towels to remove any excess moisture. Season the fish with salt and pepper on both sides.

Heat a glug of olive oil in a nonstick frying pan over medium-high heat. Once the oil is hot, add the hake fillets, skin-side down, and cook for 4–5 minutes or until the skin is crispy.

Continued →

← *Hake continued*

Gently flip the fillets and cook for a further 3–4 minutes or until the fish is cooked through, and flakes easily. Transfer the fish to a plate and keep warm.

In the same pan, melt the butter over medium heat. Continue to cook, swirling the pan frequently, until the butter starts to brown and gives off a nutty aroma. This usually takes about 3 minutes.

Add the minced garlic, grated ginger and peas to the browned butter and cook for about 30 seconds or until fragrant. Stir in the soy sauce, honey, if using, and lemon juice, then cook for a final 1 minute. Be careful as the brown butter might splutter when adding the liquids. Taste and add whichever seasoning station ingredients you feel like today.

When ready to serve, arrange the hake fillets on individual serving plates, divide the peas between the plates along with some steamed jasmine rice. Spoon over the ginger-soy brown butter sauce, and serve.

SEA BREAM

MACKEREL

HAKE

MONKFISH

HADDOCK

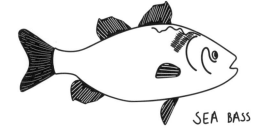
COD

SEA BASS

PERKEDEL
made with LEFTOVER POTATOES

We've all been there, right? A fridge full of spare boiled potatoes that you just don't know what to do with. Potatoes get thrown away far too often, they're high up on the list of the most frequently wasted foods. So, let's talk about perkedel, those incredible little Indonesian potato fritters that are seriously the best thing you can do with leftover spuds. This recipe is perfect for turning those neglected taters into something everyone will love, including kids. What's so great is that you can use up all those boiled potatoes, skin and everything, by simply mashing them and you're halfway there. Adapt the other ingredients to suit whatever else you have in the house.

SERVES 5, AS A SNACK

FOR THE FRITTERS
1 lb 2 oz (500 g) starchy potatoes, (like russets) cooked and roughly mashed
3½ oz (100 g) ground pork (optional, or a vegan meat alternative)
2 sprigs of fresh cilantro, finely chopped
2 tbsp crispy fried shallots
1 tbsp cornstarch
½ tsp salt, or to taste
½ tsp ground white pepper
Vegetable oil, for frying
1 egg, beaten
Sweet Chile Sauce (page 49), to serve (optional)

FOR THE SIMPLE DIPPING SAUCE (OPTIONAL)
3 fresh red or green bird's eye chiles, finely chopped
1 tbsp kecap manis (sweet soy sauce)
2 tbsp black vinegar (or malt vinegar)
Lime juice, sugar or salt, to taste

In a large bowl, combine the mashed potatoes with the ground pork, if using, cilantro, crispy fried shallots, cornstarch, salt and white pepper. Mix everything thoroughly with your hands.

Lightly oil your palms and shape the potato mixture into balls about the size of a golf ball, then flatten into patties about ½ in (1.5 cm) thick. Place them on a tray and chill in the fridge, uncovered, for at least 1 hour and up to a day ahead. This helps to firm up the fritters and prevents them from falling apart during frying. If preparing a day ahead, cover before refrigerating.

When ready to cook, fill a large frying pan with vegetable oil to the depth of about 1 in (3 cm). Heat the oil over medium heat until hot. Working in batches, dip each fritter in the beaten egg to coat, then carefully lower them into the hot oil. Fry the fritters for 2–3 minutes on each side, or until crisp and golden—keep an eye on them as the cooking time will vary based on their size. Transfer the fritters to a tray or plate lined with paper towels to drain any excess oil, and repeat to cook the rest.

Meanwhile, make the dipping sauce (if using) by combining the chopped chiles, kecap manis and vinegar in a small bowl. Taste and add lime juice, white sugar or salt, to taste.

Serve the fritters immediately, with the simple dipping sauce, or sweet chile sauce, or simply on their own.

CREAM CHEESE BAGELS WITH PICKLES
made with LEFTOVER MILK

I'm a self-confessed pickle addict, I've even taken a jar of pickles to the movies to eat as a snack. If you're as crazy about pickles as I am, then you're going to love this. Honestly, it's a game-changer. We're talking about turning leftover milk—yes, the regular stuff sitting in your fridge—into lusciously creamy cheese and then—wait for it—we stack this homemade goodness in a bagel with crisp, tangy pickles, a slick of hot chile oil and a sprinkling of fresh dill for vivacious herby flavors. It's the kind of combo that pickle lovers go nuts over.

And let me tell you, transforming surplus milk into homemade cream cheese is a breeze. It's a nifty kitchen trick that's as fun as it is practical, so stop wasting your milk and make your own cream cheese—you'll feel like a no-food-waste genius. So, if you're ready to dive into a world where pickles reign supreme, then please do join me in this rather ridiculous but delicious recipe.

MAKES 2 BAGELS

FOR THE CREAM CHEESE
11½ cups (2.7 liters) whole milk
Juice of 1 large lemon or
    3 tbsp lemon juice
⅓ tsp salt

TO SERVE
2 sesame bagels, toasted
Chile Oil (page 50, or use
    store-bought)
A selection of pickles
    (see pages 159–60)
A handful of fresh dill

YOU WILL ALSO NEED
Sieve or colander lined with
    cheesecloth or clean,
    thin tea towel

Pour the milk into a large pot and bring to a rolling boil over medium-high heat. Once boiling, add the lemon juice, then immediately turn off the heat. Allow the milk to rest for a few minutes to curdle. You will observe curds forming and a yellowish liquid, known as whey, separating.

After a few minutes, the curds should be fully formed. Strain the curdled milk through the lined sieve/colander to separate the curds from the whey. Alternatively, use a slotted spoon to transfer the curds to a bowl, leaving the whey in the pot.

Rinse the curds thoroughly with cold water to remove any residual whey. Squeeze the curds well to remove as much remaining whey as possible.

Transfer the strained curds to a food processor or blender and add the salt. Blend for 1–2 minutes (time may vary based on your machine's power) until you achieve a light and fluffy cream cheese. Your homemade cream cheese can then be stored in an airtight container in the fridge for up to 4 days.

When you're ready to eat, layer up each toasted sesame bagel with the cream cheese, chile oil, all the pickles you desire and a sprinkling of fresh dill.

BAKWAN JAGUNG (SWEETCORN FRITTERS)
made with LEFTOVER BEANSPROUTS

You only need to turn around for a few minutes and beansprouts begin to look a bit sad. They have a short shelf life and turn to mush quite easily. We tend to cook them only in stir fries, but there's so many other things they can be used for to finish up the full bag. I adore this recipe for bakwan jagung, turning any extra veg into little sweetcorn fritters.

SERVES 4, AS AN APPETIZER

2½ cups (400 g) corn kernels (frozen or canned)
1 garlic clove, peeled
1 in (3 cm) piece of ginger, peeled and roughly chopped
4 scallions, finely sliced
½ red onion, peeled and diced
1 tsp ground white pepper
4 tbsp all-purpose flour
2 tbsp sweet potato flour (or cornstarch if you don't have it)
2 large eggs, lightly beaten
1 fresh green chile, finely chopped
1 fresh long red chile, finely chopped
A handful of beansprouts
1 tsp salt, or to taste
Vegetable oil, for frying
Green Chile Chutney (page 48) mixed with mayonnaise, to serve (I like a ratio of ⅓ chutney to ⅔ mayonnaise but you can mix it to your taste)

Place half of the corn kernels in a food processor with the garlic and ginger, then blend to a coarse paste.

In a large mixing bowl, combine the corn paste, the remaining whole corn kernels, the sliced scallions, diced red onion, white pepper, all-purpose flour, sweet potato flour, beaten eggs, chopped green and red chiles, beansprouts and salt. Mix everything together until well combined.

Heat a generous amount of vegetable oil in a frying pan over medium heat, until hot. Working in batches to avoid overcrowding the pan, drop in about 1½ tablespoons of the corn batter for each fritter. Flatten the batter slightly to form fritters, then fry on low-medium heat until crispy and golden brown on the outside. This usually takes 3–4 minutes. Carefully flip the fritters and fry the other side until golden brown and cooked through (another 3–4 minutes). Transfer the fritters to a tray or plate lined with paper towels to drain any excess oil, and repeat to cook the rest.

Serve the fritters while hot with the Green Chile Chutney-mayo.

IN A PICKLE

Pickles have gained cult status recently. There are t-shirts and tote bags with pickles on them, and even Instagram pages dedicated to pickles. They often get pigeon-holed as the familiar cucumber pickle, which is not to be snubbed, but there is a whole world of pickles out there to be enjoyed. Pickling is also such a great tool to have under your belt when cooking. If you've got something that is just about to be thrown out, why not pickle it and store it in a jar to add to that salad or stir through a sauce? When you have a selection of pickles to reach for, 'current you' has a lot to thank 'former you' for. Stop wasting veggies and set about pickling lots of pleasures for 'future you."

SIMPLE PICKLING LIQUID

MAKES 1 BATCH

2/3 cup (150 ml) white vinegar
2 tbsp white sugar (adjust to taste for sweeter pickles)
½ tsp salt

OPTIONAL FLAVORINGS
½ tsp mustard seeds
1 tsp black peppercorns
1 tsp coriander seeds
1 tsp cloves
2 fresh or dried makrut lime leaves
1 garlic clove, peeled and smashed
½ tsp chile flakes

In a pot, combine the vinegar, sugar and salt with 2/3 cup (150 ml) of water and any of the optional flavorings. Slowly bring to a boil, stirring continuously, until the sugar and salt crystals have dissolved. Remove the pot from the heat and let the pickling liquid cool slightly.

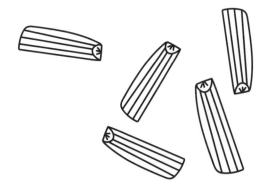

PICKLED PINK ONIONS

2 red onions, peeled and thinly sliced
1 quantity of Simple Pickling Liquid (see opposite)

Pack the sliced onions into a sterilized jar and pour the hot pickling liquid over them in the jar, making sure they are fully submerged. Leave the jar to cool to room temperature, then seal and refrigerate.

The pickled onions will be ready to eat after a few hours and can be stored in the fridge for several weeks.

SIMPLE PICKLED CARROTS

3 carrots, peeled and sliced into long matchsticks
1 quantity of Simple Pickling Liquid (see opposite)

Pack the carrot sticks into a sterilized jar and pour the hot pickling liquid over them in the jar, making sure they are fully submerged. Leave the jar to cool to room temperature, then seal and refrigerate.

The pickled carrots will be ready to eat after 24 hours and can be stored in the fridge for up to 1 month.

PICKLED CUCUMBER RELISH

2 cucumbers, finely diced
2 garlic cloves, peeled and minced
1 fresh red chile, finely chopped
2 tbsp fresh dill, chopped
1 quantity of Simple Pickling Liquid (as opposite, but made with 3 tbsp white sugar and 1 tsp salt)

Mix the cucumbers, garlic, chile and dill in a heatproof bowl. Pour the hot pickling liquid over the vegetables and mix well. Leave to cool to room temperature, then transfer to a sterilized jar, seal and refrigerate.

The relish will be ready to eat after 1 hour and can be stored in the fridge for up to 1 month.

ACHAR

2 carrots, peeled and cut into thin batons (about 2 in/5 cm long)//
1 cucumber, seeds removed and cut into thin batons (2 in/5 cm long)//
2 tbsp white sugar//
2 tbsp salt//
1 cup (250 ml) white rice vinegar//
½ cauliflower (approx. 9 oz/250 g), cut into small florets//
10 green beans, topped and tailed, halved//
5½ oz (150 g) white cabbage, washed and cut into bite-sized squares//
¼ cup (60 ml) vegetable oil

SPICE PASTE//
6 banana shallots//
1–1½ in (3–4 cm) piece of fresh turmeric or 1 tsp ground turmeric)//
1–1½ in (3–4 cm) piece of fresh ginger//
1 fresh long red chile//
4 tbsp chile powder//
2 tbsp water//
scant ½ cup (100 ml) white vinegar or rice wine vinegar, plus extra to taste//
1 cup (240 ml) water//
1 cup (200 g) white sugar, plus extra to taste//
½ tsp toasted belacan (optional)

TOPPINGS//
1¾ cups (250 g) roasted peanuts, crushed//
1 tbsp white sesame seeds//
Salt

Begin by preparing the vegetables. Place the carrots and cucumbers in a bowl, toss them with 1 tablespoon of both the sugar and the salt, then set aside.

Heat a generous 2 cups (500 ml) of water in a pot, add the remaining tablespoons of salt and sugar and the vinegar. Blanch the cauliflower florets for 1 minute, then add the green beans and cabbage for a further 1 minute until softened. Lay them all on a tray and pat dry with a clean dishcloth. Drain the carrots and cucumbers, then place them with the cauliflower, green beans and cabbage.

Blend all of the ingredients for the spice paste in a food processor until smooth.

Heat the vegetable oil in a wok and cook the paste mixture for 5–6 minutes on medium-low heat until fragrant. Add extra oil if necessary.

Toss all the vegetables together with the spice paste until everything is coated. Transfer to a sterilized jar, cover and leave to sit overnight in the fridge before eating. Before serving, you can add extra sugar, salt or vinegar, to taste. Top with crushed roasted peanuts and sesame seeds for each serving.

ARE YOU GOING TO EAT THAT PICKLE?

KAYA CROISSANT-AND-BUTTER PUDDING
made with LEFTOVER PASTRIES

There's no good reason for throwing away pastries. They make the most amazing base for bread pudding, in fact, I'd argue that it turns a bottom-of-the-barrel-quality pastry into the most delicious dessert. Of course, the kaya (coconut jam) influence is the addition here—the coconut just rounds everything off. It's also one of the simplest bakes on this planet. Please never waste a croissant again and instead make this dreamy eggy bake.

SERVES 3-4

5 stale croissants
3 eggs
12 oz (320 g) can of coconut cream
1 tsp pandan extract
½ cup (80 g) coconut sugar
1 cup (100 g) raspberries,
    fresh or frozen
¾ cup (100 g) coconut flakes
3 tbsp Kaya (coconut jam,
    see page 210)
Confectioners' sugar, for dusting
Clotted cream or whipped cream,
    to serve

Preheat the oven to 350°F (180°C).

Roughly tear the stale croissants into pieces and drop into a baking dish.

In a bowl, whisk together the eggs, coconut cream, pandan extract and coconut sugar until well combined. Pour this mixture into the dish over the torn croissants and leave them to soak for 10–15 minutes.

Scatter the raspberries over the top of the pudding, gently push them into the mixture, then place the dish into the hot oven and bake for 15–20 minutes, until golden on top.

Meanwhile, toast the coconut flakes in a dry frying pan over medium heat until golden, tossing every so often. Leave to cool.

Once the pudding is cooked, leave it to cool for about 5 minutes before dolloping the Kaya on top, then dusting with confectioners' sugar and scattering over the toasted coconut flakes. Serve with clotted cream or whipped cream.

BURNED TOAST ICE CREAM
made with STALE BREAD

There are so many things that can be made from the last slices of a stale loaf. For starters, stale bread can be frozen—I find it actually helps with its staleness. I can't quote the exact science, but it must be something to do with the ice crystallizing in the bread and reviving the slice when it's toasted. Anyway, after toasting, it's a far superior slice to the way it was before.

If you're like me and lead a busy lifestyle, you'll often burn your toast in the morning. I know this will resonate with some of you, while others will have nailed their toaster settings. But I live with a slightly dodgy toaster, which I'm rather attached to as I refuse to throw out an appliance just because it's slightly less than 100% perfect. It tends to cook one side of the toast more rapidly than the other, so occasionally I end up with burned toast. One particular day, my toast was incinerated. Rather than consign this inedible slice of toast to the trash, in fact, I did the opposite. I whipped out my ice-cream machine and made a burned toast ice cream. The blackened toast flavor goes perfectly with the sweet, creamy frozen custard and doesn't make it taste that burned at all. It just makes it rather nutty and delicious.

It doesn't surprise me that bread is one of the nation's top wasted food items, but before you throw out that bread, save those stale slices, over-toast them until charred and make this delicious ice cream.

SERVES 2–4

1¼ cups (300 ml) heavy cream
1¼ cups (300 ml) whole milk
1 tbsp honey
1 vanilla bean
4 egg yolks
½ cup (100 g) sugar
3 slices of stale bread

In a pot, combine the heavy cream, whole milk and honey. Split the vanilla bean lengthwise and scrape the seeds into the pot, then add the empty pod. Gently heat the mixture over medium-low heat, stirring continuously, until warm but not boiling.

In a separate bowl, whisk together the egg yolks and sugar until light and creamy.

Gradually add the warm vanilla-infused cream to the egg yolk mixture, whisking continuously to prevent the yolks from cooking. Pour the ice-cream mixture back into the pot and cook over low heat, stirring continuously, until it is the consistency of custard and thick enough to coat the back of a spoon. Make sure the mixture doesn't boil. Remove from the heat.

Toast the slices of bread until they are brown-black. Once cooled, tear or cut the toast into small pieces, place in a food processor and process to fine breadcrumbs.

Remove the vanilla pod from the custard, then stir in the toasted breadcrumbs. Transfer the ice-cream mixture to a bowl and chill in the fridge for 1 hour.

Once chilled, transfer the ice-cream mixture to a freezerproof container and put it into the freezer. Churn the ice cream with a spatula every 30 minutes for the next 4 hours. (If you're using an ice-cream maker, follow the manual for your machine. Once churned, transfer the ice cream to a freezerproof container and freeze until it reaches your preferred texture.)

PISANG GORENG (BANANA FRITTERS)
made with BROWN BANANAS

Move over banana bread, hello banana fritter era. When bananas are browning or blackened, in the West, we tend to make banana bread. When my Amah's bananas go bad, she makes these fritters. I suggest you wait until the bananas are blackened and smooshy until you use them—the more over-ripe, the better. When the bananas are fully ripened, you don't need to use as much sugar. Pisang goreng are such tasty morsels, and so simple to make. I have these for breakfast, just like my Amah serves them—and they're glorious.

SERVES 2–3

½ cup (75 g) frozen shredded coconut (available in the freezer section of supermarkets), defrosted
6 very ripe bananas (with skin blackened)
1¼ cups (150 g) all-purpose flour
⅓ cup (50 g) rice flour
1–2 tbsp white sugar (more if your bananas are not fully ripened, less if they are blackened)
½ tsp salt
¼ tsp baking soda
½ tsp ground cardamom
½ tsp ground nutmeg
Scant 1 cup (200 ml) canned coconut milk (I use Chaokoh, which is the best one for this recipe if you can find it)
Vegetable oil, for deep-frying
Confectioners' sugar, for dusting

Preheat the oven to 400°F (200°C). Spread the shredded coconut over a baking sheet and toast in the hot oven for 5–6 minutes, or until golden. Keep a close eye on the coconut as it can burn easily. Once toasted, set the coconut aside and allow to cool. Turn off the oven.

To make the batter, peel two of the bananas and mash them in a large mixing bowl until smooth. Sift in both of the flours, then add the sugar, salt, baking soda, ground cardamom, ground nutmeg and two-thirds of the toasted coconut. Stir well to combine. Gradually pour in the coconut milk, stirring continuously, to form a smooth batter. It should be thick enough to coat the banana pieces but not feel overly dense.

Fill a deep-fryer or large, heavy-based pot no more than two-thirds full with oil. Heat the oil to 350°F (180°C). Meanwhile, line a tray or plate with paper towels and keep a spider strainer or slotted spoon on hand.

Peel the remaining bananas and cut them into halves or thirds, depending on their size. If the bananas are very large, you may want to slice them in half lengthwise too.

Working in batches so you don't overcrowd the pan, dip the banana pieces into the batter using your hands until well coated, then carefully lower them into the hot oil. (If there are too many bananas in the fryer at once, the oil temperature will drop and they won't get crispy.) Fry the bananas for 3–4 minutes, turning once for even cooking, or until golden and crispy, then remove from the oil using a slotted spoon. Transfer the banana fritters to the lined tray or plate to drain any excess oil. Allow to cool for a couple of minutes, then serve dusted with confectioners' sugar and sprinkled with the remaining toasted coconut.

COOK WHEN
NOBODY'S WATCHING

Cook When Nobody's Watching

Cooking for oneself is a nurturing act of self-care, a ritual that sustains and comforts the soul. My culinary self-education began in my teenage years with humble, carby, after-school snacks. Some of my most memorable meals have been casually enjoyed on the sofa, immersed in a favorite show—at that stage in life, it was usually re-runs of *Sex and the City*, *Friends* or *Ready, Steady, Cook*. The salty instant noodles my mom would buy from Chinatown, brands my friends had never seen before, embellished with bits of bacon, a handful of greens and a generous swirl of shrimp chile crisp oil. Or masala spiced beans on toast with scallion, ginger and garam masala, although often with an imbalance of spices as my cooking skills were at the development stage. A take on the classic Italian carbonara using the frowned-upon cream. At this point, I didn't realize that Elmlea cream is not real heavy cream, hence my spaghetti dishes were often terrible at that age.

Nowadays, my self-nourishment looks a little different; sometimes it's simply about needing greens. A dish I make repeatedly (which has no name) involves wok-frying any greens that are in the fridge—celery, choi sum, spinach, kale—with an abundance of diced garlic (at least 4 cloves) and sesame oil, tossing it in a mix of soy sauce, sugar and vinegar and then spooning it over some steamed jasmine rice with a soy-cured egg yolk on top, all finished with chile crisp oil. Served in a deep bowl, you can use your chopsticks to smoosh all of the components together, the golden egg yolk covering each grain of perfectly steamed rice, with the salty balance of the sauce flavoring the irony greens. This is one of my regular comfort foods. It's not something I'll be remembered for, but it's my safe, healthy, comforting place that I visit frequently.

    Adversity often drives us to seek solace in food, sometimes as a comfort, other times as a crutch. Through teenage heartbreak, work blows and real adult loss, food has always been there. Sometimes in the sense of overeating, but sometimes in the sense of soul nourishment. After a painful break up in my early twenties, I remember being brought back to life by indulging in a hot steamy bowl of Chinese tomato egg drop soup: ribbons of silky eggs layered into salty chicken broth, with sweet tomatoes stewed in the mixture and an umami hit of soy sauce, topped with scallions and white pepper. This is one of life's saviors for me, a bowl of humble goodness that costs little to make. As humans, we get so connected to inanimate objects and give them life, from children with teddies, to antique collectors with trinkets, to musicians with their guitars. I feel this way about the bowls of goodness we cook for ourselves; I romanticize food and I see value in it. I think of the late Amy Winehouse, someone I listen to often in the kitchen. She wrote a song, "Cherry," which is a love letter she penned to her guitar, as if it had its own soul. I imagine that when she played her guitar, whether in times of despair or joy, it pulled out emotions that needed to be released. For me, cooking and creating food embody this strong alter ego with its own brain, sometimes stronger than my own, to pull me through tough times. Oh, and be sure to sing to your pots and pans, your neighbors will wonder what's going on, but it's worth it. Trust me.

I've also had some of my most happy meals on my own, like the time I nailed my mom's grilled char siu recipe, the nasi lemak I made for myself the evening I signed the publishing deal for this very book, the fish pie made one Sunday from scraps I had in the freezer while watching *Frasier*, the crushed tomatoes on toast I had in Jerez while the sun was rising over the Spanish city. Some of my fondest meals have been on my own. Cooking for oneself is the foundation from which we learn to cook for others. It's a personal celebration, an art form, a peaceful solace. The "*Ratatouille* moment" of culinary revelation is so often a solo experience that later transforms into a shared anecdote. In today's connected world, we often share these moments on social media, a platform that, at its best, can celebrate the quiet triumphs of our domestic lives.

To those who claim to be bad cooks, I suggest starting by practicing five dishes you love until you've mastered them. Cooking isn't about showcasing your skills to impress others; it's about nurturing oneself. This chapter is a collection of the dishes I savor in solitude, though now I'm sharing them a bit more publicly. They are cosy concoctions, perfect for curling up with under a blanket—some that have simmered for hours, some that are quick comforts. These dishes, each with their own name and story, serve as my culinary companions through life's ups and downs. From a bowl of frozen dumplings to a simple pasta reminiscent of a morning spent with a past love, each recipe is steeped in personal history and emotion. Cooking for oneself is a spiritual practice, akin to Buddhist teachings of mindfulness and nourishment. It's about the food that feeds not just our bodies but our spirits.

In cooking these recipes, they are not just to tell my own story—I invite you to reflect on your own cooking and self-nourishment. By all means adopt some of my personal favorites into your cooking ritual, and definitely adapt them to make them your own—I'm not a stickler for rules. These recipes are more than just sustenance; they are a celebration of the self, a testament to the joy of solitary dining and the profound satisfaction that comes from knowing you can cater to your own needs with the same love and care you would offer to others. This is a self-love chapter.

MASALA BEANS WITH POACHED EGGS

There's nothing more satisfying than baked beans. Even when I'm feeling a bit lazy, it's always worth taking the time to whip up this dish of masala beans. It's one of life's greatest go-to comfort foods. Of course, you can pimp up baked beans however you see fit by adding in whatever you like in terms of protein (I like an egg, but you could also add pancetta or bacon), but this is the perfect base for a lazy breakfast, lunch or dinner. Childhood beany happiness on toast.

SERVES 1–2

FOR THE MASALA BEANS
2 tbsp ghee or olive oil
½ onion, peeled and finely diced
4 garlic cloves, peeled and minced
2 tsp tomato paste
1 tsp ground cumin
1 tsp ground coriander
½ tsp ground turmeric
2 tsp garam masala
2 tsp light brown sugar, plus a pinch, or to taste
½ tsp chile powder
1 large tomato, diced
1 x 14 oz (400 g) can of cannellini beans, drained and rinsed
Salt and freshly ground black pepper

FOR THE POACHED EGGS
1 tbsp distilled malt vinegar
2 large eggs

TO SERVE
2 slices of sourdough bread
A few fresh cilantro leaves

To make the masala beans, heat the ghee or olive oil in a pot over medium heat. Add the diced onion and fry for 2–3 minutes or until translucent. Add the minced garlic and cook for a further 1 minute, or until fragrant.

Stir the tomato paste into the onion and garlic and allow it to caramelize for a few seconds. Next, stir in all the ground spices, the brown sugar and chile powder and cook for 2–3 minutes to allow the flavors of the spices to be released.

Add the diced tomato to the pan and cook until it breaks down and becomes saucy. Fold in the cannellini beans, then add the pinch of sugar and season with salt and pepper to taste. Simmer the beans for 5–10 minutes. If the mixture begins to look dry, add a little water.

Meanwhile, poach the eggs. Bring a large pot of water to a gentle simmer and add the vinegar. Crack one of the eggs into a small bowl. Vigorously stir the water in one direction to create a gentle whirlpool, then gently slide the egg into the center. Poach the egg for 3–4 minutes for a runny yolk. Using a slotted spoon, remove the egg from the water and place it on paper towels to drain. Repeat with the second egg.

While the eggs are poaching, toast the sourdough slices until golden and crunchy.

When ready to serve, spoon the masala beans into individual serving bowls. Place a poached egg on top of the beans, season and scatter over a few cilantro leaves. Serve with the toasted sourdough on the side.

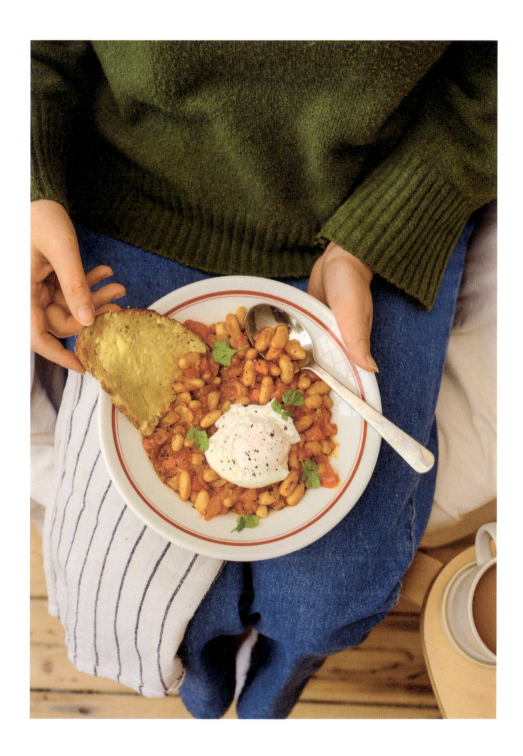

XO BUTTER CORN

Childhood memories of sweetcorn never fade. Those days when it was just me and a cob, relishing each sweet, juicy burst from the kernels. And then the inevitable toothpick dance that followed. Now, take that memory, then give it an edge. My XO butter-drenched corn is in recognition of matured palates—a blend of umami-rich XO sauce with a kick of chile. It's about transforming the simple into the sublime, and honoring a classic while giving it a new lease of life with the bold, savory notes of XO sauce. Each bite is a balance: sweetness meets the sea, heat meets comfort. It's sweetcorn reinvented for those of us who've never outgrown our love for it.

SERVES 1–2

2 ears fresh corn, husks removed
A small handful of finely chopped fresh chives
Lime wedges, for squeezing over

FOR THE XO BUTTER

11 tbsp (150 g) unsalted butter, at room temperature
6 garlic cloves, peeled and minced
¼ cup (60 ml) XO sauce (or crispy chile oil)
3 tbsp honey
3 tbsp light soy sauce

First, make the XO butter. Combine the softened butter with the garlic, XO sauce, honey and soy sauce. If you only have salted butter, that's fine, just reduce the amount of soy sauce. Mix everything well.

Boil the corn-on-the-cobs in a pan of salted water for 5 minutes to kickstart the cooking process. Drain and allow the corn to cool down slightly for about 5 minutes.

Meanwhile, preheat the broiler to medium-high heat (you can also do this on the grill). Once the broiler is hot, rub the corn all over with half of the XO butter and place them directly under the broiler. Cook, turning occasionally, until the kernels are tender and charred in spots. This usually takes about 10 minutes.

As soon as the kernels are nicely charred, remove the corn from the oven and slather them with the rest of the XO butter while they're still hot. Allow the butter to melt and coat the corn evenly. Finish by sprinkling over some finely chopped chives and a squeeze of lime juice.

AYAM PENYET
SMASHED CHICKEN

You've heard of smashed cucumber, but have you heard of smashed chicken? The process of bruising food to release flavors feels quite primal. Here, the idea behind smashing the crispy chicken skin means that the fragrant sambal permeates both the outside and inside of the chicken. This is traditionally deep-fried, but I've adapted it to give the option of oven-roasting, as I don't always have the patience to deep-fry on a weeknight. As this dish is something I eat at least once a week, I prefer oven-roasting—I find the satisfaction levels of the results just as high. This is a dish that has distinction between something that has a little bit of labor but that is perfectly OK when you are spending an afternoon cooking for yourself, it's not difficult at all and has the satisfaction levels of making a full roast dinner.

SERVES 1

1 chicken leg (drumstick and thigh, skin on)
Steamed rice, to serve
Cucumber slices, to serve
Lime wedges, to serve

FOR THE MARINADE
2 tbsp vegetable oil
1 tsp tamarind paste
5 garlic cloves, peeled and minced
1 in (3 cm) piece of ginger, peeled and minced
1 lemongrass stalk, cleaned, trimmed and bruised
½ tsp chile powder
Salt and freshly ground black pepper

FOR THE GREEN SAMBAL
2 banana shallots, peeled
2 garlic cloves, peeled
4 fresh green chiles, deseeded if you prefer less heat
A small bunch of fresh mint, leaves picked
A small bunch of fresh cilantro
1 tsp tamarind paste

First, make the marinade. Mix together the vegetable oil, tamarind paste, garlic, ginger, lemongrass, chile powder and some salt and pepper in a bowl, then stir together until fully combined. Rub the marinade all over the chicken leg, making sure all the skin is fully coated. Place in a dish, cover and let the chicken marinate for at least 30 minutes, or overnight in the fridge for a deeper flavor.

To oven-roast the chicken: Preheat the oven to 400°F (200°C). Place the chicken leg on a roasting pan and roast in the hot oven for about 30–45 minutes, or until the chicken is golden and cooked through and the juices run clear.

To deep-fry the chicken: Fill a deep-fryer or heavy-based pot no more than two-thirds full with vegetable oil. Heat the oil to 325°F (160°C). Carefully lower the chicken leg into the hot oil and deep-fry for 10–15 minutes, or until the chicken is golden and cooked through and the juices run clear. If you're unsure, use a digital meat thermometer to check the internal temperature has reached at least 170°F (75°C) so you know that it is safe to eat.

While the chicken is cooking, make the green sambal. Place the shallots, garlic, green chiles, mint, cilantro, tamarind paste, palm sugar, chicken bouillon powder and salt to taste in a food processor or blender and blend until smooth. Taste and adjust the seasoning, adding lime juice for a tangy note. Balance the flavors of the sambal with more palm sugar, chicken bouillon powder, lime juice and salt to your taste.

*1 tbsp gula melaka palm sugar
(or dark brown sugar)
1 tbsp chicken bouillon powder
(or ½ chicken stock cube
crumbled with 1 tsp MSG)
Juice of 1 lime, or to taste*

Once the chicken leg is cooked, bash it with a rolling pin until smashed and flattened. Next, take a spoonful of the green sambal and rub it into the chicken so the skin and flesh underneath are saturated with the flavor.

Serve the chicken with steamed rice, cucumber slices and lime wedges for squeezing over. Finish by topping the chicken with an extra spoonful or two of the green sambal.

CHINESE SAUSAGE BUCATINI CARBONARA

Carbonara will forever be one of my favorite dishes. Call me basic, but I just love the richness of it. The Chinese sausage (lap cheong) I use is an ambient food, so I always tend to have it in the pantry. It's truly one of the finest ingredients, the smoky sweetness of it makes it taste like maple-cured bacon and works perfectly with the richness of the egg yolks. Allowing the fat to render a little releases the oils into the dish and creates the most delicious flavor.

SERVES 2

7 oz (200 g) dried bucatini (or another long pasta if you can't find bucatini)
1½ oz (40 g) Chinese sausage (lap cheong), thinly sliced at an angle
1 tbsp olive oil
4 garlic cloves, peeled and finely chopped
3 egg yolks
1¾ oz (50 g) Parmesan, grated, plus extra to serve
1 tsp light soy sauce
½ tsp kecap manis (sweet soy sauce)
Salt and freshly ground black pepper

Bring a large pot of well-salted water to a boil. Add the bucatini to the pot and cook for 8 minutes (or according to the package instructions).

Meanwhile, in a dry frying pan, gently fry the sausage over low heat until the oils are released, allowing it to get a bit crispy. Remove the sausage from the pan and set aside. Add the olive oil to the pan and fry the chopped garlic until fragrant but not browned.

Using a fork, whisk together the egg yolks, grated Parmesan, soy sauce, kecap manis and a pinch of salt in a bowl.

Once cooked, drain the bucatini, reserving some of the pasta cooking water. Add the sausage back into the pan along with the drained bucatini and toss in the garlic oil.

Slowly add a little of the pasta cooking water to the egg yolk mixture until glossy and combined. Pour this over the hot pasta and sausage and mix together.

Serve immediately with black pepper and extra Parmesan grated on top.

CHINESE-STYLE SPICY GARLIC CELERY

Celery divides people for some reason. I think that's because most of us are introduced to it in the form of sticks dipped into things, which I don't feel is its best form. Don't get me wrong, I enjoy raw celery. It has an earthy pepperiness that I find quite delicious. But I adore celery in its cooked form, especially with soy and garlic. This is a version of a common wok-fried celery dish we eat at large banquets in Malaysia. Once you get the hang of the timings, you can switch up the flavorings to whatever you fancy. If you want a more floral version, cook off some ginger. Again, it's a dish bursting with flavor and something I make for myself when I need something green with a satisfying crunch.

SERVES 1

2 tbsp Shaoxing rice wine
3 tbsp light soy sauce
1 tsp white sugar
2 tbsp vegetable oil
1 bunch of celery, sliced at an angle
5 garlic cloves, peeled and finely diced
1 tsp cornstarch mixed with 3 tbsp water to make a paste
1 tsp Malaysian crispy shrimp chile or crispy chile oil
Salt and ground white pepper

In a small bowl, mix together the Shaoxing rice wine, soy sauce and sugar.

Heat the vegetable oil in a wok over high heat. Add the celery to the hot oil and stir-fry for 1 minute, or until a little translucent.

Next, add the garlic and stir-fry for 2–3 minutes, or until fragrant.

Add the rice wine, soy and sugar mixture, then add the cornstarch paste and stir-fry until everything thickens slightly. Allow all of the flavors to come together, then taste and adjust the seasoning with salt and white pepper.

Finally, add the crispy shrimp chile or crispy chile oil and make a few last tosses. Serve immediately while piping hot.

MUM'S LAP CHEONG FRIED RICE

This is the first dish my mom ever taught me to make. I used to call it breakfast rice because we would have it in the mornings at the weekend. Mom doesn't appreciate the greasiness of most sausages in the kitchen, so this was our alternative with Chinese sausage (lap cheong). It's so incredibly simple to put together, and yet there's a subtle art to achieving that characteristic smokiness when wok-frying rice that comes from patience. Mom taught me so much of this when mastering wok hei (see page 27). Despite the frenetic appearance of wok-frying, there's a subtle calm to it that I adore — it's patience and timing that make this dish so wonderful.

SERVES 1

1 egg, beaten
1 tbsp vegetable oil
1 Chinese sausage (lap cheong), thinly sliced at an angle
2 scallions, white parts sliced into 1 in (3 cm) pieces, green parts finely sliced
¾ cup (150 g) jasmine rice, cooked and cooled
2 tbsp frozen peas
Salt and ground white pepper

FOR THE SAUCE

1 tsp light soy sauce
1 tsp dark soy sauce
1 tsp oyster sauce
A pinch of MSG

Combine all of the ingredients for the sauce with a teaspoon of water in a small bowl or jug, then set aside.

In a nonstick pan, scramble the egg over medium heat with a pinch each of salt and ground white pepper, then set aside.

When ready to cook, place a wok over medium heat. Once hot, add the vegetable oil to coat the bottom of the wok. Add the sliced sausage and white parts of the scallions to the wok and stir-fry for 2 minutes, or until fragrant.

Add the cooked rice and the frozen peas, then immediately pour in the sauce. Turn up the heat to high and wok-fry all of the ingredients until all of the sauce has been incorporated and everything is smoky.

Add the scrambled egg and green parts of the scallion to the wok, then briefly mix everything through.

Spoon the rice into a bowl and then invert it onto a plate and serve immediately.

GOCHUJANG MAC 'N' CHEESE

In writing this book, I committed to making an honest account of my life, loves and soul… even if those truths damn me. I adore the red-boxed mac 'n' cheese from my childhood. In fact, as a kid, I remember copying my adopted sisters who would cook the mac 'n' cheese from one box and then use the package of cheese powder from a second box as a lurid orange, Parmesan-like dusting. Now, in my older years, I obviously love spice. Here, gochujang gives an element of sweet spiciness while the addition of kimchi brings a gorgeous bitterness set against the salty cheese. What's more, the gochujang turns the cheese sauce an orange shade reminiscent of that mac 'n' cheese from our childhoods. Enjoy this dish on happy days, sad days, time-of-the-month days. You name the day, this mac 'n' cheese will be there for you.

SERVES 1

3½ oz (100 g) dried macaroni
2 tsp butter
1 tsp vegetable oil
1 garlic clove, peeled and finely chopped
1 tsp all-purpose flour
¼ cup (60 ml) whole milk
1 tsp gochujang (Korean chile paste), add more or less depending on how spicy you like things
1¾ oz (50 g) mozzarella, grated
1¾ oz (50 g) Cheddar, grated
¾ oz (20 g) Parmesan, grated
1 tsp Dijon mustard
scant ½ cup (100 ml) heavy cream
1 tbsp kimchi
Salt and freshly ground black pepper
Chopped fresh chives, Korean chile powder and sesame seeds, to garnish (optional)

Bring a large pot of well-salted water to a boil. Add the macaroni and cook it for 2 minutes less than stated on the package instructions.

Meanwhile, place a large nonstick saucepan over medium-low heat. Once warm, add the butter and vegetable oil. Allow the butter to melt and brown a little and develop a nutty flavor, then fry off the garlic for a few seconds in the pan.

Now add the flour and gently whisk it into the butter and oil. Cook out the mixture for at least 2–3 minutes until the flour has made a roux.

Whisking continuously, pour one-third of the milk into the pan with the roux. Once that has been completely combined with the roux, add the remaining two-thirds of the milk and continue whisking to make a smooth sauce.

Add the gochujang, all three cheeses and the Dijon mustard to the pan, then whisk into the sauce. Continue cooking, stirring continuously, over medium-low heat until all the cheese has fully melted and the sauce thickens.

Next, stir in the cream for extra richness, then season the sauce with salt and pepper to taste. Finally, add the kimchi to the sauce and stir in.

Once ready, drain the macaroni and add it to the pan with the kimchi-cheese sauce. Stir to make sure that all the macaroni is fully coated. Serve, garnished with chives, chile powder and sesame seeds if you like. Enjoy piping hot!

MEE HOON GORENG

Mee hoon goreng is a dish of spicy, stir-fried rice vermicelli that originates from Indonesia but is also found in Malaysia, Brunei and Singapore. Each region has their own unique way of flavoring the fine rice noodles, which are the main component common to all the recipes. Lighter in texture compared to thicker noodles, when stir-fried, rice vermicelli absorbs those smoky, spicy, aromatic flavors very well. This is a perfect recipe for using up any leftovers you have in the fridge—as long as you've got the punchy spice paste correct, then the recipe is highly adaptable. Even after the memory of Christmas dinner has faded, any leftover hearty cabbage leaves would work well folded into the noodles, as would the bitter leaves of Brussels sprouts or any shredded, gamey, roasted meats. No matter what else I throw in, I do like to include both the onion and beansprouts in the noodles as they give the dish a good base texture, but the other ingredients can be swapped in and out.

This is a breakfast staple in my house as it reignites you during those bleary, cold winter mornings with a warming hit from the smoky chile, yet it doesn't leave you feeling overly full due to the lightness of the noodles. For self-nourishing purposes, add a crispy fried egg with a runny, golden yolk on top. And for those of you who enjoy chile, I've attached an optional garnish of pickled chile padi (bird's eye chiles pickled in malt vinegar), which gives the dish an extra kick. The pickled chiles can be kept in a jar in the fridge to be used on eggs, rice or stir fries. Similarly, the spice paste keeps really well in the freezer. Make a double batch, then once it is fried, use one quantity for the mee hoon goreng and freezer the other half. Put the paste into ice-cube trays and place them in the freezer. Allow the cubes of paste to freeze and then transfer them to another freezer-proof container for up to three months, to use as and when you're craving another portion. Simply defrost before using.

Recipe overleaf →

SERVES 1

← *Mee Hoon Goreng continued*

7 oz (200 g) dried rice vermicelli noodles
¼ cup (60 ml) vegetable oil
1 onion, peeled and thinly sliced
3½ oz (100 g) roast turkey, shredded
1¾ oz (50 g) cooked cabbage
1¾ oz (50 g) cooked Brussels sprouts
3½ oz (100 g) beansprouts
Crispy fried egg (see page 94), to serve

FOR THE SPICE PASTE

5 shallots, peeled and roughly chopped
6 garlic cloves, peeled and roughly chopped
2 fresh long red chiles, deseeded and roughly chopped
10–12 dried red chiles, soaked in warm water for 20 minutes, then drained
2 tsp dried shrimp or 2 tsp salted black beans (available online or in most Asian supermarkets. If you can't find either, use a little extra fish sauce during seasoning)
2 tbsp vegetable oil

FOR THE SAUCE

2 tsp kecap manis (sweet soy sauce)
2 tsp fish sauce
2 tsp light soy sauce
1 tsp sesame oil
Salt, to taste

FOR THE CHILE PADI (OPTIONAL)

Fresh red and green bird's eye chiles, sliced into thin rounds
Malt vinegar, to cover

Prepare the chile padi a few days ahead, if making. Place the sliced chiles in a sterilized jar. Pour in enough malt vinegar to cover the chiles, seal and set aside to pickle at room temperature for at least 3 days before using. After 3 days, store it in the fridge.

Boil a kettle of water. Break the noodles into a heatproof bowl and cover with boiling water. Soak the noodles for 2 minutes less than stated on the package instructions. (They should be slightly undercooked as they will be stir-fried before serving.) Drain and leave to cool.

To make the spice paste, place all of the ingredients in a food processor or blender and blend to a fine paste.

Combine all of the ingredients for the sauce in a small bowl or jug and set aside.

Heat the vegetable oil in a wok over medium heat until a little smoky, then add the spice paste and sliced onion and fry until the paste is fragrant and the onion has softened.

Add in the noodles, all of the leftovers (turkey, cabbage and Brussels) and the sauce. Keep tossing all the ingredients in the wok until all of the ingredients are well combined and warmed through. The noodles will absorb the sauce, so continue to stir-fry them until they're no longer wet and just dry enough to become a little smoky.

When ready to serve, add the beansprouts to the wok and toss them to warm through. Make sure they're the last ingredient added so that they retain their bite and don't overcook.

Serve the noodles piping hot, piled into a bowl with a crispy fried egg on top. If you want that extra kick of chile heat, add a teaspoon of chile padi on top of the fried egg.

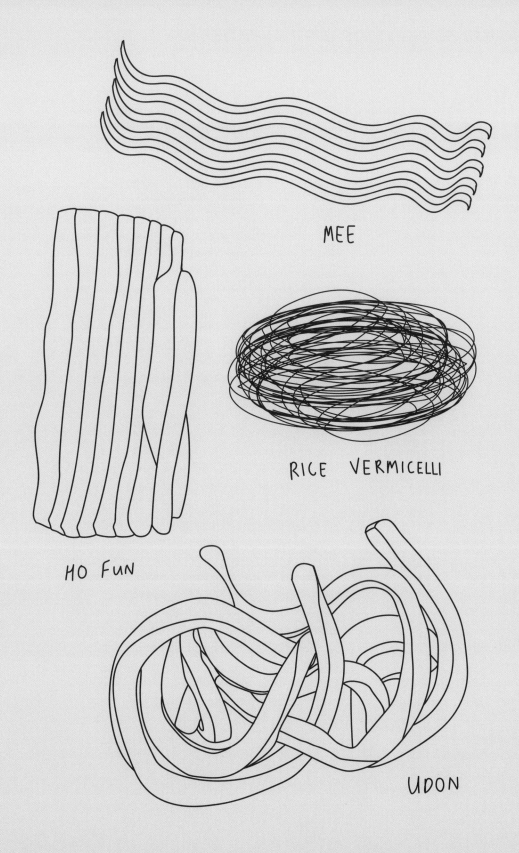

MAGGI GORENG WITH CRISPY FRIED EGGS

No matter what mood I'm in, instant noodles always soothe me. A popular street food, Maggi goreng is one of my favorite solo-cooking snacks. This is a common street food served in hawker stalls in Malaysia and I adore that there's no hiding people's love for instant noods. It's literally stalls proudly serving noodles that have been embellished with sambal, eggs, shrimp, chicken—you choose your toppings and it's ready in minutes. This instant delight really can be adapted to include whatever you crave with it.

SERVES 2

2 packages of instant noodles (I recommend Maggi brand or Indomie)
2 tbsp vegetable oil
2 garlic cloves, peeled and minced
1 small onion, peeled and sliced
1 small red pepper, deseeded and sliced into strips
1 small green pepper, deseeded and sliced into strips
1 carrot, cut into long matchsticks
2 eggs
A handful of beansprouts
1 scallion, chopped into 1–1½ in (3–4 cm) chunks, plus extra to garnish (optional)
Salt and freshly ground black pepper

FOR THE SAUCE

2 tbsp light soy sauce
1 tsp dark soy sauce
1 tbsp oyster sauce
1 tsp chile sauce or Sambal Oelek (page 46)
A pinch of sugar (optional)

TO SERVE (OPTIONAL)

2 crispy fried eggs (see page 85)
A drizzle of chile crisp oil
Crispy fried shallots (optional)

Boil a kettle of water. Set aside the package of flavoring that comes with the noodles for another recipe. Break the noodles into a heatproof bowl and pour over boiling water, then leave for 3–4 minutes until they are slightly al dente. (They should be slightly undercooked as they will be stir-fried before serving.) Drain the noodles and set aside.

Combine all of the ingredients for the sauce in a small bowl or jug, then set aside.

Heat the oil in a wok or large frying pan over medium-high heat. Add the garlic and onion and stir-fry until fragrant. (If you're adding any meat or tofu, add it now and stir-fry until slightly underdone.) Next, add the peppers and carrot and stir-fry for 2–3 minutes.

Push the veggies to one side of the wok, then crack the eggs into the other side. Cook, stirring continuously, until the eggs are lightly scrambled. Once almost cooked, mix the scrambled eggs into the vegetables.

Add the cooked noodles to the wok, pour in the sauce and season with salt and pepper to taste. Toss everything together until all the ingredients are well mixed, coated in the sauce and the noodles are heated through.

Add the beansprouts and the scallion chunks to the wok with the noodles and give it a final quick toss.

Serve the noodles hot, piled into bowls with an optional crispy fried egg on top. Drizzle with some chile crisp oil and garnish with a few extra slices of scallions or some crispy fried shallots, if you like.

STEAK AU SICHUAN POIVRE

There's a quiet satisfaction in selecting a special cut from the butcher or fishmonger for a solo supper; a sort of private ritual. I always relish those moments, walking home with something glorious tucked under my arm, anticipating the pleasure of cooking it just for me. With its reputation as a shared meal for romantic diners, steak has been pigeonholed as a dish for two. In my kitchen, however, it's a solo affair and so the steak doesn't have to share the spotlight. Cooking for one frees you from certain constraints: no need for a massive, unwieldy pan to fit two steaks, no juggling timings to suit different tastes, it's just you giving your undivided attention to the sizzling single steak in the pan, and cooking that steak to your own definition of perfect doneness.

In this take on the French classic, steak au poivre, Sichuan peppercorns bring a nuanced, tingling heat that complements the richness of the meat. I've always found steak au poivre to be reminiscent of beef in black bean sauce—salty umami flavors with rich meat. This is a self-indulgent hybrid. In fact, this dish is excellent when you swap the steak with fried oyster mushrooms that have been marinated in a little bit of soy sauce and kecap manis (sweet soy sauce) and left to caramelize a little; you'll also need to use vegetable stock instead of beef. It's a vegetarian dream. Topped with a soy-cured egg yolk, this dish bridges the gap between classic French technique and bold Asian flavors, all the while celebrating the act of cooking for oneself as an indulgence in its own right.

Recipe overleaf →

SERVES 1

1 fillet steak
Sea salt flakes
2 tsp black peppercorns, lightly crushed
Vegetable oil
1 tsp Sichuan peppercorns, lightly crushed
½ banana shallot, peeled and finely chopped
¾ in (2 cm) piece of ginger, peeled and grated
5 garlic cloves, peeled and crushed
3 tbsp Shaoxing rice wine
1 tbsp light soy sauce
1 tsp rice wine vinegar or cider vinegar
scant ½ cup (100 ml) beef stock
A pinch of MSG
1 tbsp cold butter

SEASONING STATION (OPTIONAL)
Light soy sauce, salt, vinegar, stock

FOR THE SOY-CURED EGG YOLK
scant ½ cup (100 ml) light soy sauce
2 tbsp rice wine vinegar
1 egg yolk

TO SERVE
Steamed rice
Chopped fresh chives
Steamed greens

← *Steak continued*

Well ahead of when you want to eat, cure the egg yolk. Combine the soy sauce and rice wine in a small bowl, then carefully lower in the egg yolk. Depending on how firm you prefer the yolk, cure it for between 1 and 8 hours at room temperature: 1 hour for lightly cured, 2–3 hours for medium and 4–8 hours for firm. Store the cured egg yolk in the fridge if you are not using it immediately.

About 30 minutes before cooking, take the steak out of the fridge to allow it to reach room temperature. Season the steak generously with the sea salt flakes and 1 teaspoon of the black peppercorns.

Heat a glug of vegetable oil in a frying pan over medium-high heat. Once hot, sear the steak in the pan to your preferred level of doneness. Transfer the steak to a plate or board and set aside to rest.

In the same pan, toast the Sichuan peppercorns and the remaining 1 teaspoon of black peppercorns in the same oil until they start to pop and release their aromas.

Reduce the heat to low, add the shallot, ginger and garlic to the pan, then fry until softened and fragrant. Deglaze the pan with the Shaoxing rice wine, then add the soy sauce, vinegar, beef stock and MSG. Allow the mixture to simmer and the flavors to meld together, then adjust the seasoning to taste with whichever seasoning station ingredients you feel like today.

Finish the sauce by swirling in the cold butter for richness and a glossy sheen.

Spoon some of the peppercorn sauce over the resting steak, reserving plenty for finishing the dish.

When ready to serve, spoon the steamed rice into a serving bowl. Slice the steak into strips and drape them over the rice, then spoon over the rest of the peppercorn sauce. Nestle the soy-cured egg yolk into the bowl and top with some chopped chives. Serve with any steamed greens of your choosing.

I'M JUST MAKING A WEE TREAT FOR MYSELF

SWEET AND SOUR PINEAPPLE MEATBALLS

There is a concept in Malaysia called economy rice. It's a system whereby you get a plate of rice and then the hawker stalls offer different dishes like curry chicken, stir-fried celery and fried fish to top up your plate until you are satisfied. It's a cost-effective way of sampling lots of delicious dishes. That was where I first fell in love with these meatballs. They're so incredibly flavorful, with the pineapple adding the extra tanginess the rich meatballs need. The secret to this recipe is thoroughly browning the meatballs so they gain an almost crispy texture on the outside.

SERVES 2–3

FOR THE MEATBALLS

1 lb 2 oz (500 g) ground pork, 20% fat
5 garlic cloves, peeled and finely diced
1½ in (4 cm) piece of ginger, peeled and finely diced
3–4 scallions, finely sliced
1 tbsp chicken bouillon powder
2 tbsp light soy sauce
1 tbsp sesame oil
Vegetable oil, for frying

FOR THE STIR-FRY

1 red pepper, deseeded and chopped
1 green pepper, deseeded and chopped
1 onion, peeled and sliced
10 garlic cloves, peeled and diced
5½ oz (150 g) pineapple chunks, canned or fresh

FOR THE SWEET AND SOUR SAUCE

½ cup (150 g) ketchup
2 tbsp light brown sugar
6 tbsp white vinegar
3 tsp cornstarch
Salt, to taste

TO SERVE

Steamed rice
Sesame seeds

First, make the meatballs. Place the ground pork, garlic, ginger and scallions in a bowl. Add in the chicken bouillon powder, light soy sauce and sesame oil, then use your hands to bring it all together and the flavors to infuse the meat. Roll the pork mixture into tight balls about the size of a golf ball, place them on a tray and cover with plastic wrap. Chill in the fridge to allow them to firm up for at least 1 hour and up to 12 hours.

When ready to cook, prep all the stir-fry ingredients, and make the sweet and sour sauce by combining all the ingredients in a small bowl or jug with ⅔ cup (150 ml) of water. Set aside.

Heat up a good amount of vegetable oil in a large wok. Working in batches, add the pork meatballs to the wok and fry until deep golden brown on the outside. Transfer to a plate and set aside.

Next, add all the stir-fry ingredients to the wok and stir-fry in the same oil until fragrant.

Pour the sweet and sour sauce into the wok, then return the meatballs to the pan along with any juices from the plate. Allow everything to simmer and the sauce to thicken. Taste and adjust the seasoning to how you like it.

When ready to serve, fill a bowl with steamed rice and ladle over the meatballs, veggies and sauce. Scatter over a few sesame seeds to finish.

SAMBAL EGGPLANT AND GREEN BEANS

This is truly one of the dishes that makes me wonder whether I could become permanently vegetarian or even vegan. I've always thought that it would be easier for me to go veggie in Asia, where the abundance of veg and the flavors that support its cooking make for a broad repertoire of meat-free dishes. In Asian culture, chiles aren't used in a macho way to show off our tolerance to heat, they're used to flavor a dish and bring out its smokiness or sweetness. In this dish, the sambal actually helps the eggplant taste better. The eggplant is the star of the show, but the supporting cast really makes for a stellar performance. I've used Chinese eggplant in this recipe, but if you can't find one then any regular eggplant will do. Obviously, they come in a range of sizes so just make sure you have enough for one portion. Serve this dish with steamed rice and some crispy garlic for one of the best weeknight meals you could ever ask for.

SERVES 1

1 Chinese eggplant
   (or a common globe eggplant)
Vegetable oil, for stir-frying
7 oz (200 g) string beans, trimmed
3 tbsp Sambal Oelek (page 46)
1 tbsp kecap manis (sweet soy sauce)
1 tsp palm sugar (or dark brown sugar)
A pinch of MSG
1 tsp salt
Steamed rice, to serve
Store-bought crispy fried garlic,
   to serve

SEASONING STATION (OPTIONAL)
Salt, sugar, lime juice

First, prepare the eggplant. Dice it into bite-sized chunks about 1–1½ in (3–4 cm) long.

Heat a generous glug of vegetable oil in the base of a wok or large frying pan over medium heat. Once hot, add the eggplant in batches and stir-fry until golden. Transfer to a plate lined with paper towels to soak up any excess oil.

Using the oil left in the wok, stir-fry the green beans. Return the eggplant to the wok along with the Sambal Oelek, kecap manis, sugar, MSG, salt and a scant ½ cup (100 ml) of water. Stir-fry over high heat for about 5 minutes, or until everything is cooked through.

Taste and adjust to your taste with the seasoning station ingredients. Serve with steamed rice alongside and scattered with crispy fried garlic.

LEARNINGS FROM
THE MOTHERLAND

Amah and Gōng Gong in Molaka, sometime in the nineties

Learnings from the Motherland

In the quiet hour between 5am and 6am, as the sun caresses the horizon, Melaka's temperature hovers at a comfortable 80°F (27°C), offering a temporary respite from the relentless heat that dominates the rest of the day. Being so close to the equator, Malaysia is a land of perpetual warmth, but these early mornings hold a special charm. They marked the beginning of a new day in my grandparents' pre-war house, the very place my mother and her 13 siblings spent their childhood. It was a spacious home with generously-sized bedrooms, split into rooms for the boys and rooms for the girls, each furnished with many double beds. Their living conditions weren't cramped, but rather it made for a joyous, sociable upbringing. At the heart of the house, there was a large opening for ventilation—a functional architectural feature that also served as a lightwell. As a child, I adored this unique element as it allowed us to feel simultaneously indoors and outdoors. It was a rare luxury, and one that couldn't be replicated in my home country of Scotland.

At this early hour, my Gōng Gong (grandfather) would commence his daily ritual—a tranquil stroll through the city of Melaka. A creature of habit, he sported a simple ensemble: white vest, shorts, brown sandals and his signature gold-rimmed aviator glasses. He was a kind and family-oriented man, always overjoyed when his grandchildren paid a visit. At precisely 5:30am, he would summon me to accompany him on these peaceful expeditions. Our morning rambles weren't filled with chatter but were instead marked by serenity, a time for contemplation. My grandfather encouraged silence, not in a domineering manner, but in a way that fostered appreciation and mindfulness. As an adult who now values mindfulness, I've come to regard these walks as my grandfather's way of imparting conscious meditation. Silently absorbing the heartbeat of Melaka, those walks instilled in me the importance of mindfulness. This practice continues to play a significant role in my life, even when it comes to food. Each meal is an opportunity to savor and appreciate the flavors, an act of mindfulness that enhances the overall experience.

With hands clasped behind his back, Gōng Gong ambled through the streets, his gaze sweeping across the architectural wonders of Melaka. The city was dotted with traditional Baba-Nyonya houses, masterpieces of Chinese-Malay architecture. These houses featured rows of wooden-shuttered windows designed to keep the stifling heat at bay and welcome the cooling breeze. We weaved through the winding streets, tracing the path of the famous Melaka River that meandered through the heart of the city. On the riverbanks, giant monitor lizards would bask in the morning sun. Whenever we encountered them, my grandfather would pause, allowing me to join him in observing these magnificent creatures for extended periods. As a tomboyish child with a fascination for frogs, insects and all things reminiscent of *Jurassic Park*, I couldn't contain my excitement. Growing up in Glasgow, where a gray squirrel was the creature you'd sight most frequently, these monitor lizards were like a trip to Disneyland for me. I would occasionally break our silence by exclaiming, "Diles!"—mistakenly thinking they were crocodiles. Their immense size and resemblance to Komodo dragons only added to the confusion. It was astonishing to witness such exotic creatures in the heart of a bustling city, mere feet away from local cafés serving oyster omelets and noodles. To this day, these majestic reptiles still inhabit Melaka, though the city has evolved around them, with some now residing near a shiny H&M outlet.

Despite their formidable appearance, I've grown fond of these ancient beasts, finding them strangely endearing. Reflecting on this, I realized how much of my identity has been shaped by my experiences in Malaysia. It made me ponder the profound impact of a place thousands of miles away from Glasgow on my sense of self. Being of mixed heritage, I've come to appreciate how seemingly insignificant details from my childhood contribute to the person I've become. One of the first street foods that left an indelible mark on me was the humble chicken satay, known as sate ayam. While it's a dish we encounter frequently in the West, in Malaysia it takes on a whole new dimension. Skewers of succulent meat are expertly arranged over a sizzling barbecue at outdoor hawker stalls. Watching their preparation is an exciting spectacle—the smoke from the grills mingles with the hot evening air, the lively night market echoes with shouts of orders, and skilled stall owners deftly fan the smoke to control the oxygen and maintain the perfect heat. The aroma of fat dripping from pork and chicken onto the coals is nothing short of intoxicating. And then there is the taste—the fragrant marinade of spices, the sweet caramelization of the skewers and the rich peanut sauce. This peanut sauce is a far cry from anything that has seen the inside of a jar. It's made from deep-fried peanuts, cooked to a golden hue, combined with spices and blended into a buttery, nutty delight. For me, this dish is a portal to Malaysia, akin to the magical food experiences portrayed in the movie *Ratatouille*.

Food has a unique power to reignite cherished memories, easing the ache of longing. During one winter lockdown, my mother and I yearned for authentic satay. We braved the cold, setting up a fire pit in the front yard of our family home, where a makeshift grill held beef satay skewers. It was our attempt to capture the essence of Malaysia in a snowy front garden in chilly Glasgow. In conversations with my mixed-heritage friends, we often express a yearning to revisit the "other" places we hail from, as if we are rechargeable batteries seeking to plug into various power sources. When travel isn't possible, food is the connection that refuels these batteries. Which is why I find it so important to absorb as much as possible when I am in Malaysia. The experiences of and lessons from the country of my heritage, particularly those shared with my beloved grandfather, have all contributed to my sense of self. They remind me that our identities are shaped by countless small, seemingly insignificant details, which collectively define the whole person we become. My journey, woven with mindfulness and monitor lizards and flavored by the rich tapestry of Malaysia, is a testament to the beauty of cultural diversity and the profound influence of our roots.

A lot of my learning has come from hawker centers. These open-air food halls are more than mere eating spots; they are the pulsating heart of the Malaysian dining tradition. Each stall is a window into the expertise of the hawker owner and their background. They vary in offerings from dishes to their origin. These are lively places. The clatter of utensils cuts through the sounds of chatter. The smells that hit you vary from stall to stall—from Cucur Udang (shrimp fritters, see page 228) to Rojak (a savory-sweet fruit salad, see page 242). In these communal hubs, an array of dishes brings people from all walks of life together, and it really celebrates the shared language of food. Malaysian hawker stalls are cultural sanctuaries rather than mere food outlets, as the term "street food" seems too commercial to capture their authentic charm.

The affordability of the food is just one of the draws; it's the reason why modern homes often forgo large kitchens. My Aunt Nancy and Uncle Leong are connoisseurs of these markets; they have become my invaluable guides to the shining gems of these food centers all over the country. Dining out is a family affair for my aunt and uncle and, through their eyes, I've come to appreciate making a journey for a specific taste, whether it's for the creamiest durian or the juiciest pork chop with gravy. They introduced me to the wonders of roti canai (buttery, flaky flatbread), served right off the grill at a roadside rest stop, an experience that redefined my understanding of the perfect dish. This casual mode of dining, perched on petite red stools, taught me volumes about how I like to eat—I'm not bothered by fancy chairs and starched linen, money cannot buy atmosphere. In fact, I mirrored the casual dining offered by hawker stalls when I opened my first street-food stall in Glasgow. It was down a narrow alleyway and, for the first few months, all I could afford was a paper sign saying "Julie's Street Kitchen" taped to the wall.

I watch in awe of the wizardry of these hawker chefs, hand-stretching roti dough to thin perfection and masterfully wok-tossing mee goreng, the embers catching alight from the burner to create that magical wok hei (the breath of the wok, see page 27). It's this immersive experience that has deepened my love for cooking. It's not just about the plate that's delivered in front of you; it's a living, breathing, hands-on culinary education that unfolds before your eyes. These are not fancy kitchens with induction stoves and combi ovens, rather these stalls rely on the bare minimum of equipment. I find strength in that style of cooking. My laid-back attitude towards having the "best" equipment comes from watching exceptional food being produced from very little at these hawker stalls. At my first restaurant, we had a small prep bench and a back stove with space for three portable induction burners—the entire kitchen was smaller than some people's pantry, but somehow we made it work. The chefs I employed had the open-mindedness to cook with me in a kitchen of tiny proportions on makeshift prep benches.

During my childhood, Amah's (grandmother's) cooking was a constant throughout the time I spent in Malaysia. Her presence in the kitchen was synonymous with the warmth and busyness of the family home. She is a pillar of the Melaka market community, cherished by a network of friends cultivated over decades of daily excursions for the freshest ingredients at the local market. The market has a vibrancy of color across all of the fruit and vegetable stalls. There are a few stalls that sell hot youtiao (wheat-flour donuts), deep-fried to order. I've often related that smell to the sugared donuts sold on a Sunday morning in Glasgow's Barras market, famously fried fresh. There's something so enticing about the smell of these fried treats while you're among so many other delicious ingredients. I adored going with Amah and other family members to the market. Immersed in the unfamiliar, I would wander through the market holding someone's hand, completely awe-struck by this land of newness.

Once we were back home, Amah would artfully whip up sambal shrimp, fish head curry and a medley of seasonal vegetables into aromatic feasts that filled our home with the rich scents of chile, garlic and belacan. I vividly recall the beautifully set table, adorned with a practical, yet stylish, wipeable cloth and safeguarded by mesh domes to keep the flies out. Her crockery collection—each piece a canvas of intricate designs—sitting precariously in a cabinet full of many beautiful utensils, speaks to her aesthetic sensibility. The same hands that conjure culinary magic sew her wardrobe from Batik fabrics, a rainbow of colors and patterns, each stitch imbued with her creativity and self-reliance. Any time I wore solely black clothing, she would encourage me to change, to celebrate color and its vibrancy.

Amah's spirit is famous within the community; her spirituality draws friends and neighbors seeking enlightenment. Locals would visit the house to seek her guidance, and that still happens to this day. Her matriarchal influence is a spectacle of wisdom and strength. Her palm readings, always insightful and occasionally humorous, reveal layers of our potential futures. When she read my palm, her laughter was a prelude to a playful prophecy, "You will marry a rich old man for his money." Yet here I am at 32, my life's narrative unfolding in contrast to her light-hearted predictions. To this day, I wonder whether that was an accurate palm reading, or rather Amah manifesting that I'll assist everyone to early retirement. Beyond her laughter lies a deep respect for her spiritual guidance, rooted in Buddhism, that imbues our mornings with the sacred scent of incense. It's this incense that transports me back to her porch in Melaka, in anticipatory delight of her breakfast spread—noodles, fresh fruits and soya milk. And occasionally indulging my young Western palate with whatever chocolatey cereal was popular there, with shelf-stable milk.

From Melaka to Glasgow, the creations of my Amah have woven a rich tapestry through our family's history and into my mom's cooking. Her skillfully crafted "Love Letters"—delicately thin cookies rolled into scrolls, embossed with intricate designs—as well as the tender "kuih," soft, sweet morsels of rice

Me and my cousins with Amah and Gōng Gong, in their home in Melaka, 2002

flour perfumed with the lush green of pandan leaves. These delights are not mere confections; they are the storied chronicles of our heritage, whispered through recipes passed from one generation to the next.

Embodying Amah's adventurous spirit, my mother ventured to the UK at the tender age of 18. With her heart set on a career in healthcare, she arrived in Leeds to study, her English at an almost-there stage, but her resolve unwavering. Her tenacity and resilience are qualities I strive to embody daily. When language faltered, her culinary creations spoke volumes, her dishes becoming the dialect of her affection, the cuisine of connection. She raised me to feel pride in our rich, mixed heritage, never dwelling on the challenges but celebrating the triumphs of being an Asian woman in 1980s' Glasgow. As a health visitor, my mother's empathy and boundless kindness became her signature, her generosity of spirit a beacon in the community. Her path crossed with that of my father at a famous pub in Glasgow, The Ubiquitous Chip, an encounter blossoming into love, anchoring her to Glasgow as her chosen home. Her kitchen, a crucible of creativity, earned her acclaim among those fortunate to taste her culinary creations. Her char siu roast pork, anointing the grill with its sweet and savory fragrance, served alongside slices of cucumber and crystallized ginger, demonstrated her gastronomic genius.

In our culture, food is the currency of love. My mother transcended even this tradition, her words and dishes intertwining to form a language of love that was uniquely hers. She cultivated a community of friends, an extended family of sorts, who filled the void of distant relatives with their warmth and kinship. At the core of it all was her innate ability to orchestrate feasts effortlessly, the matriarchal lineage of culinary wisdom flowing through all of us in quite a spiritual fashion. Our family's saga has always been one of matriarchal strength, a legacy I carry with immense pride. A rich blend of origins form the roots of my culinary knowledge: the ancestral teachings of Malaysia, the cherished recipes my mother brought with her to Scotland as she bravely established a new life, and the observances from my childhood visits back to the land that feels home.

Embracing the lessons from the Motherland, I have woven them into the fabric of my own identity. Whether through traditional dishes or innovative fusions, my cooking is a dialogue of self-expression, a celebration of my mixed heritage that stands confidently on the plate. It's an authenticity that resonates with every slightly modified recipe, and ones that remain exactly traditional. Because the make up of authenticity involves respecting tradition and our ancestors' teachings in order to create new dishes. This chapter takes traditional learnings from Malaysia that have helped to shape me as a chef. And learnings that I find extremely important to pass on. Gatekeeping has never been a trait of mine—and I certainly won't be gatekeeping any of these recipes.

KAYA TOAST
with SOFT-BOILED EGGS

Kaya toast is one of Malaysia's key breakfasts. It's gained cult status. Kaya is a green, thick luscious jam that spreads so well on toast and should be eaten with big, thick slabs of butter in-between. It's unbelievably delicious and goes best with thick, store-bought white bread. It is dunked in rich soft-boiled eggs that are salted with dark soy sauce and made fragrant with white pepper. If I could have only one jam for the rest of my life—it would be kaya. It's made similarly to crème pâtissière but flavored with pandan leaf. I'm not going to sugar-coat this, it's a labor of love. The kaya needs to be stirred for a long time, think the love, care and attention a risotto needs. However, the work is incredibly satisfying when you try the kaya. If you don't have enough time to make it, then I recommend Madam Chang's Kaya—this is sold by an independent retailer and it is delicious. But if you do have time to make your own, jar it up and keep it in your fridge. It's the perfect snack.

SERVES 1–2

FOR THE KAYA (COCONUT JAM)
4 frozen pandan leaves, defrosted, plus 2 extra tied into a knot
½ cup (100 g) sugar
4 large egg yolks
A drop of pandan essence
scant 1 cup (200 ml) coconut cream

TO SERVE
2 eggs
Dark soy sauce, to taste
Ground white pepper, to taste
Thick slices of white bread, toasted
Thick slabs of butter, softened

To make the kaya, blend the 4 pandan leaves in a juicer or food processor with about 3½ tablespoons of water (you might need more if it isn't liquefying into a watery paste). Pour through a fine mesh sieve so just the green juice is left and none of the leaves. Whisk the sugar and egg yolks together in a heatproof bowl until pale yellow.

Place the bowl over a pot of simmering water or double boiler, making sure the water doesn't touch the bottom of the bowl. Cook and whisk the mixture, stirring continuously for a minute or two, then add the pandan juice, pandan essence, remaining pandan leaves and coconut cream and continue to cook and whisk until it thickens to a jam-like consistency. This may take up to 1 hour, but remain patient as it's completely worth it. Once thickened, let the coconut jam cool. You should have a thick, glossy, pale green curd that will keep in a sealed sterilized jar in the fridge for up to 5 days.

When ready to serve, boil a pot of water and keep it on a rolling boil. Carefully place the eggs in the pot using a spoon, then put a lid on top. Remove after 5–6 minutes and crack them open into a bowl. Season with dark soy sauce and ground white pepper.

Meanwhile, toast the white bread and spread thickly with butter, then top with a generous layer of kaya. Dunk the kaya toast into the eggs; the contrast is delicious between the sweet coconutty kaya and the rich, salty eggs.

SINGAPORE CHILE CRAB

I first tasted Singapore chile crab at a hawker center in Singapore. I had gone out for dinner with my cousins, and collectively we decided to indulge in Singapore chile crab. Donning plastic bibs, we devoured the most divine-tasting crab I've ever eaten. I'll never forget it. It's one of those food memories that brings back immense joy: the air was warm, my cousins and I were having such a good time, and the crab itself was so sizeable. Part of the joy of eating crab in this way is that you have to work hard to extract the meat. I believe this effort makes you savor the dish even more. I've always thought that if all the crab meat was shelled and served with the sauce, it just wouldn't be as satisfying.

I then had the pleasure of serving this dish in my Glasgow restaurant to two friendly food heroes, known for their kindness and love of fun, and tasty food—The Hairy Bikers, Si King and Dave Myers. They visited my first restaurant, Julie's Kopitiam, in 2022, and we filmed a beautiful episode of *The Hairy Bikers Go Local,* where they traveled around the west coast of Scotland. I cooked for them, then they gathered local ingredients and made one of the most incredible meals I've ever had. That week I was in a flurry, wondering what I could possibly cook that would be good enough for two joyous souls that I so hugely respected. My fishmonger came to my rescue with a beautiful crab caught in Tarbert. It was a biggie, and had been freshly caught that morning. I cooked it with this luscious, thick, rich sauce, slick with egg gravy. A feast fit for two kings. Dave Myers sadly left this world in February 2024. He was a true inspiration and he left his beautiful mark on the world. Many of his close friends and family describe a good day, full of fun and love, as a "Dave Day" so I would like to dedicate this recipe to Dave, his lovely wife Lil, and wonderful Si. Thank you for all of your love, may every day that we eat Singapore Chile Crab be a Dave Day.

Recipe overleaf →

SERVES 4

1 large fresh brown crab (weighing around 2 lb 4 oz/1 kg)
A fresh handful of cilantro leaves, chopped, to garnish
Steamed white rice, to serve
Fried mantou or brioche buns, to serve

FOR THE SPICE PASTE
1 tbsp belacan
5 shallots, peeled and roughly chopped
1 head garlic, cloves peeled and roughly chopped
4 in (10 cm) piece of ginger, peeled and roughly chopped
8 dried red chiles, soaked in warm water for 20 minutes, drained, deseeded if you prefer less heat
4 dried ancho chiles or any other smoky dried chiles, soaked in warm water for 20 minutes, drained, deseeded for less heat
2 tbsp soybean paste

FOR THE SAUCE
¼ cup (60 ml) canola oil
1 cup (250 g) tomato paste
Scant 1 cup (120 g) ketchup
3 tbsp distilled malt vinegar
White sugar, to taste
Salt, to taste
1 large egg, beaten

SEASONING STATION (OPTIONAL)
Salt, sugar, MSG, chile oil

← *Crab continued*

Prepare the crab by separating the legs and claws from the body. Gently crack them with a mallet to allow the sauce to penetrate during cooking, but don't shatter the shells completely, ensuring that the brown meat remains intact. Set aside in the fridge while you make the paste and sauce.

In a dry pan over medium heat, toast the belacan until lightly golden and fragrant.

Place the toasted belacan in a food processor or blender, add the rest of the ingredients for the spice paste and blend to a fine paste. Make sure everything is well-combined and the paste is free of any lumps.

Next, use the spice paste to make the sauce. Heat the canola oil in a large pot with a lid over medium heat, add the paste and fry gently, stirring frequently, until it has caramelized. This usually takes at least 10 minutes.

Stir the tomato paste into the paste in the pot and cook briefly to deepen the flavor. Add the ketchup and vinegar along with 1 cup (250 ml) of water. Leave the sauce to simmer for a few minutes and then taste and adjust the seasoning with sugar and salt as necessary.

Add all the crab pieces to the sauce in the pot, cover with a lid and steam for 15–20 minutes or until the crab meat is cooked through. This cooking time is based on a 2 lb 4 oz (1 kg) crab, but adjust the time based on the size of your crab. Once cooked, remove the crab pieces and set aside.

Take the pan off the heat and let the sauce cool for 2 minutes. Slowly stir in the beaten egg, whisking vigorously to thicken the sauce. At this stage, season to your taste with the seasoning station ingredients. If you want it spicier, a chile oil will do the trick here.

Arrange the crab pieces on a large serving dish or platter, placing the legs and claws at the bottom, and the main body of the crab on top. Spoon generous amounts of the sauce over the crab and then garnish with fresh cilantro. Serve with steamed rice and mantou or brioche buns for mopping up the sauce.

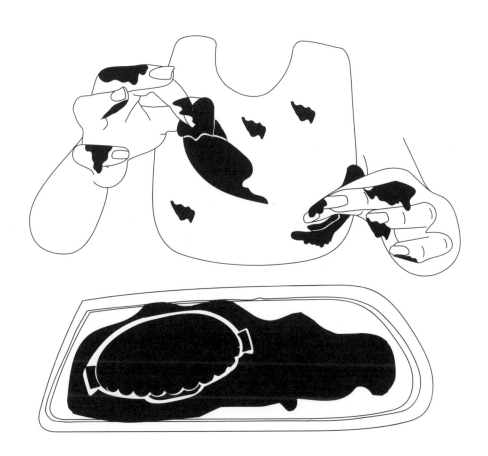

CHAR KUAY TEOW
BIG FAT NOODLES

I've never had a tattoo, but if I were to get one, it would read "big fat noodles." This phrase echoes from my childhood—it was the call from my mom that dinner was ready, and what awaited us was big fat noodles (see page 7). It wasn't until I grew older that I discovered "big fat noodles" referred to char kuay teow, a dish famously cherished in Malaysia, where there are many regional variations. You've got the Penang version, which is beautifully smoky, and then there are other variations from around Malaysia that I've yet to explore, particularly from the east side of the country. It's one of those incredible dishes that's not only deeply satisfying to make but also quite distinctive—a dish that has become somewhat mainstream, akin to pad Thai.

I believe char kuay teow stands as one of the best noodle dishes in the world. Typically served on banana leaves to enhance its aromas, char kuay teow boasts a recognizably smoky flavor achieved by frying to perfection. Generations of aunties and uncles who run the hawker stalls work tirelessly, ensuring that the flavor intensity is just right, the shrimp are succulent, and the noodles are tender, complemented perfectly by the egg. The beansprouts add a bit of crunch to a dish that is otherwise soft, comforting and utterly delightful. Definitely consider cooking this on a weeknight. It's surprisingly easy to whip up and is a dish you'll never regret making.

Recipe overleaf →

SERVES 2–4

← *Char Kuay Teow continued*

1 lb (450 g) fresh wide rice noodles (ho fun noodles — fresh noodles are best, but you can use 8 oz/ 225 g dried noodles)
2 Chinese sausages, sliced diagonally
¼ cup (60 ml) vegetable oil, plus extra for frying the noodles
10 garlic cloves, peeled and minced
12 raw jumbo shrimp, peeled and deveined
4 Thai fishcakes, finely sliced
1 tbsp Shaoxing rice wine
10 Chinese garlic chives, cut into 2 in (5 cm) slices
2 large eggs, lightly beaten
7 oz (200 g) beansprouts

FOR THE SAUCE
2½ tbsp light soy sauce
2½ tbsp dark soy sauce
1 tbsp kecap manis (sweet soy sauce)
1 tbsp fish sauce

SEASONING STATION (OPTIONAL)
Light soy sauce, chile oil, lime juice, fish sauce

If you're using dried noodles, soak the noodles in cold water for 45 minutes, or until completely soft. Drain and set aside.

Meanwhile, make the sauce. Combine all of the ingredients for the sauce in a bowl or jug and set aside.

Heat a very large wok (you don't want to overcrowd it) over medium-low heat. Once hot, add the sliced sausages and fry to render the fat. This should take around 2 minutes. Leaving the fat in the wok, transfer the sausage slices to a plate and set aside.

Add the vegetable oil to the fat already in the wok, then toss in the garlic, shrimp and fishcake slices. Stir-fry until fragrant.

Increase the heat to high, then add the Shaoxing rice wine to the wok to get the temperature of the wok up to very high. Continuing to move everything around the wok, add in the noodles, folding them into the other ingredients.

Move everything into the center of the wok and pour over the sauce. Now add an extra 1½ tablespoons of vegetable oil around the wok to get everything hot again.

Add the chopped garlic chives to the wok. Mix them in thoroughly but don't break up the noodles. Once the noodles are frying, create a space at the bottom of the wok and add a final 1 tablespoon of vegetable oil with the lightly beaten eggs. Stir the eggs around for 10–15 seconds to lightly scramble them. Gently mix the eggs through all the other ingredients, then fold the beansprouts into the mixture. At this stage, add whichever seasoning station ingredients you feel like today.

The key is to ensure the char kuay teow isn't dry; if it is, add a little water and re-fry. To gain the flavor of wok hei (see page 27) in this dish, use a blowtorch around the noodles until they blacken a bit under the heat, do this for about 30 seconds, then toss and repeat the same method with a new section. Serve piping hot.

AHMA'S HOUSE FISH HEAD CURRY

My Ahma. Mother to nine children, grandmother and now great-grandmother, too. Her traditional Nyonya-style house is always vibrant with the hustle and bustle of multiple generations of our family buzzing in and out. She often brings us fish head curry from the local market. In the West, fish heads are widely disregarded and discarded, whereas in Malaysia they are treasured. Beautifully soft and flavorful, but in scarce supply due to the fish's anatomy, fish cheeks are a rare and cherished treat. Ahma's house is where I learned of this almost sacred meat.

SERVES UP TO 3

FOR THE SPICE PASTE
6 banana shallots, peeled and roughly chopped
2 lemongrass stalks, cleaned, trimmed and roughly chopped
6 dried red chiles, roughly chopped
2 fresh long red chiles, roughly chopped
1½ in (4 cm) piece of galangal, peeled and roughly chopped
4 garlic cloves, peeled and roughly chopped
1½ tbsp belacan
3 tbsp Malaysian curry powder (see page 21)

FOR THE CURRY
Vegetable oil
15 fresh curry leaves
1 tbsp mustard seeds
2 lb 4 oz (1 kg) fish heads, chopped
3 tomatoes, chopped
1 eggplant, diced into chunks
6 okra, left whole
3 tsp tamarind paste
1–2 tbsp fish sauce

TO SERVE
Steamed rice

First, make the spice paste. Place all the ingredients for the paste in a food processor or blender and blend until smooth.

Heat enough vegetable oil to cover the base of a large sauté pan over medium heat. Add the curry leaves and mustard seeds and warm until the seeds are popping and have released their fragrant aromas. Immediately add the spice paste to the pan and fry until cooked through, adding a little more oil if necessary, so the paste doesn't burn.

Next, add the fish heads to the pan and lightly season with salt. Fry the fish heads for 1 minute on each side in the paste, then transfer them to a plate and set aside.

Add the chopped tomatoes, eggplant chunks and whole okra to the pan. Stir in the tamarind paste along with 3½ cups (800 ml) of water. Season with the fish sauce and a little more salt to taste. Simmer everything for 20 minutes, then return the fish heads to the pan and simmer for a further 5 minutes, or until the flesh on the fish is white.

Ladle the curry into bowls and serve alongside some steamed rice.

SAMBAL MACKEREL IN BANANA LEAF

There's something very special about cooking food in banana leaves. It develops an unbelievable amount of fragrance. Meat and fish soak up the flavor of the leaves but also absorb any marinade you add to the parcel. In Malaysia, we eat lots of food from banana leaves; in most cases, it acts as the plate. I'm fascinated by how the human brain works when we eat in a certain way, from fine dining off one-of-a-kind ceramics to the daily newspaper that wraps your fish dinner. For me, fish and chips always taste better when eaten from newspaper. Likewise for this dish, eating it straight from the banana leaf is so satisfying. You can find banana leaves in the freezer section of Asian supermarkets, in a big wrap of three or four leaves. Simply defrost before use.

SERVES 2–4

4 banana leaves, defrosted, to wrap the fish fillets
Vegetable oil, to brush the banana leaves
4 mackerel fillets, skin on, cleaned, deboned and patted dry
Sambal Belacan (page 47), to spread over the fish fillets
Salt, to taste
Fresh cilantro leaves, to serve
Lime wedges, to serve

First, prepare the banana leaves. Gently wipe the leaves clean with a damp cloth, then pass them quickly over an open flame. Alternatively, heat the leaves in a pan for a few seconds on each side. (This makes them more pliable and releases their aromatic oils.) Brush the shiny side of the leaves with a little vegetable oil. (This prevents sticking and adds a subtle flavor.)

Lightly season the mackerel fillets with a little salt. If your Sambal Belacan is already quite salty, reduce the amount of salt used here for seasoning. Spread a generous layer of the sambal over both sides of each mackerel fillet.

Place a mackerel fillet, sambal-side up, in the center of an oiled banana leaf. Fold the leaf around the fish to create a neat parcel, folding in the sides first and then the top and bottom. Secure the parcel either with toothpicks or tied with string. Repeat for the other parcels.

Preheat the broiler to medium-high. Place the banana-leaf parcels under the broiler and cook for 10–12 minutes, flipping them over halfway through. The cooking time may vary depending on the thickness of the mackerel fillets and the intensity of your broiler. The banana leaves should be charred and impart a smoky flavor to the fish and sambal.

Carefully unwrap the banana leaf from each parcel to expose the cooked mackerel. The sambal should be aromatic and slightly caramelized on top of the fish.

Garnish the fish with a few fresh cilantro leaves and serve with lime wedges on the side for squeezing over to provide a zesty contrast.

BIHOON UDANG
Shrimp RICE NOODLES

The last time I had the privilege of visiting my grandmother's kitchen, it was alive with the sounds of her cooking. That day, she was preparing a special lunch for her friends. On the menu was bihoon udang to start, and a bowl of ripe cherries to finish. I adore this noodle dish because of its simplicity. It can be tweaked to be vegetarian or vegan by substituting the oyster sauce for kecap manis (sweet soy sauce) and the proteins for any veggies you fancy.

SERVES 2

7 oz (200 g) dried rice vermicelli noodles
2 tbsp vegetable oil
6 garlic cloves, peeled and minced
1 onion, peeled and thinly sliced
1 carrot, grated
3½ oz (100 g) cabbage, shredded
3½ oz (100 g) cooked chicken thigh meat, shredded (optional)
3½ oz (100 g) raw jumbo shrimp, peeled and deveined (optional)
2 eggs, lightly beaten
2 tbsp light soy sauce
1 tbsp oyster sauce
A pinch of MSG
Salt and freshly ground black pepper

SEASONING STATION (OPTIONAL)
Lime juice, salt, chile oil

TO SERVE
Crispy fried egg (see page 94, optional)
Scallions, chopped
Fresh long red chiles, sliced

Boil a kettle of water. Break the noodles into a heatproof bowl and pour over boiling water. Soak the noodles for 2 minutes less than stated on the package instructions. (They should be slightly undercooked as they will be stir-fried before serving.) Drain and leave to cool.

Heat the oil in a wok or large frying pan over medium heat. Add the garlic and onion, then stir-fry for 2 minutes, or until the onion has softened and the garlic is fragrant.

Increase the heat to high, add the carrot and cabbage, then stir-fry for 2–3 minutes. If using the chicken and shrimp, add those now. Stir-fry until the shrimp have just turned pink.

Push all of the veggies, chicken and shrimp to one side of the wok, then pour the beaten eggs into the other side. Cook, stirring continuously, until the eggs are scrambled. Once cooked, mix the scrambled eggs with the rest of the stir-fry ingredients.

Add in the noodles, soy sauce, oyster sauce and MSG. Keep tossing all the ingredients in the wok and stir-fry for a further 2–3 minutes, or until everything is well combined and warmed through. The noodles will absorb the sauce, so continue to stir-fry until they're no longer wet and just dry enough to become a little smoky. Taste and adjust the seasoning with salt and pepper.

Serve the noodles piping hot, piled into bowls with a crispy fried egg on top, if using. Add whichever seasoning station ingredients you feel like today. Scatter over a few chopped scallions and sliced chiles.

FRAGRANT COCONUT RICE

Inspired by the famous podcast, *Off Menu*, like many others I have given a lot of thought to my favorite appetizer, main course, side dish and dessert. When it comes to *Off Menu*, I was late to the party, so I ended up lying and telling people that I had listened to it when I hadn't. I've no idea why it took me so long, but once I had listened to one episode, I was like a dog with a bone. I spent the next three months catching up on all episodes, back-to-back. Those two giggle bombs, James Acaster and Ed Gamble, ended up being my sole listening throughout 2020. My thoughts about my *Off Menu* main dish have remained constant throughout the years. Whenever I envision my last day on this beautiful earth and my final meal, it is always nasi lemak. Here's why...

"Nasi" means rice, while "lemak" essentially means fatty and rich. Nasi lemak features rich, coconut rice flavored with pandan leaves and other aromatics to make it super fragrant and delicious, served with some incredible accompaniments. You can have sotong kunyit, turmeric squid; beef rendang, the famously rich beef curry; or ayam goreng, fried chicken. Nasi lemak is typically served with a set of sides too, including sambal, cucumber, crispy fried anchovies and a hard-boiled egg (as pictured opposite). Sometimes, nasi lemak also comes with acar pickle, a delightful relish that includes pineapple, curry paste and peanuts. But despite the fact that all of these incredible-sounding sides and accompaniments have serious star quality themselves, the leading element of nasi lemak is the humble rice. Even though it's really just rice infused with coconut milk, it truly is one of life's greatest pleasures. Treasure this recipe and etch it into your memory because it's the best coconut rice you'll find.

SERVES 4–6

2¼ cups (450 g) jasmine rice

1 x 14 oz (400 ml) can of coconut milk (I use Chaokoh; if your coconut milk has a lower fat content, use a mixture of half coconut milk and half full-fat coconut cream)

1 tsp salt

2 tbsp vegetable oil

4 fresh pandan leaves, tied into a knot (in terms of flavor, there is no substitute for pandan, however, for a fragrant, herbal rice, use 2 lemongrass stalks)

¼ cup (60 ml) full-fat coconut cream

Begin by thoroughly rinsing the rice. Using the "claw" method (see page 26), rinse the rice at least three times in cold water until the water pretty much runs clear.

Combine the rice, coconut milk, salt and vegetable oil with a scant ½ cup (100 ml) of water in a bowl, stirring until well mixed. (If using half milk half cream, leave the cream for now and use 1¼ cups/300 ml of water.) Transfer to a large sauté pan with a wide opening. (The wide pan prevents the natural sugars in the coconut milk from burning.) Nestle in the pandan leaves and bring to a bubble over medium heat. Cover the pan with a lid and leave it over medium heat for 10 minutes, or until all the water has been absorbed.

Now, add the coconut cream to the pan and stir through the rice grains. Turn off the heat, cover the pan again, then leave the lid on for a further 5 minutes. Taste and adjust the seasoning with more salt, if needed. Serve.

CUCUR UDANG
SHRIMP FRITTERS

I adore traveling and always have. Of course, food is a key factor in what draws me to a country. While I was in Cádiz, in the south of Spain, exploring the local sherry and trying flamenco dancing with friends, I rediscovered this dish of shrimp fritters called tortillitas de camerones. I wonder whether this dish has any connective roots to cucur udang, from when the Portuguese colonized Melaka. Within Malaysia's colonization, there has been a huge crossover with foods. The two types of fritters are both incredibly simple: the shrimp have to be on the outside and the fritters themselves are very flat. They're salty-delicious.

SERVES UP TO 5,
AS A SNACK OR SIDE

Scant 1 cup (125 g) rice flour
⅓ cup (40 g) white wholewheat flour (or all-purpose flour)
½ tsp baking soda
A pinch of ground turmeric
1 large egg
15 whole raw small-medium shrimp, peeled and deveined
15 whole raw small-medium shrimp with shells on, deveined
A handful of fresh garlic chives (or regular chives), chopped
A handful of beansprouts
Vegetable oil, for deep-frying
Salt and ground white pepper
Sambal Oelek (page 46), to serve

First, make the batter. In a large mixing bowl, combine the rice flour, white wholewheat flour, baking soda and turmeric. Crack the egg into the bowl, whisk it into the flour mixture and then gradually add ¾ cup (180 ml) of water, little by little, to form a smooth batter. The consistency should be similar to a pancake batter; it should coat the back of a spoon but not be too thick.

Fold the peeled and shell-on shrimp, chopped garlic chives and beansprouts into the batter. Season with a pinch each of salt and white pepper.

Fill a deep-fryer or large, heavy-based pot no more than two-thirds full with oil. Heat the vegetable oil to 340°F (170°C). Meanwhile, line a tray or plate with paper towels and keep a spider strainer or slotted spoon on hand.

Working in batches so that you don't overcrowd the pan, spoon the batter into the oil to form small fritters. (If there are too many fritters in the fryer at once, the oil temperature will drop and they won't go crispy.) Deep-fry for 3–4 minutes on each side, or until golden, crispy and cooked through. Transfer the shrimp fritters to the lined tray or plate to drain any excess oil.

Once they are all cooked, serve the fritters immediately while hot with Sambal Oelek for dipping.

GARLICKY GREEN BEANS

This is absolutely perfect as a side dish for dinner, but I also have it simply with some steamed jasmine rice and a fried egg for a quick lunch. I adore the texture of green beans and how they absorb salty flavors so well. I'm sure you've gathered from the other recipes in this book that I use an abundance of garlic. The "jarlic"—pre-chopped garlic in a jar—won't do here. It holds an acrid flavor from the agents used to preserve it, which I don't think you can disguise even by adding other flavors. The beauty of this dish lies in its simplicity; it only uses a few ingredients, but steals the show every time.

SERVES 1-2, AS A SIDE

10½ oz (300 g) string beans
2 tbsp vegetable oil (or any other neutral oil)
7–8 garlic cloves, peeled and finely sliced
Sesame oil, to serve

FOR THE SAUCE
1 tbsp light soy sauce
1 tsp sugar
1 tbsp Shaoxing rice wine (or sherry or white wine)

SEASONING STATION (OPTIONAL)
Light soy sauce, vinegar

First, make the sauce. Combine the soy sauce, sugar and Shaoxing rice wine in a bowl or jug. Set aside.

Trim the tops and bottoms off the green beans.

Heat the vegetable oil in a wok over medium-high heat. Once it's hot, throw in the green beans and stir-fry for 1–2 minutes.

Make a space in the center of the wok and add in the garlic. Allow the garlic to sit in the hot oil for about 30 seconds–1 minute, then move the beans and garlic around the wok again.

Pour the sauce over the beans in the wok and stir-fry for a further 1–2 minutes. Add whichever seasoning station ingredientas you feel like—a bit more soy sauce if you want it salty, or vinegar if you want an acidic kick. Serve immediately, drizzled with a little sesame oil.

KANGKUNG BELACAN
WATER SPINACH WITH SHRIMP PASTE

Kangkung is also referred to as water spinach, but perhaps more poetically, it's sometimes known as morning glory. It's hard to put an exact finger on what is so good about this specific veggie. It's quite similar in flavor to spinach, but with longer stems. The leaves absorb flavor so well, and here the belacan (fermented shrimp paste) just drives it to an unctuous, salty level while chile wraps it all up with a heady kick. If you can't find the kangkung itself, I suggest using spinach with the stems still on. Don't bother with the bagged stuff from supermarkets, try South Asian supermarkets, which often have spinach with the stems still on. It's a great cheap substitute. I often drape this kangkung belacan over steamed white rice and top it with a fried egg for lunch. It's truly the best veggie of them all… in my eyes. Give it a try.

SERVES 2, AS A SIDE

14 oz (400 g) kangkung (water spinach)
1 tbsp belacan
2 tbsp vegetable oil
10 garlic cloves, peeled and minced
1 tbsp Sambal Oelek (page 46)
1 tbsp light soy sauce
1 tbsp dark soy sauce
1 tsp sugar
A pinch of MSG

SEASONING STATION (OPTIONAL)

Light soy sauce, salt, Sambal Oelek, lime juice

Thoroughly wash the kangkung to remove any dirt or grit. Shake off the excess water, then cut the kangkung into 2 in (5 cm) lengths, separating the stems from the leaves as the stems take longer to cook.

Heat a frying pan over low heat. Add the belacan to the pan and toast it until fragrant. Let the belacan cool.

Heat the vegetable oil in a wok or large frying pan over medium-high heat. Add the minced garlic and the sambal, then stir-fry until aromatic but not burned.

Add the toasted belacan to the wok and mix it into the sambal and garlic. Stir-fry everything for 1 minute, or until all the aromatics are well combined.

Add the kangkung stems to the wok first as they take longer to cook. Stir-fry the stems for about 2 minutes, then mix in the light and dark soy sauces, the sugar and MSG, ensuring the stems are well coated.

Now add the kangkung leaves, tossing quickly as they will wilt and cook within 1 minute. Taste and adjust with whichever seasoning station ingredients you feel like today. The belacan and soy sauces are already salty, so season sparingly. Serve immediately.

OYSTER OMELET WITH WILD GARLIC

I'll never forget the first time I tried an oyster omelet. It was in Melaka, right in the middle of all that buzz and history. It went all crispy at the edges but kept the oysters juicy on the inside. My mom has never been one for raw oysters—she says they're too slimy for her—but give her a cooked oyster and she's all smiles. Now, Scotland has oysters by the bucket-load. Last year, I got my fill at the Stranraer Oyster Festival. Sure, the weather was typical Scottish dreich, but hey, that didn't put a damper on anything. I was there tossing pans with the likes of Michael Caines and Felicity Cloake. What a crew! We had a good laugh, all while whipping up some amazing food. Those gray skies didn't stand a chance against the good times we had. This recipe? It's a little memento from that weekend—a crispy, tasty, wrap-up of good vibes and even better company. It's a taste of Scottish waters and, every time I make it, it's like being back at Stranraer with the gang, cooking and joking, no matter the drizzle or chill in that wee tent.

SERVES 2–3, AS A SIDE

6–8 medium shucked oysters
2 tbsp vegetable oil
4 large eggs, beaten
3½ oz (100 g) wild garlic leaves
    (optional)
½ tsp fish sauce, or to taste
3 tbsp Sambal Oelek (page 46)
    or preferred chile paste, to serve

FOR THE BATTER

¾ cup (90 g) tapioca flour
¼ cup (30 g) all-purpose flour
3 tbsp sweet potato starch
    (or potato starch)
1 tsp fish sauce
1 tsp light soy sauce
1 tsp sesame oil
¼ tsp ground black or white pepper
¼ tsp salt

First, make the batter. In a mixing bowl, whisk together all the ingredients for the batter with 1¼ cups (300 ml) of water until well combined and smooth.

Drain any excess liquid from the oysters and gently pat them dry with paper towels.

Heat a nonstick frying pan over medium heat and add the vegetable oil. Stir the batter to redistribute any starch that has settled, then ladle in enough batter to form a thin layer across the pan. Cook until crispy and then break the batter into large chunks once set.

Carefully pour in a quarter of the beaten eggs over the set batter, then cook until just solidified but still retaining some moisture. Add your oysters and add the remaining beaten eggs gradually, mixing them together after each addition.

Stir in the wild garlic, if using, and the fish sauce and cook for another 3–4 minutes without stirring (to let it crisp up), until the oysters are just cooked. Serve with the Sambal Oelek alongside.

Learnings from the Motherland

PENANG HOKKIEN MEE
SHRIMP NOODLE SOUP

This is one of Malaysia's culinary gems, one of the country's most exceptional broths. Particularly in George Town, Penang, this dish stands out for its rich, aromatic essence, the combination of sweet seafood and salty pork. Using shrimp heads to create the broth might seem laborious, however, this infuses the soup with its distinctive, robust flavor. Dedicating a day to creating this guarantees kitchen smugness. This recipe makes a large batch of broth, which can be frozen for up to a month.

SERVES 3–4

FOR THE BROTH
2 tbsp vegetable oil
2 lb 4 oz (1 kg) shrimp heads and shells
10 shallots, peeled and chopped
5 garlic cloves, peeled and chopped
2–3 dried red chiles, soaked in warm water for 20 minutes, drained, deseeded
10½ oz (300 g) pork ribs or a chicken carcass
1 oz (30 g) rock sugar (or brown sugar), plus extra to taste
1 tbsp salt, plus extra to taste
1 tsp tamarind paste
1–2 limes, cut into wedges

TO SERVE
14 oz (400 g) dried yellow egg noodles (or rice noodles if gluten-free)
7 oz (200 g) dried rice vermicelli noodles
3–4 tbsp Sambal Belacan (see page 47), depending on heat
7 oz (200 g) raw shrimp, peeled
7 oz (200 g) pork loin, thinly sliced (optional)
2 handfuls of spinach or water spinach (kangkung), blanched
7 oz (200 g) beansprouts, blanched
2 hard-boiled eggs, peeled and halved
Crispy fried shallots, to garnish
Red chile slices, to garnish

First, prepare the shrimp broth. Heat the vegetable oil in a large pot over medium heat. Add the shrimp heads and shells, then fry them until fragrant and well colored. Transfer to a plate and set aside.

Add the shallots, garlic and soaked chiles to the same pot and fry until fragrant. Return the shrimp heads and shells to the pot, then add 8½ cups (2 liters) of water. Submerge the pork ribs or chicken carcass in the water, then add the rock sugar, salt and tamarind paste. Bring to a boil, then reduce the heat and simmer, uncovered, for 1–2 hours to allow the flavors to develop. Skim off any impurities that rise to the top of the broth during cooking.

Once the broth has cooked, strain the liquid through a sieve. Discard the shrimp heads and shells and pork ribs or chicken carcass. You might need to add more water if the broth has reduced by more than a third, then check the seasoning and add salt, sugar or lime juice to taste.

Prepare both types of noodles according to the package instructions. Drain and set aside.

Bring the clear broth to a boil, add the Sambal Belacan, then the shrimp and pork loin slices, if using. Cook for about 5–10 minutes, or until the shrimp and pork loin slices are cooked through.

When ready to serve, place a portion of the egg noodles and rice vermicelli noodles into each bowl. Divide the cooked shrimp, pork loin slices, spinach and beansprouts among the bowls, then ladle over the hot broth. Add half a hard-boiled egg to each bowl and garnish with crispy fried shallots, slices of red chile and a lime wedge on the side for squeezing over.

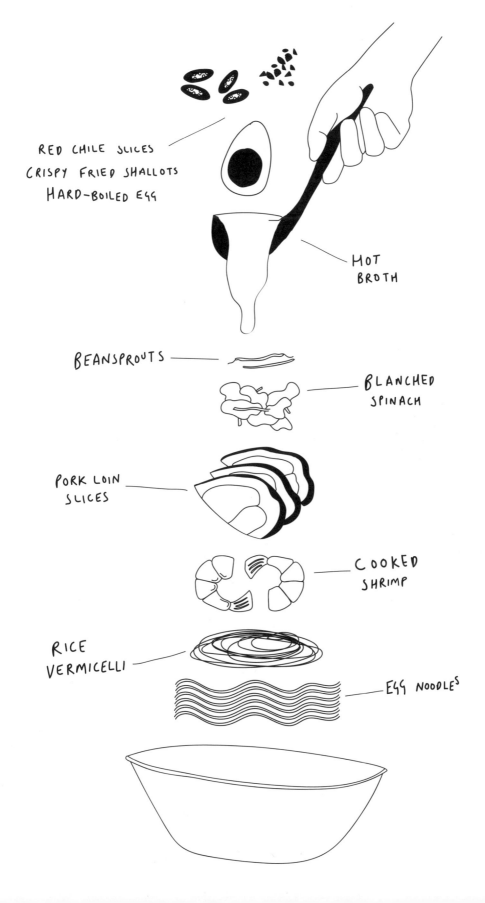

SATE DAGING
BEEF SATAY SKEWERS

For me, there's something magical about satay. It was one of the very first dishes I tried at a hawker stall as a child. Sate daging, commonly known as beef satay, transports me back to the lively evenings at Jonker Street night market in Melaka. The streets bustle with people, since the local culture is to meet up with friends around food. The simple pleasure of this dish lies not only in its preparation but also in the flood of memories it prompts—the sweet aromas of meat juices sizzling on the charcoal grill, the buzzing atmosphere of the market and the warmth of family around.

Proper sate daging, in my opinion, is best cooked over a charcoal grill. The infusion of smokiness from the charcoal into the skewered, marinated beef creates a flavor symphony that's hard to replicate. However, during those chilly months, when firing up the outdoor grill might not be the most appealing prospect, a trusty cast-iron grill pan over high heat works wonders in capturing that distinctive smokiness.

MAKES 10–12 SKEWERS

14 oz (400 g) beef tenderloin, cut into bite-sized chunks (roughly 1 in/3 cm cubes)
Vegetable oil, for brushing
Peanut Sauce (page 52), to serve

FOR THE PASTE

4½ oz (125 g) shallots, peeled and roughly chopped
6 garlic cloves, peeled and chopped
2 fresh long red chiles
1 in (3 cm) piece of galangal, peeled

FOR THE MARINADE

Juice of 2 limes
1¾ oz (50 g) gula melaka palm sugar, shaved (or 3½ tbsp dark brown sugar)
2 tbsp ground coriander
1 tbsp ground cumin
¼ cup (60 ml) light soy sauce
6 tbsp kecap manis (sweet soy sauce)
1½ tsp salt

First, make the paste. Place all the ingredients for the paste in a food processor or blender and blend until smooth.

Next, make the marinade. Combine all of the ingredients for the marinade in a bowl and mix together thoroughly. Once combined, stir the paste into the marinade.

Add the beef to the bowl with the marinade and massage the mixture into the meat. Cover with plastic wrap and leave to marinate in the fridge for at least 3 hours, but preferably overnight.

Place 10–12 wooden skewers into a tray filled with water and let them soak for at least an hour or even overnight (to stop them from burning).

Once the beef has marinated, assemble the skewers. Thread the chunks of beef onto the skewers, dividing the meat equally among the skewers until all the meat has been used up.

Heat a cast-iron grill pan over high heat until very hot, then brush the pan with a little oil. Add the beef skewers to the pan and cook for 2 minutes on each side until seared on the outside. Use a cloth when turning the skewers as they will be very hot.

Serve the beef skewers immediately while hot with the Peanut Sauce alongside.

ROJAK

A word that translates as "mixture" in Malay, rojak is so much more than just a salad; it's a medley of tastes and textures, of sweet fruits and salty shrimp. It's divine. Growing up, rojak was a refreshing, cooling treat that we would eagerly await as a respite from the relentless heat and humidity. Fast-forward to summer 2023 in London, with the temperature hitting a scorching 91°F (33°C). I was at Carousel, an amazing event space that hosts guest chefs from all over the world to cook, and where I was kindly invited to cook. I was ready to bring a piece of my childhood to the bustling capital. Serving rojak at my pop-up was like coming full circle—from those memories of finding solace in its refreshing crunch, to watching the faces of Londoners light up as they discovered its unique flavors. My lovely friend Clare Finney attended that night, and gave me her book that had just been published, *Hungry Heart*. After service, I read her beautiful memoir in my hotel bed. She spoke of foods that gave her comfort growing up and it brought me such joy, as I had just served my own taste of home that night in the middle of London.

SERVES 3-4

FOR THE DRESSING

3 tbsp tamarind paste
3 tbsp gula melaka palm sugar (or dark brown sugar)
1 tbsp light soy sauce, or to taste
1 tbsp cooking caramel (black soy sauce); or use 1 tbsp kecap manis and only 1 tbsp gula melaka sugar
1 fresh small long red chile, deseeded and finely chopped (adjust to taste)
1 fresh red bird's eye chile, deseeded and finely chopped
1 tsp belacan, toasted (optional)
1 tsp lime juice, or to taste

FOR THE SALAD

1 small celeriac (celery root), peeled
1 cucumber, peeled and deseeded
1 ripe mango, peeled and stoned
1 pineapple, peeled and cored
7 oz (200 g) firm tofu, cubed and fried
2 tbsp chopped salted roasted peanuts, to serve

First, make the dressing. Combine the tamarind paste, sugar, light soy sauce and cooking caramel in a small saucepan over low heat. Heat, stirring continuously, until all the sugar crystals have dissolved. Mix in the chopped chiles, then stir in the toasted belacan, if using. Continue to heat, stirring continuously, until the dressing thickens to a sticky consistency.

Remove the pan from the heat and add the lime juice. Taste and adjust the balance of flavors with more soy sauce and lime juice as needed. Leave the dressing to cool.

Cut the celeriac, cucumber, mango and pineapple into bite-sized cubes of uniform size for a consistent texture to the salad, similar in size to the cubes of tofu. Place all the diced salad ingredients in a large salad bowl and gently toss together.

Immediately before serving, drizzle the cooled dressing over the ingredients in the salad bowl and toss to ensure every cube is well coated. Liberally sprinkle the salad with the chopped peanuts.

SAMBAL MUSSELS

Sambal Lala, or chile clams, is a beloved dish in Malaysia, a staple in the vibrant culinary landscape of Melaka. Its rich, spicy flavors have captivated many, including myself, and inspired by my Scottish roots, I've added a twist to this traditional recipe. Scotland is renowned for its abundant and sustainable mussel populations, making them one of the most environmentally friendly shellfish options available.

My fondest memories of mussels are intertwined with visits to my adopted Grandad's (my seanair, in Scottish Gaelic) house near Loch Melfort. We would stroll along the beach, picking fresh mussels to pair with wild garlic for a truly local feast. These sambal mussels blend those cherished moments from my Scottish heritage with the culinary traditions of my Malaysian roots. This dish is an homage to both my Grandad and my Amah, my grandparents from different sides of the globe. Their influences and the fusion of their cultures in my life inspired this recipe, bridging the gap between Malaysia and Scotland in a delicious and meaningful way.

SERVES 4–6

2 lb 4 oz (1 kg) fresh mussels in shell
Scant 1 cup (200 ml) canola oil
²⁄₃ cup (150 ml) tamarind water
3 tbsp kecap manis (sweet soy sauce)
2 tbsp gula melaka palm sugar
   (or dark brown sugar)
3½ oz (100 g) wild garlic leaves
Lime juice, to taste
½ bunch of fresh Thai basil
   leaves, torn, to serve
Salt, to taste
Fragrant Coconut Rice
   (page 227), to serve

FOR THE SPICE PASTE

7 banana shallots, peeled
   and roughly chopped
15 garlic cloves, peeled
20 dried red chiles, soaked in
   warm water, drained and
   mostly deseeded (depending
   on how spicy you like it)

First, prepare the mussels. Begin by carefully scrubbing the mussels and de-bearding each one. Wash and clean the shells. Discard any that are open or don't close with a sharp tap.

Next, make the spice paste. Place the shallots, garlic, dried and fresh chiles, lemongrass and toasted Sambal Belacan in a food processor or blender, then blend to a fine paste. Transfer to a bowl and stir in the sugar and salt.

When ready to cook, place a large wok over high heat. Once hot, add half of the canola oil to coat the bottom of the wok and allow it to reach medium heat. Add the spice paste to the wok and stir-fry over medium-low heat for 15 minutes, moving the paste continuously so it doesn't burn. Now, add in the rest of the canola oil. If the paste looks like it's getting too dry, add a little more oil. The ideal state is when the oil has split from the sambal and risen to the top.

Add the tamarind water, kecap manis and palm sugar to the wok, allow it to reduce for about 2 minutes, then season to taste with salt.

Reduce the heat to medium, add the mussels to the wok and toss them in the sauce, then cover with a lid. Steam them and check them after 3–4 minutes—once they have opened up, then they are ready to be served.

- 3 fresh long red chiles, roughly chopped
- 3 lemongrass stalks, cleaned, trimmed and roughly chopped
- 1 heaped tbsp Sambal Belacan (page 47), toasted
- 2 tbsp gula melaka palm sugar (or dark brown sugar)
- 1½ tbsp salt

Discard any that do not open.

Add the wild garlic to the mussels in the wok, then toss everything together to ensure it is all well coated in the sauce.

Squeeze the lime juice to taste over everything, scatter over the torn basil leaves and give it a final stir. Serve piping hot alongside Fragrant Coconut Rice.

NOT TOO SWEET

The first time I tried chocolate, in the house that I grew up in, 1992

Not Too Sweet

The first time I ate chocolate I adored it, and smeared it all over my face. That love carried on, but not in quite the sense it did for other kids at my age. It was a love that was to fade a little before it developed into something different over the years. When I was a child, Easter presented a conundrum that baffled many around me—I would eagerly collect my pastel-wrapped chocolate eggs, not for consumption, but for trade. Where my friends saw a chocolate haven, I saw currency to barter for salty bags of chips. Much to my mother's amusement, my friends would come over and I would hand out my Easter eggs. This penchant for the less sweet side of life has its roots in my Malaysian heritage, where desserts are indeed treasured, but not consumed with the frequency that characterizes the Western three-course meal. Our sweets are interludes rather than grand finales. In fact, the ultimate compliment is hearing that something is indeed "not too sweet"— that is the spoken marker of the perfect dessert.

In our household, an overly sweet dessert was a rare occurrence. My mother, with her discerning palate, always favored subtlety and balance over heavy-handed sweetness, and it's a sensibility that has woven its way into my own tastes. I've come to appreciate that a perfect dessert need not overwhelm the taste buds with sugar; rather, it should dance gracefully between the notes of sweet, perhaps with a touch of sour or a hint of bitterness. Like chocolate with tart berries, or creamy rice pudding with mango... and don't even get me started on sorbets. I love sorbets, they're just perfect.

It was at The Scullery, my first job in the professional cooking world, where my affinity for desserts blossomed. Laurie MacMillan, the head chef with a keen eye for potential, saw beyond the resumé of a novice. She entrusted me with the task of crafting crémeux and pavlovas—a gesture that spoke volumes. In the heat and hustle of the kitchen, where desserts were often relegated as an afterthought, Laurie's recipes were always perfection and a great way to learn. A well-worn trope in the culinary world is this notion that the precision and artistry of crafting desserts are somehow better suited to the "gentler sex," as if the delicate piping of chocolate work or the handling of pastry are not made for the macho hands that sear steaks. In Laurie's kitchen, she dismantled those archaic beliefs one dessert at a time. Being a woman did not define my role, skill did. Laurie's confidence in me was not just empowering; it was a clarion call to shatter the glass ceiling, one sweet masterpiece at a time. Her trust was not misplaced—the desserts I made became more than just a final note to a meal; they broke molds.

Each crémeux that set flawlessly and probed to the correct temperature, every pavlova that held its airy structure, was a small victory. (Of course, sometimes there were collapsed meringues, because everyone is human.) But Laurie was fantastic, not just for my burgeoning skills, but for the recognition that the dessert station was no less challenging, no less important than any other part of the kitchen. Laurie's belief in training was a gift that transcended the kitchen; it instilled a confidence that shaped not only my career but my very approach to cooking and life. It was under her mentorship that I learned the true art of dessert-making—not as a mere process of combining ingredients to create something sweet, but as a craft of balancing flavors, textures, and most importantly, breaking the sweet ceiling of culinary stereotypes.

Unlike the other recipes in this book, I do request precision when dessert-making. It's a science to be respected. There's an undeniable allure to the accuracy required; it's a meticulous dance of exact measurements and perfect timings. This discipline of precision, which I have cultivated over countless hours, has become my sanctuary. It was during my intense preparation for *MasterChef* that the rigors of pastry-making became my world. Night after night I practiced, coaxing flour and butter into shortcrust, puff and choux, ensuring that each batch was better than the last. These pastries weren't just potential components of my competition dishes, they were my silent allies on the battlefield of the invention test. Each fold and roll imbued me with a quiet confidence. I figured that if I could memorize these three pastry recipes, maybe I'd get past that initial round.

Then came the moment that tested every fiber of my being… the chocolate-orange fondant. Live on camera, with the relentless tick of the clock in my ears and the crew watching for the jeopardy of a failing mission, I watched in horror as my first batch of fondants curdled before my eyes. I was looking at chocolate scrambled eggs, and now so were the camera crew. It felt like watching a ship slowly sink. But surrender was not an option. To the backdrop of a frantic heartbeat, I rallied my composure, diving back into the process with a fervor fueled by the minutes on the countdown clock. And as the ovens hummed, out came a fondant that was silky, molten and triumphant—a dish that was as much my savior as it was the cause of my near downfall. To this day, the dichotomy of chocolate fondants haunts and delights me in equal measure. There's a flicker of PTSD each time I whisk eggs into chocolate, a flashback to that moment of near defeat. Yet it also, when successful, provides a rush of elation. Eating them is a full-circle moment, a bite that's fraught with memories but ultimately brings me back to the joy of what made me fall in love with the art of the dessert in the first place. Hence why in true fashion, if you fall off your bike, the best thing you can do is get right back on it and try again.

In this chapter, I explore lots of different themes and stories, as desserts have become deeply personal to me. These are not-so-sweet creations for those who, like me, look for a well-balanced dessert that isn't drowning in lashings of maple syrup or salted caramel, but rather gives you that "Oooh" feeling of sinking into a couch, or taking your bra off after work. A satisfying feeling. These are desserts made for savoring, for lingering over conversation as the evening winds down. These are desserts that, quite simply, are just sweet enough.

GULA MELAKA STICKY TOFFEE PUDDING

My mom has always been a great baker, and what's more, she's managed to perfect her baking by eye. This sticky toffee pudding is one of her very best desserts. I tweaked Mom's original recipe for serving to customers in my first restaurant, and it soon became a cult classic. Gula melaka palm sugar has an unparalleled flavor, with rich, treacly notes and the deep fragrance of molasses. An ingredient that's famously associated with my mom's hometown, Melaka, gula melaka is now widely available online and in Asian supermarkets. If you can't find gula melaka, then a mix of regular palm sugar and dark brown sugar will do just fine. The gula melaka sauce is so unctuous that it speaks for itself. It's incredible on ice cream, too. Make it now and thank me later!

SERVES 6

FOR THE PUDDING

7 oz (200 g) pitted dates, finely chopped
Scant 1 cup (200 ml) boiling water
7 tbsp (100 g) butter, softened
½ tsp vanilla bean paste
5½ oz (150 g) gula melaka palm sugar, grated (or a mix of palm sugar and dark brown sugar)
3 large eggs, beaten
1½ cups (175 g) self-rising flour, sifted
1 tsp baking soda
Toasted coconut flakes, to serve (optional)

FOR THE GULA MELAKA

1 x 14 oz (400 ml) can of coconut milk
10½ oz (300 g) gula melaka palm sugar, grated; or 7 oz (200 g) palm sugar and ½ cup (100 g) dark brown sugar
3 green cardamom pods

Put the chopped dates in a heatproof bowl and pour over the boiling water. Leave to soak for 30 minutes.

Preheat the oven to 400°F (200°C) and line a deep 9½ in (24 cm) round cake pan with parchment paper.

Using an electric stand mixer or whisk, beat together the butter, vanilla bean paste and grated sugar until the mixture is light, fluffy and a few shades paler in color.

Gradually add the beaten eggs to the bowl, little by little, beating continuously. Next, gently fold in the sifted flour and baking soda. Finally, add the chopped dates and the soaking water to the bowl, gently folding everything together. Scrape the batter into the lined cake pan and level with a spatula.

Place the cake pan in the hot oven and bake for about 30 minutes, or until a toothpick inserted into the center comes out clean. Remove from the oven.

Meanwhile, make the gula melaka. Pour the coconut milk into a saucepan and add the grated sugar. Warm the coconut milk over medium heat until the sugar has melted. Add the cardamom pods and simmer over low heat for 10 minutes, or until thickened. Remove and discard the cardamom pods.

Once cooked, turn the pudding out and serve the dessert topped with the toasted coconut flakes, if using, and the gula melaka sauce alongside for pouring over.

PAVLOVA WITH MANGO CREAM AND PANDAN CURD

I'm not the biggest dessert fan, but there's one dish I cherish… and that's a pavlova. My second father figure, Jim, passed away while I was writing this very book. He was full of love, generosity and laughter. There are many things he taught me, one of which was how to give a strong handshake, and another was how to make a beautiful pavlova. One of the strongest food memories I have of him is the pavlova that he used to bring over when my mom was hosting one of her dinner parties. It was piled high with fruits of the forest and perfectly whipped cream, the pavlova itself was chewy and decadent, with the best gloss on the outside. We miss you, Jim. And we hope wherever you are, you're munching blissfully on that delicious pavlova and washing it down with a coffee with two sweeteners. In this recipe, I've layered the meringue with mango cream and pandan curd. It's also delicious with frozen cherries and chopped pistachios instead of the pandan curd, if you don't feel like making that.

SERVES 4–6

FOR THE MERINGUE
4 large egg whites, at room temperature
1 cup (200 g) superfine sugar
1 tsp distilled malt vinegar
1 tsp cornstarch

FOR THE MANGO CREAM
1 ripe mango, peeled, pitted and roughly chopped
1 cup (240 ml) heavy cream
2 tbsp confectioners' sugar

FOR THE PANDAN CURD
3 large egg yolks
½ cup (100 g) granulated sugar
1 cup (225 ml) coconut milk
3–4 fresh pandan leaves (tied into a knot) or 1 tsp pandan extract
4 tbsp (60 g) unsalted butter, cubed

TO SERVE
Sliced mango
Toasted coconut flakes

Preheat the oven to 300°F (140°C) and line a baking sheet with parchment paper.

First, make the meringue. In a spotlessly clean and grease-free bowl, whisk the egg whites until soft peaks form. (Any traces of grease will prevent the egg whites whisking to their full volume.) Gradually add the superfine sugar, whisking between each addition until stiff and glossy peaks form. Gently fold in the vinegar and cornstarch.

Spoon the meringue mixture onto the lined baking sheet in circular motions to create peaks and spread it to a thickness of 2 in (5 cm). Place the baking sheet in the hot oven and bake for 45 minutes, or until crisp on the outside. Turn off the oven, open the door slightly and leave the meringue inside to cool completely.

Next, prepare the mango cream. Place the chopped mango in a blender and bleend until smooth. In a bowl, whip the cream with the confectioners' sugar until it forms soft peaks. Gently fold the mango purée into the whipped cream. Chill in the fridge until ready to use.

Now make the pandan curd. In a heatproof bowl, whisk together the egg yolks and sugar until combined. Add the coconut milk and pandan leaves or extract.

Continued →

← *Pavlova continued*

Place the bowl over a pan of simmering water, ensuring the water doesn't touch the bottom of the bowl. Add the butter, cube by cube, while stirring continuously, until the mixture thickens enough to coat the back of a spoon. This usually takes about 10 minutes. Once thickened, remove and discard the pandan leaves and let the curd cool. Chill in the fridge until ready to use.

When ready to assemble the pavlova, spoon or pipe the mango cream onto the cooled meringue base. Using a pastry bag fitted with a star tip, pipe the pandan curd on top of the mango cream in a flower pattern.

Serve the pavlova immediately, topped with sliced mango and toasted coconut, or store in the fridge for up to 1 hour before serving.

HIBISCUS AND POMEGRANATE POSSET

Hibiscus is Malaysia's national flower. It's a beautiful pink flower on a large stem with little yellow pollen pods. It's stunning to look at, but it also has quite a sour, floral taste when dried and used in teas. I was making possets one day when it occurred to me that hibiscus would be a delicious addition to this creamy dessert. Hibiscus makes everything so unique in flavor with its floral notes, and not to mention it gives the posset a gorgeous pale pink color.

SERVES 4–6

2½ cups (600 ml) heavy cream
¾ cup (150 g) sugar
2 tbsp dried hibiscus flowers
scant ½ cup (100 ml) pomegranate juice, freshly squeezed and strained
Zest of 1 lemon
2 tbsp lemon juice
Seeds of 1 pomegranate, to decorate

Pour the cream into a large pot and add the sugar and hibiscus flowers. Gently heat the cream mixture over low heat, stirring continuously, until all the sugar crystals have dissolved. Remove the pot from the heat and leave the cream mixture to cool for 5 minutes, so the hibiscus flavor intensifies.

Strain the cream mixture through a fine sieve into a large measuring cup. Discard the hibiscus flowers. Stir the pomegranate juice and lemon zest into the cream mixture, then add the lemon juice and whisk thoroughly.

Divide the mixture among 4–6 individual serving glasses or ramekins and leave to cool to room temperature. Chill in the fridge for at least 2–3 hours, or until the posset is set. It should have a firm but creamy texture.

Just before serving, decorate each posset with a small handful of fresh pomegranate seeds.

RASPBERRY AND SESAME BLONDIES

I love to offer up food that makes people feel at ease, and that is abundant. It's just my natural cooking style. Whenever I have friends over, I invariably reach for a sheet pan recipe. This one is so incredibly simple to make and really does sate any chocolate cravings. It's my offering to a certain Milkybar Kid, who I was obsessed with when I was younger. Of course, the raspberries are there in order to add a little sharpness and make sure that everything is not too sweet.

MAKES 16

1 stick (115 g) unsalted butter, plus extra for greasing
1 cup (200 g) light brown sugar
1 large egg, beaten
2 tsp vanilla extract
1 cup (125 g) all-purpose flour
½ tsp baking powder
¼ tsp salt
about 1 cup (170 g) white chocolate chips
⅓ cup (50 g) sesame seeds (toasted for a nuttier flavor, if you like)
about 1 cup (100 g) fresh or frozen raspberries

Preheat the oven to 375°F (195°C) and lightly grease and line an 8 in (20 cm) square cake pan with parchment paper.

In a saucepan, melt the butter over medium heat. Remove the pan from the heat and stir in the brown sugar until well combined.

Let the mixture cool slightly, then beat in the egg and vanilla extract until smooth.

In a bowl, sift together the flour, baking powder and salt. Gradually add the flour to the pan with the butter and egg mixture, stirring until just combined.

Fold in the white chocolate chips and most of the sesame seeds, reserving a few to sprinkle on top.

Scrape the batter into the prepared pan, spreading it evenly. Scatter the raspberries randomly across the batter, gently pressing them into the batter, then sprinkle the remaining sesame seeds over the top. Place the pan in the hot oven and bake for 25–30 minutes, or until the edges are golden and a toothpick inserted into the center comes out with just a few moist crumbs.

Let the blondies cool completely in the pan before cutting them into squares.

SICHUAN DARK CHOCOLATE CRÉMEUX
with PEANUT BRITTLE

At my first job as a chef, I was put in charge of making this dessert. I was so determined to get it just right and figure out all of the nuances of a pastry chef in a professional kitchen. My boss, Laurie MacMillan, was and still is my kitchen hero. She taught me how to dance in a kitchen, both metaphorically and literally; she's so full of joy and encouragement. This is a recipe I dedicate to Laurie, for believing in a novice chef and allowing them to flourish. Of course, with my taste buds not loving anything too sweet, here dark chocolate is my friend. I've added a twist with a little Sichuan pepper in here. This dessert is perfect for dinner parties, simply make the chocolate crémeux in advance and then when ready to eat, serve with the peanut brittle shards and some extra whipped cream, if you so desire.

SERVES 4–5

FOR THE CHOCOLATE CRÉMEUX
7 oz (200 g) dark chocolate (minimum 70% cocoa solids), finely chopped
1¼ cups (300 ml) heavy cream
scant ½ cup (100 ml) whole milk
1 tsp vanilla extract
3 egg yolks
¼ cup (50 g) sugar
¼ tsp Sichuan pepper powder

FOR THE PEANUT BRITTLE
1 cup (200 g) sugar
¾ cup (100 g) unsalted peanuts, roughly chopped
A pinch of sea salt
½ tsp baking soda

Place the finely chopped chocolate in a heatproof bowl and set aside.

Combine the cream, milk and vanilla extract in a large saucepan and bring to a simmer over medium heat.

Meanwhile, in a separate bowl, whisk together the egg yolks and sugar until pale and slightly thickened, then stir in the Sichuan pepper powder.

Once the cream mixture is hot, very slowly pour it over the egg yolk mixture, little by little, whisking continuously to prevent the eggs from scrambling.

Return the custard mixture to the saucepan and cook over low heat, stirring continuously with a wooden spoon or spatula, until the mixture reaches 170°F (75°C) and is thick enough to coat the back of a spoon.

Pour the hot custard through a sieve into the bowl with the chopped chocolate. Let it sit for 1 minute to melt the chocolate, then stir everything together until smooth and glossy. Pour the chocolate custard into 4 or 5 individual serving dishes or glasses. Tap gently to remove any air bubbles and then cover the surface with plastic wrap to prevent a skin from forming. Chill in the fridge for at least 4 hours, or until set.

Continued →

← *Crémeux continued*

To make the peanut brittle, heat the sugar in a heavy-based pot over medium heat until it begins to melt around the edges. Once it starts to liquefy, gently tilt the pan until all the crystals have melted and the sugar has turned a deep amber color (don't stir with a spoon as this risks the sugar crystallizing).

Quickly stir the chopped peanuts and a pinch of sea salt into the pot with the caramelized sugar. Keep an eye on the heat to ensure the caramel doesn't burn.

As soon as the peanuts are coated in caramel, stir in the baking soda until the mixture foams and lightens in color. Immediately pour the peanut brittle mixture onto a silicone baking mat or greased baking pan. Using a silicone spatula, flatten the peanut brittle to your preferred thickness. Let the brittle cool completely and then break into shards by bashing with a rolling pin.

Take the crémeux out of the fridge 5 minutes before serving and place some of the peanut brittle shards on top for decoration.

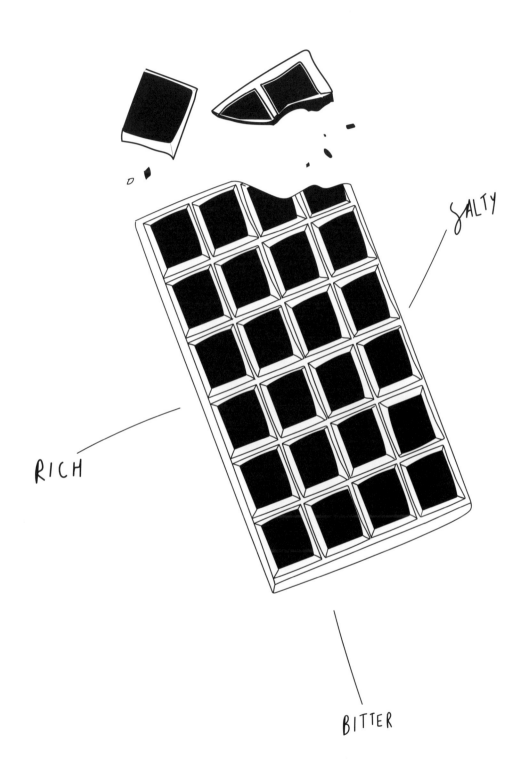

HOMEMADE PEACH AND MANGO PIES

There's a chain of fast-food restaurants in Asia that serves a certain pie that I adore. This recipe brings back childhood memories of waiting impatiently for that sweet fruit filling to cool down enough so that you could actually eat it, rather than burn your mouth on the molten lava inside the pie. If you're a fan of the squirty whipped cream that comes in an aerosol can, then that works really well here for that all-too-familiar flavor. If not, freshly whipped cream cuts through the sweetness here.

MAKES 4

1 x 12 oz (320 g) ready-rolled all-butter puff pastry sheet (or ¾ x 1 lb package – you can use excess to decorate), at room temperature
1 egg, beaten, to glaze
Vegetable oil, for deep-frying
Confectioners' sugar, for dusting (optional)
Freshly whipped cream or squirty whipped cream topping, to serve

FOR THE FRUIT FILLING

2 ripe peaches, peeled, pitted and finely chopped (or canned peach slices or halves)
1 ripe mango, peeled, stoned and finely chopped (or canned mango slices)
¼ cup (50 g) white sugar (reduce the amount if you're using canned fruit)
1 tsp vanilla extract
½ tsp ground cinnamon
A pinch of salt
2 tsp lemon juice
1 tbsp unsalted butter
1 tbsp all-purpose flour, plus extra for dusting

First, make the fruit filling. In a pot, combine the chopped peaches and mango with the sugar, vanilla extract, cinnamon and salt. Place the pot over medium heat and cook the fruit until tender, but not mushy. This should take about 5–7 minutes for fresh fruit and about 5 minutes for the canned fruit, until the sugar has dissolved.

Stir the lemon juice and butter into the fruit mixture. Once the butter has melted, sprinkle in the flour to thicken the mixture. Cook for a further 1 minute. Remove from the heat and let the fruit filling cool completely.

Lightly dust a clean work surface with a little flour. Unroll the puff pastry sheet on the work surface and cut it into 4 equal rectangles.

Spoon a good amount of the fruit filling onto one side of each pastry rectangle, leaving a ½ in (1 cm) border around the edge. Brush the edges with the beaten egg. Fold the clean pastry over the filling to enclose it, then use the tines of a fork to seal the edges of each pastry parcel.

Fill a deep-fryer or large, heavy-based pot no more than two-thirds full with oil. Heat the oil to 350°F (180°C). Meanwhile, line a tray or plate with paper towels and keep a spider strainer or slotted spoon on hand.

Working in two batches so that you don't overcrowd the pan, carefully lower the pies into the hot oil. Deep-fry the pies for 5–7 minutes, or until golden and flaky. Transfer the pies to the lined tray or plate to drain any excess oil. Repeat with the remaining pies.

Allow the pies to cool for 10 minutes before serving. Dust the pies with confectioners' sugar for extra sweetness, if you like, then serve with a dollop or squirt of whipped cream on each pie.

PANDAN LEAF PANNA COTTA
with GULA MELAKA

This was the number one best-selling dessert in my first restaurant. I was just 27 when I opened that little restaurant. Nervous and in need of a partner-in-crime, I employed my first ever member of staff, Derek. He would take my ideas and formulate them into workable recipes for a restaurant. Derek had worked in Glasgow's best fish restaurant, Crabshakk, where he had learned a huge amount. He's an incredible chef with a joyous, happy outlook on life. This panna cotta was the brainchild of myself and Derek, and to this day, it's still one of the desserts that I'm most proud of. I wanted to make this dessert because I just knew that something about the herbaceous, vanilla-green flavor of pandan would go so well in a jiggly panna cotta. At the end of a busy night's service at the restaurant, I would often run across the road and buy a package of ginger nuts. I'd take a panna cotta home, then scoop it up with those cookies while watching TV. I encourage you to do the same!

SERVES 4

FOR THE PANNA COTTA

3 oz (75 g) fresh pandan leaves (or an extra ½ tsp pandan extract)
²⁄₃ cup (150 ml) canned coconut milk (I use the Chaokoh brand)
1¼ cups (300 ml) heavy cream
3 tbsp sugar
½ tsp pandan extract
1 vanilla bean, split lengthwise and seeds scraped out (or 1 tsp vanilla bean paste)
1½ tsp unflavored gelatin powder (bloomed in 2 tbsp cold water for at least 1 minute)
Vegetable oil, for greasing
Confectioners' sugar, for dusting

FOR THE GULA MELAKA

1 x 14 oz (400 ml) can of coconut milk (I use the Chaokoh brand)
1½ cups (300 g) gula melaka palm sugar (or 1⅓ cups/275g dark brown sugar with a few whole green cardamom pods)

Place the pandan leaves and the coconut milk in a blender and blend, then pass through a fine sieve into a bowl until only the liquid is left.

Combine the cream, sugar, pandan extract and vanilla seeds or vanilla bean paste in a saucepan and, whisking frequently, slowly bring to a simmer. Once it has been simmering for 1 minute, add the pandan-coconut milk and bring it back to a simmer, ensuring the mixture doesn't catch on the base of the pan.

Strain the panna cotta mixture into a heatproof bowl. Add the bloomed gelatin to the bowl, whisking continuously until dissolved.

Place the bowl with the panna cotta mixture over another bowl filled with ice and cold water to create an ice bain marie. Whisk frequently as the panna cotta mixture will set at the coldest parts of the bowl, for around 2 minutes, or until everything is combined.

Lay out 4 pudding cup molds. If you plan to turn the panna cotta out of the molds, rather than serve them in the pots, grease each one with a drop of vegetable oil and then dust the molds with a little confectioners' sugar.

Transfer the mixture to a large measuring cup and divide it evenly among the molds. Cover the tops with plastic wrap to stop a skin from forming. Allow to set in the fridge, ideally overnight or for around 4 hours.

To make the gula melaka, slowly heat the coconut milk and sugar in a pan, then allow this mixture to simmer for 5–10 minutes, or until everything is combined. Allow to cool to room temperature.

To unmold the panna cottas, simply get some boiling water in a bowl and dip the molds in the boiling water for a second, then tip the molds upside down to release the panna cotta onto plates. Serve with the gula melaka. When stored in the fridge, the panna cotta and gula melaka will both last for up to 3 days.

DRINKS

When in Malaysia, one quickly learns that hydration is not just a necessity; it's a way of life. The practice of drinking hot water with meals is woven deeply into the culture, a concept that might seem counterintuitive in a tropical climate, but it is, in fact, rooted in both tradition and science. Hot water aids digestion by helping to break down the food in your stomach more efficiently, allowing your body to absorb nutrients better. It also challenges the belief that cold drinks are the best way to cool down in hot weather. Surprisingly, sipping on something warm can actually encourage your body to regulate its internal temperature more effectively, leaving you feeling cooler in the long run.

My love for Malaysian drinks started early. I have fond memories of my mom taking me for iced Milo, a popular malted milk drink that holds a special place in the hearts of Malaysians. It's rich, chocolatey and refreshing—especially when paired with a simple, comforting plate of Kaya Toast (page 210) in the morning. As I developed the menus for my restaurants, I knew I wanted to capture the essence of these drinks, selecting each one with care and intention.

Take, for example, at my first restaurant Julie's Kopitiam, a ginger and turmeric tea. Infused with local Glasgow honey, it's a warm, soothing antidote to a spicy plate of sambal, offering a perfect balance to the bold flavors. Or the teh serai, a delicate lemongrass tea that we crafted by simply using the fragrant tips of the lemongrass plant. These teas aren't just beverages; they're thoughtfully chosen companions to the dishes they accompany, each one simple yet profound in its ability to complement the food. In Malaysia, the variety of drinks available is as diverse as the country itself. From the robust and aromatic kopi O (black coffee) to the sweet and creamy teh tarik (pulled tea), each drink tells a story of the land and its people. There's the rich, almost dessert-like bandung, a rose syrup and milk concoction, and the tangy, refreshing assam boi, a drink made with dried plums that's perfect for a hot day. Whether it's a classic beverage or a modern twist, these drinks are more than just a way to quench your thirst—they're a celebration of flavor and culture.

And then, there's the simple joy of making your own tea. The act of boiling water, selecting your ingredients, and letting them steep is a ritual that connects you to the essence of the drink. Whether it's a calming cup of chamomile or a vibrant ginger brew, the process is as satisfying as the drink itself. It's a reminder that sometimes the simplest things, done with care and attention, can bring the greatest pleasure.

KOPITIAM TURMERIC GINGER TEA

SERVES 2

1 in (3 cm) piece of ginger
1 in (3 cm) piece of fresh turmeric
1–2 tsp honey, or to taste
A tiny pinch of freshly ground black pepper (optional)

Rinse the ginger and fresh turmeric under cold running water. There is no need to peel them, just make sure they're clean. Thinly slice or grate both, then place in a small saucepan. Pour over 2 cups (480 ml) of water and bring to a boil over medium-high heat. Once boiling, reduce the heat to low and let it simmer gently for 10–15 minutes. The longer it simmers, the more intense the flavor will be. (When I'm working from home, I leave this in a pot all day and heat it up with more hot water and honey, as needed.)

Once simmered, remove the pan from the heat and strain the tea through a fine-mesh strainer into a mug or teapot. Discard the ginger and turmeric.

While the tea is still warm, stir in the honey until it dissolves completely. If you like, add a tiny pinch of black pepper to the tea before serving.

Note: Black pepper contains a compound that can significantly boost the absorption of curcumin (the active component in turmeric) by the body.

Not Too Sweet

PEACH ICED TEA

SERVES 3-4

4–6 black tea bags, depending on desired strength
1 x 14 oz (400 g) can of peaches in light syrup or juice
½ cup (100 g) sugar, adjust to taste (optional)
Ice cubes, to serve

Bring 4¼ cups (1 liter) of water to a boil in a large pot. Remove the pot from the heat, add the black tea bags and let them steep for about 5 minutes for a strong tea base. Remove and discard the tea bags.

Drain the peaches, reserving the syrup or juice from the pot. Place the peaches in a blender, then blend to a smooth purée. If the peaches are in syrup and you prefer a sweeter tea, add a little of the reserved syrup when blending the peaches. Alternatively, if your peaches are not in syrup and you prefer a sweeter tea, dissolve the sugar in the hot brewed tea, adjusting the amount based on your preference and the sweetness of the peaches.

Pour the tea into a large heatproof jug and stir in the peach purée until well combined. Taste and adjust the sweetness, adding more syrup or sugar as needed. Allow the peach tea to cool to room temperature, then chill in the fridge until thoroughly cold.

To serve, fill tall glasses with ice cubes and pour over the chilled peach tea.

PINEAPPLE PEEL ICED TEA

SERVES 3-4

Peel of 1 pineapple
2 black tea bags
A few slices of ginger
1 tsp ground turmeric
Maple syrup, to taste
Ice cubes, to serve

Start by thoroughly washing the pineapple peel, then place the peel in a large pot and add 4¼ cups (1 liter) of water to cover it. Add the tea bags, ginger and turmeric. Bring the mixture to a boil, then reduce the heat and let it simmer, uncovered, for 30–45 minutes.

After simmering, strain the liquid to remove the peel, tea bags and ginger. Sweeten the tea with maple syrup to your taste, stirring well to ensure it dissolves. Allow to cool, then add ice to serve.

ASAM BOI
SALTED PLUM DRINK

SERVES 3–4

5–6 asam boi (dried salted plums, available online)
2–3 tbsp white sugar, or to taste
A pinch of salt (optional, depending on the saltiness of the plums)
Juice of 1 lime, or to taste
Ice cubes, to serve

If you prefer the drink to be less salty, rinse the asam boi under cold running water to remove any excess salt from the surface.

Bring 4¼ cups (1 liter) of water to a boil in a large pot. Add the asam boi and sugar to the pot. (If you're unsure about the sweetness, start with less sugar as you can always add more later.) Reduce the heat and simmer the mixture, uncovered, for 15–20 minutes. The plums will soften and the liquid will take on a rich flavor.

Taste and adjust the sweetness, adding more sugar as needed. If the drink is too salty, add more water to dilute it. If the plums haven't provided enough saltiness, stir in a pinch of salt. Remove the pot from the heat and let the liquid cool for a few minutes.

Stir in the lime juice for a refreshing tangy kick, adjusting the amount to your taste.

Strain the drink into a jug. Discard the plums and any seeds. Allow the asam boi drink to cool to room temperature, then chill in the fridge until thoroughly cold.

To serve, fill tall glasses with ice cubes and pour over the chilled asam boi drink.

HOT LIMAU

SERVES 1

Juice of 1–2 limes, or to taste
1–2 tsp light brown sugar, or to taste
1 cup (240 ml) hot water (not boiling)
A few lime slices, to garnish (optional)
Ice cubes, to serve

Squeeze the juice from the fresh limes until you have 2 or 3 tablespoons. Strain the juice to remove any seeds or pulp, if preferred.

In a heatproof glass or mug, combine the lime juice and brown sugar. Pour the hot water into the glass or mug, stirring to mix all the ingredients well. Garnish with lime, if you like, and add a few ice cubes before serving.

A Love Letter to Those Who Have Inspired Me

Reflecting on my origins, I attribute much of my culinary education to the influential women in my life. It began with my mother, whose joy for cooking and belief in its social significance were infectious. Along my journey, I have encountered many remarkable women who have all left indelible marks on my professional growth.

In the early 2010s, Glasgow's culinary scene was nascent and female head chefs were a rarity. After my stint on *MasterChef* in 2014, I left retail with a fervent desire to delve deeper into the hospitality industry. My first opportunity came at The Scullery, a charming establishment reminiscent of a Parisian bistro, nestled in Glasgow's West End. There, I met Laurie MacMillan, a head chef who would play a pivotal role in my career. Despite my lack of experience, Laurie, hailing from Fife and with a delightful accent, embraced me with patience. Her extensive experience at the renowned Balbirnie Hotel had endowed her with immense culinary wisdom and a heartening laugh. Under Laurie's mentorship, I learned the intricacies of kitchen management, from the importance of making fries from scratch, to cleaning out fryers, to using an industrial can opener, to passing a health and safety visit... everything from the basics of operating industrial equipment to crafting stocks and sauces. But beyond those skills, she instilled in me the significance of humor and composure, especially when faced with the inevitable challenges of kitchen life. In this kitchen, giggles were essential.

My next notable encounter was Rachna Dheer, the owner of an Indian street-food kitchen in central Glasgow. Her vibrancy and culinary prowess brought a slice of Mombai to my home city, introducing innovative dishes all cradled in the iconic Mortons roll, a local favorite famed for its crispy crust and soft interior: keema pau, vada pav, bhurji pao. I took her guidance on selecting premium spices, particularly the Supreme brand of garam masala, which is darker in color, richer in flavor and has the perfect balance of supporting spices to make it the star ingredient that it is. Small teachings like this have stayed with me. She exemplified the art of celebrating one's culture through cuisine, a lesson that has profoundly influenced my approach to food.

Rosie Healey of Gloriosa introduced Mediterranean culinary delights to Glasgow, inspiring me to infuse my own restaurant with vibrant colors and flavors.

Pam Brunton of Inver, renowned for her joyous demeanor, was recently recipient of Scotland's first green Michelin star, demonstrating the beauty of her culinary passion.

My dear friend Tatenda, with her expertise in pairing wines with diverse cuisines, has shown me the exquisite interplay between flavors and cultures.

Liz Seabrook, who I met on a photoshoot, has a unique talent for capturing the essence of our industry's most celebrated figures. She has taken every single photo you see in this book. She's been a constant cheerleader of my career and, more importantly, is one of my most beloved friends.

These individuals, among others, represent the diverse talent across the culinary industry, whose backgrounds vary and whose contributions transcend traditional gender roles, including those who are non-binary and carving their own paths across Glasgow.

Their collective influence has shaped my philosophy: that the food and drink world should be one of inclusivity and progression. I see it as essential in the rise of the underrepresented in our industry. It's this conviction that fuels my dedication to honor those from all walks of life who have made significant impacts, often from the humblest beginnings.

Index

A
achar 160
Ahma's house fish head curry 221
apples
    green apple and green bean kerabu 108
asam boi drink (salted plum drink) 273
ayam penyet: smashed chicken 176

B
bakwan jagung (sweetcorn fritters) made with leftover beansprouts 156
banana leaves
    sambal mackerel in banana leaf 222
bananas
    pisang goreng (banana fritters) made with brown bananas 167
beansprouts
    bakwan jagung (sweetcorn fritters) made with leftover beansprouts 156
    char kuay teow: big fat noodles 217
beef
    beef shank rendang 121
    sate daging: beef satay skewers 241
    steak au Sichuan poivre 193
buns, rolls & bagels
    chaat masala potato fritter in a morning roll 61
    cream cheese bagels with pickles made with leftover milk 154
    crispy chicken burger: the one with fish sauce caramel 79
    crispy chicken burger: the one with sambal, mayo, cucumber and a fried egg 77
    sambal halloumi morning buns 94
burgers
    crispy chicken burger: the one with fish sauce caramel 79
    crispy chicken burger: the one with sambal, mayo, cucumber and a fried egg 77
butter
    Sichuan brown butter eggplants 80
    Xo butter corn 175

C
cabbage
    bihoon udang: shrimp rice noodles 225
    crispy chicken burger: the one with sambal, mayo, cucumber and a fried egg 77
cakes
    raspberry and sesame blondies 261
cannellini beans
    masala beans with poached eggs 172
carrots
    achar 160
    simple pickled carrots 159
cashews
    cashew chicken stir-fry made with leftover celery 146
    orange and cashew chicken 74
celeriac (celery root)
    rojak 242
celery
    Chinese-style spicy garlic celery 180
chaat masala potato fritter in a morning roll 61
char kuay teow: big fat noodles 217
Cheddar
    grilled cheese sandwich with tamarind onions 86
    gochujang mac 'n' cheese 185
chicken
    ayam penyet: smashed chicken 176
    bihoon udang: shrimp rice noodles 225
    cashew chicken stir-fry made with leftover celery 146
    crispy chicken burger: the one with fish sauce caramel 79
    crispy chicken burger: the one with sambal, mayo, cucumber and a fried egg 77
    curry leaf chicken legs with salted egg yolk sauce 93
    fragrant soy roast chicken 107
    goodbye buttermilk chicken, hello tea-brined crispy fried chicken 70
    grilled lemongrass chicken thighs with peanut sauce 116
    orange and cashew chicken 74
chiles
    base curry paste 42
    chile crisp puttanesca 64
    green chile chutney 48
    Julie's kopitiam chile oil 50
    salad dressing 39
    sambal mussels 244
    sambal oelek 46
    simple sambal 45
    Singapore chile crab 212
    sweet chile sauce 49
Chinese sausages *see* sausages
chocolate
    raspberry and sesame blondies 261
    Sichuan dark chocolate crémeux with peanut brittle 263
choi sum
    clam-orous noods 132
chop suey eggplant with Thai basil 68
chutney
    green chile chutney 48
clams
    clam-orous noods 132
    clams with Chinese sausage and samphire 82
coconut cream
    beef shank rendang 121
    Kaya croissant-and-butter pudding made with leftover pastries 163

Kaya toast with soft-boiled
  eggs 210
coconut milk
  beef shank rendang 121
  fragrant coconut rice 226
  gula melaka sticky toffee
    pudding 253
  pandan leaf panna cotta with
    gula melaka 268
  Pavlova with mango cream and
    pandan curd 254
  pisang goreng (banana fritters)
    made with brown
    bananas 167
condiments 36
corn
  bakwan jagung (sweetcorn
    fritters) made with leftover
    beansprouts 156
  Xo butter corn 175
crab
  chile crisp puttanesca 64
  Singapore chile crab 212
cream
  burned toast ice cream made
    with stale bread 164
  hake in ginger-soy brown
    butter made with leftover
    cream 148
  hibiscus and pomegranate
    posset 258
  pandan leaf panna cotta with
    gula melaka 268
  Pavlova with mango cream and
    pandan curd 254
  Sichuan dark chocolate
    crémeux with peanut
    brittle 263
cream cheese bagels with pickles
  made with leftover milk 154
croissants
  Kaya croissant-and-butter
    pudding made with leftover
    pastries 163
cucumber
  cucumber and crystallized
    ginger salad 109

pickled cucumber relish 159
rojak 242
cucur udang: shrimp fritters 228
curry leaf chicken legs with
  salted egg yolk sauce 93
curry paste
  base curry paste 42

D
dates
  gula melaka sticky toffee
    pudding 253
desserts
  gula melaka sticky toffee
    pudding 253
  hibiscus and pomegranate
    posset 258
  homemade peach and mango
    pie 267
  pandan leaf panna cotta with
    gula melaka 268
  Pavlova with mango cream and
    pandan curd 254
  Sichuan dark chocolate
    crémeux with peanut
    brittle 263
dhal
  garlic dhal 103
dressings
  black tahini dressing 53
  salad dressing 39
drinks
  asam boi drink (salted plum
    drink) 273
  hot limau 273
  kopitiam turmeric ginger
    tea 271
  peach iced tea 272
  pineapple peel iced tea 272
dumplings
  mushroom and potato pot
    stickers 89
  pork and shrimp
    dumplings 126

E
eggs
  curry leaf chicken legs with
    salted egg yolk sauce 93
  Kaya croissant-and-butter
    pudding made with leftover
    pastries 163
  Kaya toast with soft-boiled
    eggs 210
  Maggi goreng with crispy fried
    eggs 190
  masala beans with poached
    eggs 172
  nasi goreng with smoked
    mackerel 85
  oyster omelet with wild garlic 234
  sambal halloumi morning buns 94
  Sichuan dark chocolate crémeux
    with peanut brittle 263
eggplants
  Ahma's house fish head
    curry 221
  chop suey eggplant with
    Thai basil 68
  sambal eggplant and green
    beans 198
  Sichuan brown butter
    eggplants 80

F
fish
  Ahma's house fish head curry 221
  hake in ginger-soy brown butter
    made with leftover cream 148
  nasi goreng with smoked
    mackerel 85
  sambal mackerel in banana
    leaf 222
fritters
  bakwan jagung (sweetcorn
    fritters) made with leftover
    beansprouts 156
  chaat masala potato fritter in a
    morning roll 61
  cucur udang: shrimp fritters 228
  perkedel (potato fritters) made
    with leftover potatoes 152

Index 279

pisang goreng (banana fritters)
    made with brown bananas 167

G
garlic
    garlic dhal 103
    garlic udon in sesame and chile oil 67
    garlicky green beans 231
    oyster omelet with wild garlic 234
    sambal belacan 47
ginger
    cucumber and crystallized ginger salad 109
    kopitiam turmeric ginger tea 271
gochujang
    gochujang ketchup 140
    gochujang mac 'n' cheese 185
green beans
    garlicky green beans 231
    green apple and green bean kerabu 108
    sambal eggplant and green beans 198
gula melaka
    gula melaka sticky toffee pudding 253
    pandan leaf panna cotta with gula melaka 268

H
hake in ginger-soy brown butter made with leftover cream 148
halloumi
    sambal halloumi morning buns 94
hibiscus and pomegranate posset 258

I
ice cream
    burned toast ice cream made with stale bread 164

K
kangkung belacan: water spinach with shrimp paste 232
Kaya 210
    Kaya croissant-and-butter pudding made with leftover pastries 163
    Kaya toast with soft-boiled eggs 210
kerabu
    green apple and green bean kerabu 108
kopitiam turmeric ginger tea 271

L
lamb
    spiced leg of lamb 138
lemongrass
    Ahma's house fish head curry 221
    ayam penyet 176
    basic curry paste 44
    beef shin rendang 121
    fragrant coconut rice 226
    grilled lemongrass chicken thighs with peanut sauce 116
    peanut sauce 52
    pineapple curry with lime leaves 112
    sambal belacan 47
    sambal mussels 244
    sticky tamarind shrimp 118
lentils
    garlic dhal 103
lime leaves
    pineapple curry with lime leaves 112
limes
    hot limau 273
Lunar New Year deep-fried oysters 140

M
mackerel
    nasi goreng with smoked mackerel 85
    sambal mackerel in banana leaf 222

Maggi goreng with crispy fried eggs 190
mango
    homemade peach and mango pie 267
    Pavlova with mango cream and pandan curd 254
    rojak 242
masala beans with poached eggs 172
meatballs
    sweet and sour pineapple meatballs 197
mee hoon goreng 187
meringue
    Pavlova with mango cream and pandan curd 254
milk
    burned toast ice cream made with stale bread 164
    cream cheese bagels with pickles made with leftover milk 154
mushrooms
    mushroom and potato pot stickers 89
    mushroom sticky rice with kecap manis oyster mushrooms 137
    salt and pepper oyster mushrooms 124
mussels
    sambal mussels 242

N
nasi goreng with smoked mackerel 85
noodles
    bihoon udang: shrimp rice noodles 225
    char kuay teow: big fat noodles 217
    clam-orous noods 132
    garlic udon in sesame and chile oil 67
    Maggi goreng with crispy fried eggs 190
    mee hoon goreng 187

Penang hokkien mee: shrimp noodle soup 236

O
oil
  Julie's kopitiam chile oil 50
okra
  Ahma's house fish head curry 221
omelets
  oyster omelet with wild garlic 234
onions
  grilled chese sandwich with tamarind onions 86
  pickled pink onions 159
orange and cashew chicken 74
oysters
  Lunar New Year deep-fried oysters 140
  oyster omelet with wild garlic 234

P
pandan leaf
  pandan leaf panna cotta with gula melaka 268
  Pavlova with mango cream and pandan curd 254
pasta
  chile crisp puttanesca 64
  Chinese sausage bucatini carbonara 179
  gochujang mac 'n' cheese 185
Pavlova with mango cream and pandan curd 254
peaches
  homemade peach and mango pie 267
  peach iced tea 272
peanut sauce 52
  gado-gado 104
  grilled lemongrass chicken thighs with peanut sauce 116
  sate daging: beef satay skewers 241

peanuts
  green apple and green bean kerabu 108
  puffed rice, peanut and shrimp cracker bhel 131
  rojak 242
  Sichuan dark chocolate crémeux with peanut brittle 263
Penang hokkien mee: shrimp noodle soup 236
peppers
  chop suey eggplant with Thai basil 68
  sweet and sour pineapple meatballs 197
perkedel (potato fritters) made with leftover potatoes 153
pickles
  achar 160
  pickled cucumber relish 159
  pickled pink onions 159
  simple pickled carrots 159
  simple pickling liquid 158
pies
  homemade peach and mango pie 267
pineapple
  pineapple curry with lime leaves 112
  pineapple peel iced tea 272
  rojak 242
  sweet and sour pineapple meatballs 197
pisang goreng (banana fritters) made with brown bananas 167
plums
  asam boi drink (salted plum drink) 272
pomegranate
  hibiscus and pomegranate posset 258
pork
  Penang hokkien mee: shrimp noodle soup 236
  perkedel (potato fritters) made with leftover potatoes 153
  pork and shrimp dumplings 126

sweet and sour pineapple meatballs 197
potatoes
  chaat masala potato fritter in a morning roll 61
  mushroom and potato pot stickers 89
  perkedel (potato fritters) made with leftover potatoes 153
  spiced leg of lamb 138
puffed rice, peanut and shrimp cracker bhel 131

R
raspberry and sesame blondies 261
rempah
  nasi goreng with smoked mackerel 85
rendang
  beef shank rendang 121
rice 26
  fragrant coconut rice 226
  mum's lap cheong fried rice 182
  mushroom sticky rice with kecap manis oyster mushrooms 137
  nasi goreng with smoked mackerel 85
rojak 240

S
salad dressing 39
salads
  cucumber and crystallized ginger salad 109
  green apple and green bean kerabu 108
  rojak 242
sambal
  green sambal 176
  sambal belacan 47
  sambal mackerel in banana leaf 222
  sambal mussels 244

Index

sambal oelek 46
simple sambal 45
samphire
   clams with Chinese sausage and samphire 82
sate daging: beef satay skewers 241
sauces
   master wok sauce 43
   peanut sauce 52
   sweet chile sauce 49
   sweet dim sum dipping sauce 44
sausages
   char kuay teow: big fat noodles 217
   Chinese sausage bucatini carbonara 179
   clams with Chinese sausage and samphire 82
   Mom's lap cheong fried rice 182
sesame seeds
   black tahini dressing 53
   raspberry and sesame blondies 261
sev
   puffed rice, peanut and shrimp cracker bhel 131
shrimp
   bihoon udang: shrimp rice noodles 225
   char kuay teow: big fat noodles 217
   cucur udang: shrimp fritters 228
   Penang hokkien mee: shrimp noodle soup 236
   pork and shrimp dumplings 126
   Singapore butter shrimp 115
   sticky tamarind shrimp 118
shrimp crackers
   puffed rice, peanut and shrimp cracker bhel 131
shrimp paste
   kangkung belacan: water spinach with shrimp paste 232
   Singapore chile crab 212
Sichuan dark chocolate crémeux with peanut brittle 263
Singapore chile crab 212

skewers
   sate daging: beef satay skewers 241
soup
   Penang hokkien mee: shrimp noodle soup 236
soy sauce
   fragrant soy roast chicken 107
   master wok sauce 43
   mushroom sticky rice with kecap manis oyster mushrooms 137
   sweet dim sum dipping sauce 44
steak au Sichuan poivre 193
sweet and sour pineapple meatballs 197

T
tamarind
   grilled chese sandwich with tamarind onions 86
   sticky tamarind shrimp 118
tea-brining
   goodbye buttermilk chicken, hello tea-brined crispy fried chicken 70
tempeh
   gado-gado 104
toast
   grilled chese sandwich with tamarind onions 86
   Kaya toast with soft-boiled eggs 210
toffee pudding
   gula melaka sticky toffee pudding 253
tofu
   gado-gado 104
   rojak 242
turkey
   mee hoon goreng 187
turmeric
   kopitiam turmeric ginger tea 271

V
vegetables
   achar 160
   gado-gado 104
   see individual vegetable listings

W
water spinach
   kangkung belacan: water spinach with shrimp paste 232

X
Xo butter corn 175

Terima Kasih
Thank you

Writing a book has been a completely new experience for me. I was blessed in first landing myself with Ebury (part of Penguin Random House), a publisher who gave me the confidence to tell my story in a different way (and help me with my countless spelling mistakes). I remember my childhood books from Penguin that sat on my bedroom shelf as a little girl. And I was given not one, but two of the best editors in the business, Emily Brickell and Nell Warner. These two women supported me through all of the emotions of writing a first book, and continued to cheerlead me on when I was trying to express a million emotions with the right words. They come alongside a brilliant team, Alice King and Stephenie Reynolds in publicity and marketing. Blessed doesn't even begin to cover it. This team of women at Ebury made the journey so magical. Emily, here is a special mention to you. You have been my rock! Thank you.

I must profusely thank my mom for being the best guidance I could ever ask for, and teaching me the ways of her heritage. When I think of you, I'll always think of the scene in *The Lion King* with the pawprint, your pawprint has been a big one to fill because you are an extremely special mom. Your bravery and kindness is something that touches everyone around you and has been an inspiration. I am so proud of where I come from because of you. I can't even imagine being 17 years old and coming to the UK to create a life, and you created such a wonderful life here in Glasgow. I'm forever grateful for you. And Dad, I mean this sincerely—your beans on toast, trips to the chippy when we're too tired to cook and love of food has helped this entire journey too. All jokes aside, you have been there for me when I really needed you, and you taught me great morals and values. My Uncle Kenny and Aunty Marion, I adore you too. Thank you from the bottom of my heart.

A special mention to Katrina Bell and Donald Sloan who helped me begin this whole journey—you look after those you love in a way that is so admirable and it doesn't go unnoticed. Needless to say, the women in my life are some of the strongest, most cheerleading wonderful women I'll ever meet. I am grateful to all of you and full of endless love for you. The book itself was shot by my very best friend, Liz Seabrook—to you, my rock, I'll always be so thankful. All of the photos that you see in this book were shot by Liz, the most talented photographer and best friend I could ever ask for—you gave the pages beauty and life and it takes someone as special as you to do that.

Behind the front pages of the book, there's also my entire family to thank, related and non-related. From the hawker stall owners I've watched growing up to all the people I've worked with … everyone. Below is a small handful of the people I want to give gratitude to for this book. And I dedicate this whole book to my mom and dad. Thank you for everything.

To the best friends who come over for dinner and try my cooking, eat with me on vacation and support my every move there are so many of you, too many for space in this book but here are just a few who had a particular moment in my life with food: Dave Liddell (of course, my number one chief taster, plate scraper, bowl licker and bestie), Nadia Radmehr, Laurie MacMillan, Thomas Small, Ilona Stolte, Lisa Jahanarai, Zara Weir, Christina Riley, Disa Persson, Hannah Stewart, Prerna Menon, Paul Crawford.

To my family from Malaysia: Amah, Gōng Gong, Aunty Nancy, Uncle Leong, Uncle John, Aunty Eileen, Uncle Benny, Aunty Suzy, Uncle Alan, Aunty Huang, Aunty Pat, Lin, David, Wern, Christina, Caroline, Robin, Yee Shiang, Yee Min, Kevin, Jasper, Andrew and Arthur. Thank you for guiding me and sharing your love of our food.

To my adopted family whom I owe so much to. As mentioned a lot in this book, my closest people when I was growing up—Carol and Jim, Gillian and Susan. Thank you for giving me love and support, you are my extended family and I feel truly secure in this world having grown up with you. Having you as an extension over the years has given me more love than I can quantify.

And finally a special shout out to those who completed this book with me—you made it so special: Sonali Shah, Kristine Jakobsson, Tom Pardhy, Katrina Bell, Tegan Hendel and Lola Hoad. There's absolutely no I in team here, I couldn't have done it without you all.

Behind the Scenes of *Sama Sama*

Conversion Tables

Weights

METRIC	IMPERIAL
15 g	½ oz
25 g	1 oz
40 g	1½ oz
60 g	2 oz
75 g	3 oz
100 g	3½ oz
150 g	5 oz
175 g	6 oz
200 g	7 oz
225 g	8 oz
250 g	9 oz
275 g	10 oz
350 g	12 oz
375 g	13 oz
400 g	14 oz
425 g	15 oz
450 g	1 lb
550 g	1¼ lb
675 g	1½ lb
900 g	2 lb
1.5 kg	3 lb
1.75 kg	4 lb
2.25 kg	5 lb

Volumes

METRIC	IMPERIAL
30 ml	1 fl oz (2 tbsp)
60 ml	2 fl oz (¼ cup)
75 ml	2½ fl oz (5 tbsp)
150 ml	5 fl oz (⅔ cup)
300 ml	10 fl oz (1¼ cups)
480 ml	16 fl oz (2 cups)
600 ml	2½ cups
700 ml	3 cups
900 ml	4 cups
1 liter	4¼ cups (1 quart)
1.2 liters	5 cups
1.3 liters	5½ cups
1.4 liters	6 cups
1.5 liters	6½ cups
1.7 liters	7 cups
1.75 liters	7½ cups
2 liters	8½ cups
2.25 liters	9½ cups
2.5 liters	10½ cups
2.8 liters	12 cups
3 liters	13 cups
3.5 liters	15 cups
4 liters	16 cups (1 gallon)

Oven Temperatures

°C	FAN °C	°F	GAS MARK
140°C	120°C	275°F	Gas Mark 1
150°C	130°C	300°F	Gas Mark 2
160°C	140°C	325°F	Gas Mark 3
180°C	160°C	350°F	Gas Mark 4
190°C	170°C	375°F	Gas Mark 5
200°C	180°C	400°F	Gas Mark 6
220°C	200°C	425°F	Gas Mark 7
230°C	210°C	450°F	Gas Mark 8
240°C	220°C	475°F	Gas Mark 9

Measurements

METRIC	IMPERIAL
0.5 cm	¼ inch
1 cm	½ inch
2.5 cm	1 inch
5 cm	2 inches
7.5 cm	3 inches
10 cm	4 inches
15 cm	6 inches
18 cm	7 inches
20 cm	8 inches
23 cm	9 inches
25 cm	10 inches
30 cm	12 inches

First published in 2025 by

Interlink Books
An imprint of Interlink Publishing Group, Inc.
46 Crosby Street
Northampton, Massachusetts 01060
www.interlinkbooks.com

Published simultaneously in the United Kingdom by Ebury Press, part of the Penguin Random House group of companies whose addresses can be found at global.penguinrandomhouse.com

Copyright © Julie Lin 2025
Illustration © Lola Hoad 2025
Photography © Liz Seabrook 2025

All rights reserved. No part of this publication may be reproduced, stored in a retrieval system, or transmitted, in any form or by any means, electronic, mechanical, photocopying, recording or otherwise, without the prior written permission of the publishers.

Library of Congress Cataloging-in-Publication Data available
ISBN 978-1-62371-612-7

Quote on page 11: Lawson, Nigella, cited in "Nigella Lawson: I'm very much a survivor. Everyone should be," theguardian.com (2014)

Design: Tegan Ella Hendel
Illustration: Lola Hoad
Photography: Liz Seabrook
Food Stylist: Sonali Shah
Prop Stylist: Libby Silbermann

Color origination by Altaimage Ltd
Printed and bound China by C&C Offset Printing Co., Ltd.

This book is produced from independently certified FSC® paper to ensure responsible forest management.